EARLY INTERVENTION FOR AUTISM SPECTRUM DISORDERS: A CRITICAL ANALYSIS

EARLY INTERVENTION FOR AUTISM SPECTRUM DISORDERS: A CRITICAL ANALYSIS

By

JOHNNY L. MATSON
Louisiana State University, USA

and

NOHA F. MINSHAWI
Louisiana State University, USA

Amsterdam • Boston • Heidelberg • London • New York • Oxford
Paris • San Diego • San Francisco • Singapore • Sydney • Tokyo

ELSEVIER

Elsevier
The Boulevard, Langford Lane, Kidlington, Oxford OX5 1GB, UK
Radarweg 29, PO Box 211, 1000 AE Amsterdam, The Netherlands

First edition 2006

Notice
No responsibility is assumed by the Publisher for any injury and/or damage to persons
or property as a matter of products liability, negligence or otherwise, or from any use
or operation of any methods, products, instructions or ideas contained in the material
herein. Because of rapid advances in the medical sciences, in particular, independent
verification of diagnoses and drug dosages should be made.

British Library Cataloguing in Publication Data
A catalogue record for this book is available from the British Library.

Library of Congress Cataloging-in-Publication Data
A catalog record for this book is available from the Library of Congress.

ISBN-13:   978-0-08-044675-2
ISBN-10:   0-08-044675-2
ISSN: 1871-1294

For information on all Elsevier publications
visit our website at books.elsevier.com

Printed and bound in The Netherlands

06 07 08 09 10   10 9 8 7 6 5 4 3 2 1

Working together to grow
libraries in developing countries

www.elsevier.com | www.bookaid.org | www.sabre.org

ELSEVIER   BOOK AID
            International   Sabre Foundation

Contents

Dedication

We would like to dedicate this book to our families and the families of children with Autism Spectrum Disorders.

Chapter 1

History and Development of Autism Spectrum Disorders

Early Work by Kanner

Understanding current knowledge of disorders as complex as those on the autism spectrum requires some appreciation of the condition's history. We will begin with the original definition of autism that came from Leo Kanner in 1943, the core symptoms of which are still recognized. Kanner observed 11 children with similar patterns of behavior, including abnormal language development and use, social skills deficits and excesses, and insistence on sameness in their environment. An additional common characteristic linking these children was their disregard for or inattention to the outside world, which Kanner referred to as "extreme autistic aloneness" (p. 242). As noted, the basic definition has remained constant since that time. The stability of the definition and the unusual pattern of human behavior that it describes have, as a result, drawn a great deal of attention from professionals and parents. Thus, autism is one of the most studied and discussed topics in the broad field of developmental disabilities and mental health (Tager-Flusberg, Joseph, & Folstein, 2001).

Parent reports of the 11 children's language were similar to the language observed by Kanner himself. The autistic children developed language according to normal milestones, and began memorizing and repeating nursery rhymes, poems, and songs at a very young age (e.g. 2 to 3 years). However, as the children approached school age they did not begin asking or answering questions as most children of their age did. Kanner hypothesized that the language of these children was being used for a function other than communication (Kanner, 1943). Thus, not only was there delayed speech, but the children's language was characterized as literal and inflexible, and many of the children with autism were unable to generalize or transfer an expression from one object or situation to another. Language was also irrelevant at times, with the children repeating phrases they had previously heard, but in socially inappropriate ways. Personal pronouns were also used incorrectly. Typically, these children's speech consisted of "quoting" (i.e. echoing) something previously heard. Language such as "quoting" and "echoing" would be used over and over in the descriptions of autism, perhaps because it was such a common and persistent theme, but also because it resulted in such an unusual presentation. In addition, the children also produced nonfunctional sounds in a repetitive manner. Odd speech patterns were common, but a few of the children failed to acquire communicative speech beyond a few words. Kanner referred to this latter group as mute (Kanner, 1943).

Reports of social skills difficulties were spread throughout Kanner's original account of autism (Kanner, 1943). Parent reports of infancy and early childhood contained abundant references to their children's lack of interest in the comings and goings of the people in their homes and the social lives of other children in their neighborhoods. Parents described the children as being self-sufficient, largely oblivious to their surroundings, hypnotized, and happiest when left alone. Kanner noted in his 1943 report that the children, upon entering a room, often paid no attention to the people in the room and instead went directly to objects. When forced to interact with other people, these children often showed annoyance, resentment, and anger. The little interaction that could be elicited from the children was devoid of eye contact and reciprocity. These problem areas of social interaction and language have been underscored as one of the key elements of autism (Sevin et al., 1995).

Finally, Kanner made detailed mention of the children's insistence on sameness. Most of the children exhibited a marked limitation in spontaneous activity. Toys were played with the same way each time. Blocks were often arranged precisely by color or size, and beads were routinely strung in the same order. When these rituals were interrupted, or routines were changed, some children became uncomfortable, anxious, or angry (Kanner, 1943). Additionally, several of the original 11 children became disturbed at the sight of something incomplete or broken. Kanner noted that some of the children possessed irrational fears toward very mundane environmental stimuli. For example, riding a tricycle horrified one child, while mechanical objects, such as his mother's eggbeater, frightened another.

Kanner viewed the combination of language and social deficits, coupled with an insistence on sameness, stereotyped patterns of behavior, echolalia and obsessive behavior, as a disorder that differed from other childhood conditions. The most closely linked problem area at the time was considered to be childhood schizophrenia. However, Kanner characterized autism as an entirely different syndrome. Kanner remarked that the combination of echolalia, stereotypy, obsessiveness, and autism (i.e. focus on self) overlapped with some of the basic characteristics of schizophrenia. However, Kanner believed that the age of onset differentiated the two disorders. Childhood schizophrenia, he noted, typically began after at least two years of seemingly typical development, whereas the children Kanner described exhibited social withdrawal throughout development. Also cited as a distinction between autism and childhood schizophrenia was the low incidence of schizophrenia in the families of children with autism, compared to the high incidence of schizophrenia in the families of children with childhood schizophrenia (Eveloff, 1960). In addition, Kanner believed that the children's good rote memory, intelligent parents, and lack of physical deformity were evidence that children with autism were of average, if not above average intelligence, providing further differentiation from what he considered to be more severe forms of psychopathology (Kanner, 1943). Kanner concluded his seminal paper by stating that children with autism were born with an innate inability to develop normal affective contact with other people. This statement led to a long and widely held belief that autism was a form of emotional reactivity. Psychoanalytic theorists later went on to espouse this view.

In 1956, with a colleague named Eisenberg, Kanner further refined the definition of autism. Eisenberg and Kanner (1956) reduced the essential features of autism to just two categories of behavior: extreme aloneness and insistence on sameness. However, this definition of autism lacked the emphasis on language abnormalities present in Kanner's (1943) original description. Drawing back to the differentiation Kanner proposed in his initial writings between autism and schizophrenia, Eisenberg and Kanner (1956) included in their new definition of autism an age of onset, stating that autism occurred prior to age 2.

Beyond Kanner

Kanner is still quoted when talking about autism and the features that define the condition. While his core description remains, some refinements in the definition have occurred. With Eisenberg, Kanner provided a fairly straightforward set of symptoms and characteristics for autism (Eisenberg & Kanner, 1956). Many researchers and clinicians have since written on the topic, in an attempt to refine the definition. The efforts of Creak, Rutter, and the National Society for Autistic Children are particularly noteworthy and will be addressed in some detail below.

Creak

More than 20 years after Kanner's description of infantile autism, Creak (1961) developed a set of criteria for the identification of early childhood psychosis. Creak presented a brief list of nine characteristics that could be readily observed. Creak's nine points were: (1) gross and continuing impairment of emotional relationships, described as aloofness and difficulty playing with peers; (2) age-inappropriate lack of awareness of personal identity, including abnormal body posturing, self-injury, and personal pronoun confusion in expressive language; (3) pathological preoccupation with certain objects or their characteristics, without regard for the function of the item; (4) resistance to environmental change and effort to maintain or restore sameness; (5) abnormal perceptual experience, marked by excessive or unpredictable response to sensory stimuli, such as insensitivity to pain and temperature; (6) acute or excessive anxiety, usually triggered by changes in the environment; (7) loss of speech or failure to acquire or develop language and the occurrence of echolalia or pronoun reversal (using "you" instead of "I" when referring to oneself); (8) distorted pattern of motility, including abnormal gait, unusual body posturing, rocking, or spinning; and (9) history of serious retardation, although some intellectual functions may be normal or exceptional.

While many of his characteristics overlapped with Kanner's, Creak, like other researchers at the time (i.e. Fish, 1976), believed that these behaviors were actually a form of childhood schizophrenia. However, Creak failed to further operationalize his criteria or indicate how these behavior patterns were specific to childhood schizophrenia. As a result, Creak's nine features were incorporated into many subsequent descriptions of autism and commonly used autism assessment instruments (e.g. Krug, Arick, & Almond, 1980b; Schopler, Reichler, DeVellis, & Daly, 1980). For example, the Childhood Autism Rating Scale (CARS; Schopler et al., 1980) includes items related to abnormal use of senses and strict adherence to routines. Additionally, the DSM-IV criteria for autism, which will be discussed at length later in this chapter, incorporated many of Creak's (1963) nine points.

Rutter and Associates

Another influential researcher in the early history of autism was Michael Rutter at the University of London. In 1968, focusing on the efforts of Kanner and Creak, Rutter attempted to further clarify the definition and classification of autism. An important step in defining a new disorder was ascertaining whether the condition differs significantly from established disorders. As Kanner (1943) pointed out, an overlap existed between the characteristics of schizophrenia and autism. Additionally, it was important to determine whether autism was simply a variant of intellectual disability (ID) or a disorder unto itself. Rutter (1968) argued that autism could, in fact, be differentiated from both schizophrenia and ID.

Rutter (1968) provided a basis for the differentiation between autism and schizophrenia. In 1911, Bleuler originally used the term "autism" to describe the active withdrawal from social relations into a rich fantasy life seen in individuals with schizophrenia (Bleuler, 1950). Rutter felt that this "unfortunate choice of name" (p. 139) led to much of the confusion between the two disorders (Rutter, 1978a). Using the research available at the time, Rutter noted a number of differences between autism and schizophrenia. He cited the higher male-to-female ratio in autism over schizophrenia as one difference. In addition, Rutter believed that a higher proportion of children with autism came from parents with high socioeconomic status and above average intelligence (Lotter, 1967). This assumption later proved to be incorrect. Rather, people with financial resources were more likely to seek, and pay for, services. Also noted was the absence of delusions or hallucinations and the relatively poor intellectual functioning in individuals with autism. Finally, autism had a stable course for the most part compared to the potential for relapse and/or marked improvement in schizophrenia. Rutter deemed the lack of compelling evidence for an association between the two disorders to mean that autism was not merely a variant of schizophrenia.

While Kanner claimed that children with autism had normal intellectual functioning, Rutter pointed out that there was no empirical evidence to support Kanner's claim (Rutter, 1968). Rutter noted that children with autism typically functioned at a "mentally subnormal level" (p. 5). Researchers had generally assumed prior to these assertions that autistic features suppressed the ability to perform, thus differentiating autism from ID. However, later research supported Rutter's assertion.

In their 1967 study, Rutter and Lockyer concluded that half of the children with autism in their sample obtained intelligence quotient (IQ) scores in the mentally subnormal range on standardized intelligence tests. The IQ scores obtained for this sample were found to be both stable and good predictors of intellectual functioning later in life (Lockyer & Rutter, 1969). However, Rutter (1968) went on to point out that despite the low intellectual functioning present in many children with autism, the disorder should not be considered another form of ID. He supported his argument by highlighting the fact that not all children with autism also had ID and that the intellectual functioning of one third to one quarter of children with autism was within the normal range (Rutter & Lockyer, 1967). Finally, Rutter hypothesized that the low intellectual functioning found in some children with autism might be more a product of language deficits than global intellectual deficits (Rutter, 1968).

In 1978, Rutter stated that autism was a distinct syndrome because the behaviors observed occurred with uniformity across all subjects and were specific to autism. Thus, autism could be differentiated from other developmental disorders. Because of the high rates of comorbidity between autism and ID, Rutter believed any definition of autism must take into account intellectual functioning and developmental level. Thus, Rutter cautioned that developmental level was vital to understanding autism. He stated that autism could not be diagnosed solely on the presence of social and language impairments. Rutter gave the example of a 4-year-old child with a mental age (the measure of intelligence used at the time, as opposed to IQ, which is used today) of 6 months. Autism could only be diagnosed in this hypothetical child if the social and language deficits exhibited were abnormal for the child's mental age and showed the "special features characteristic of autism" (Rutter, 1978a, p. 144).

Rutter divided the "special features characteristic of autism" into three broad behavioral groupings. These categories of behaviors were: impaired social relations, delayed and/or abnormal language development, and insistence on sameness (Rutter, 1978b). The social deficits noted by Rutter included lack of attachment and bonding during infancy, failure to anticipate being picked up or held, and failure to seek comfort from parents. Lack of eye-to-eye gaze was also considered a prominent feature of the social deficits seen in autism. Rutter noted that the quality, as opposed to quantity, of eye-to-eye gaze was important in persons with autism. Children with autism do not use eye-to-eye gaze in the same discriminating fashion as typically developing children or avoid eye-to-eye gaze the same way highly anxious or shy children might (Rutter, 1978b).

Rutter's second category of behavior was abnormal language use. Children with autism often fail to show prelanguage skills such as waving and social imitation. While many children with autism fail to develop useful speech, those that do exhibit a number of abnormalities, such as echolalia (i.e. repeating words or phrases), rare use of gestures (e.g. lack of pointing) and pronoun reversal (e.g. referring to self in third person). In general, speech does not seem to be used as a means of social communication. Children with autism appear to talk *at* a person rather than *to* a person. For example, a child with autism may request an item without making eye contact, without using polite phrases or appropriate vocal inflection, and without appropriate affect.

The final category of behaviors Rutter proposed as essential to autism was insistence on sameness. Children with autism often exhibit rigid, inflexible patterns of play lacking in imagination. Oftentimes, a child with autism may become attached to an object, although the object's function may be irrelevant. For example, a book may be carried around constantly but never opened or read. Additionally, routines may be rigidly adhered to, with a marked resistance to change in either routine or the appearance of the environment. Rutter also noted that children with autism might develop obsessional symptoms that can take different forms, such as touching or compulsions. A child with autism may insist on touching people's faces repetitively, for example.

Rutter struggled with the inclusion of an age of onset in the diagnostic criteria. He cited research pertaining to the differences in etiology, symptomatology, and prognosis that exist between disorders with early versus late onset. While many of the disintegrative disorders that begin in late childhood and early adolescence share characteristics with autism, many of the behaviors differ significantly. As a result, Rutter agreed with Kanner on the importance of differentiating autism from late onset disorders (Rutter, 1978b). The difficulty came in creating a specific age cutoff. Without empirical data to guide the decision, Rutter felt that it was important to have a cutoff before the age of 3 because some of the "disintegrative psychoses" (1978a, p. 145) began around that age. Thus, in the absence of further data, it seemed reasonable to him to adopt the 30-month cutoff recommended by both Eisenberg and Kanner (1956) and the World Health Organization. As will become apparent in further discussion of the classification and description of autism, the concept of an age cutoff continues to be debated and modified.

Rutter's work proved to be influential in developing the definition of autism and its systematic use through the inclusion of his criteria in the DSM. However, many other researchers and groups have provided their own ideas on the relevant characteristics of the disorder. At the time Rutter published his definition of autism, the National Society for Autistic Children (NSAC), which was influential in its own right, proposed its own definition (Ritvo, 1978). A review of the NSAC approach to the diagnosis of autism follows.

National Society for Autistic Children (NSAC)

In the 1970s, parent groups became a new and very powerful contingent in the debate regarding the nature of autism. Many parents were dissatisfied with the services being offered to their children and began to form groups to lobby local and federal governments for research money and services. Parent groups have proven to be effective at expressing their concerns and interests to the research and political communities. One of the first and most influential parent groups for children with autism in the United States was the National Society for Autistic Children (NSAC). In 1978, Edward Ritvo and the NSAC proposed their own definition of autism. A review of the NSAC definition (Ritvo, 1978) and its similarities and differences with Rutter's 1978 definition follow.

Under the NSAC definition, autism consisted of four essential problem areas: (1) developmental rate; (2) response to sensory stimuli; (3) speech, language and cognitive capacities; (4) capacities to relate to people, events, and objects. Also included was an age of onset prior to 30 months. The NSAC definition paralleled that proposed by Rutter (1978a) in the age of onset criterion, as well as a focus on social and language deficits. However, the NSAC definition departed from Rutter in the inclusion of criteria based on rate of development and response to sensory stimuli.

The NSAC criterion of disturbance in the rate of development refers to disruption in the normal development of motor, social-adaptive, and/or cognitive pathways. Ritvo (1978) stated that disruption could occur within a pathway (e.g. gross motor but not fine motor milestones are met) or between pathways (e.g. a cognitive delay is evident although motor development is within normal limits). Additionally, a regression or delay can occur after a period of normal development. At least one of these disturbances in development would have had to occur for a child to meet the NSAC's original criteria for autism.

The other addition to the NSAC definition of autism was disturbances in response to sensory stimuli. These disturbances could include visual, auditory, tactile, vestibular, olfactory, and proprioceptive symptoms. Examples of visual symptoms include failure to establish or maintain eye contact, close scrutiny of visual details in the environment and prolonged examination of objects. Auditory symptoms of autism consist of no response or overresponse to sounds. Tactile symptoms include sensitivity to food textures and underreaction or overreaction to pain, touch, or temperature. Vestibular symptoms deal with over- or underreactions to gravity stimuli and preoccupation with spinning items. Another vestibular symptom is the lack of a dizzy feeling despite repeatedly turning in circles. Olfactory or gustatory symptoms include licking inedible objects, specific or restricted food preferences, and repetitive sniffing of objects. Finally, proprioceptive symptoms are behaviors such as hand flapping, gesturing, posturing, and grimacing.

The definitions provided by Ritvo and the NSAC (Ritvo, 1978) and Rutter (1978a, 1978b) were two of the most significant being debated in the 1970s. While the two definitions had many features in common, it is interesting to assess their significant differences. First, Rutter (1978a) and Kanner (1943) both emphasized the importance of insistence on sameness in differentiating autism from other disorders. The NSAC definition did not include insistence on sameness as either a defining or associated feature. However, the NSAC definition highlighted atypical development and unusual responses to sensory stimuli. Although Rutter did recognize the necessity of viewing autistic symptoms in the light of the child's developmental level, he did not use atypical development as a defining feature.

The discrepancy in criteria appeared to be at least partially motivated by politics (Schopler, 1978). This point is of importance in highlighting that research does not occur in a vacuum; research is influenced by political and cultural views. The two definitions were created for different audiences and with different intentions. Rutter's criteria were developed based on historical and scientific research and were driven by a need to clarify previous findings and provide a framework for future research (Schopler, 1978). On the other hand, the NSAC definition was intended to assist parent groups in their efforts to raise public awareness of autism and, most importantly, lobby for increased funding for badly needed treatment and research. Table 1.1 provides a comparison of the criteria discussed thus far.

Diagnostic and Statistical Manual

With Rutter's synthesis of Kanner's work, autism (called infantile autism, in order to further emphasize autism's differentiation from other mental disorders) was included for the first time in the *Diagnostic and Statistical Manual of Mental Disorders, Third Edition* (DSM-III; American Psychiatric Association, 1980). This development was significant because the manual is used by insurance companies and thus almost all mental health professionals. The DSM thus proved valuable by standardizing and popularizing one particular set of criteria for autism.

The diagnosis of autism has developed considerably since Kanner (1943). As a result, it is important to understand the evolution of the diagnosis. The changes in diagnostic criteria have affected our understanding of the disorder, its etiology and prevalence. Therefore, we will review the diagnosis of autism as defined by the *Diagnostic and Statistical Manual of Mental Disorders* and *International Classification of Diseases*.

A brief review of the nature of the *Diagnostic and Statistical Manual of Mental Disorders* may be helpful to those unfamiliar with the diagnostic manual's history. The first edition of the *Diagnostic and Statistical Manual of Mental Disorders* (DSM-I; APA, 1952), developed by the American Psychiatric Association (APA) and the New York Academy of Medicine, was intended to create a nationally acceptable nomenclature for diagnosing individuals living in inpatient units with severe psychiatric and neurological disorders (APA, 2000). Each disorder was considered a clinically significant behavioral or psychological pattern associated with distress, disability or a significantly increased risk of harm or loss of freedom (APA, 2000). DSM-I was limited in scope. Disorders included in DSM-I held a psychodynamic theoretical emphasis and no childhood disorders were included due to the

Table 1.1: Comparison of Kanner, Creak, Rutter and NSAC criteria for autism

Domains	Kanner (1943)	Creak (1961)	Rutter (1978)	NSAC (Ritvo, 1978)
Language	Delay in language acquisition	Failure to develop language	Lack of prelanguage skills	Disturbances in speech, language or cognitive capacities
	Lack of asking/answering questions	Echolalia	Pronoun reversal	Abnormalities in relating to people, objects or events
	Irrelevant speech		Rare use of gestures	Echolalia
	Failure to acquire communicative speech			
Socialization	Lack of interest in other people	Impaired relationships	Lack of bonding in infancy	
	More attention paid to objects than to people	Preoccupation with parts of objects	Lack of eye contact	
	Lack of eye contact/social reciprocity	Resistance to change		
Other	Insistence on sameness	Abnormal sensory experience	Inflexible patterns of play	Disruption in normal development
	Average/above average intelligence	Acute anxiety	Rigid adherence to routine	Abnormal response to sensory stimuli
		Intellectual disability	Obsessions or compulsions	Onset prior to 30 months
		Abnormal body movements	Onset prior to 30 months	

theoretical belief that children did not possess the ego strength necessary to have mental health conditions.

Since DSM-I, the diagnostic system has been revised four times. DSM-III (APA, 1980) was the first edition to incorporate specific diagnostic criteria for each disorder. In addition, DSM-III was based on a multiaxial system. In this system, each individual case is assessed for clinical disorders and conditions that may be a focus of clinical attention (Axis I), personality disorders and mental retardation (Axis II), general medical conditions (Axis III), psychosocial and environmental problems (Axis IV) and global functioning (Axis V). In addition, the DSM uses a categorical approach to the classification of mental disorders. This means that disorders are grouped based on similar defining features. However, a number of inconsistencies and lack of clarity in criteria brought about a revision of DSM-III, *the Diagnostic and Statistical Manual of Mental Disorders, Third Edition, Revised* (DSM-III-R; APA, 1987).

A great deal of research on psychopathology was being conducted around the time that DSM-III and DSM-III-R were in development. This research formed the fourth revision of the DSM (DSM-IV; APA, 1994). Groups of researchers and clinicians in each specialty area conducted a systematic review of published literature, reanalyzed data sets, and conducted field trials in order to arrive at the diagnostic criteria included in DSM-IV. Finally, in 2000, the APA published a text revision of DSM-IV (DSM-IV-TR; APA, 2000). The text revision was intended to correct any factual errors in DSM-IV and provide up-to-date information (APA, 2000). As noted, the DSM has, in its various revisions, become the most influential definition of mental health disorders and developmental disabilities. Published in the United States, it is the most widely used set of criteria in North America and has recently surpassed the World Health Organization's mental health criteria in use throughout Europe.

Autism first appeared in DSM-III, among a new category of disorders named Pervasive Developmental Disorders (PDD). Parents were concerned that their children be classified without implying that the disorders were traditional mental health conditions, such as schizophrenia. Thus, the term PDD was used. In order for a child to meet a diagnosis of infantile autism he or she had to exhibit a pervasive lack of social relationships and language deficits, beginning before the age of 30 months. In line with Kanner's belief that autism affected only young children, DSM-III included a diagnosis of "residual" autism for those individuals who had met the criteria for infantile autism at one point, but no longer exhibited the symptoms.

While DSM-III brought official recognition of autism by the mental health community (defined as inclusion in the DSM), there were problems with the DSM-III definition. These problems included an overemphasis on the "infantile" aspect of the disorder (Volkmar, Bregman, Cohen, & Cicchetti, 1988), overly stringent criteria, and a lack of consideration of issues associated with developmental change (Volkmar, Cicchetti, Bregman, & Cohen, 1992a). These issues were addressed in the subsequent revision, DSM-III-R (APA, 1987).

The DSM-III-R replaced infantile autism with the term autism, recognizing that individuals with autism continued to exhibit symptomatology beyond childhood. The category of "residual" autism was also removed, allowing the disorder to be diagnosed in individuals of any age or developmental level. In addition, the criteria for autism were broadened to encompass potential developmental changes. With the expansion in criteria came a high rate of false positives (Factor, Freeman, & Kardish, 1989; Hertzig, Snow, New, & Shapiro, 1990; Volkmar, Cicchetti, Bregman, & Cohen, 1992b). The criteria were too general; thus some children were diagnosed with autism but did not truly have the disorder. Clarification of these false positives, as well as the reasonable range of symptom inclusion and rationale for the use of historical information, provided the basis for the field trials for DSM-IV (Volkmar et al., 1994).

International Classification of Diseases

Since the early 1600s, physicians have attempted to classify the numerous causes of death (Knibbs, 1929). One of the first notable classification systems to accomplish this goal was the *International List of Causes of Death*, originally based on the work of William Farr on behalf of the first International Statistical Congress in 1853 (WHO, 2005). In the 1920s, the Health Organization of the League of Nations and the International Statistical Institute collaborated to publish the Fourth and Fifth revisions of the *International List of Causes of Death* in 1929 and 1938, respectively (WHO, 2005). The sixth revision of the *International List of Causes of Death* was entrusted to the World Health Organization (WHO). The WHO commission produced the first internationally agreed rules for selecting the causes of death and changed the name from the *International List of Causes of Death* to the *Manual of the International Statistical Classification of Diseases, Injuries, and Causes of Death* (WHO, 1948).

The ICD-10 (WHO, 1996), the most recent revision of the criteria, described autism as a PDD defined by abnormal or impaired development evident by age 3, with abnormalities in reciprocal social interaction and communication, and restricted, stereotyped, repetitive behavior. In order to meet the criteria for autism under the ICD-10's algorithm, a child must display at least one of three impairments in reciprocal social interaction, two of four qualitative impairments in communication and at least two of five restricted, repetitive, and stereotyped patterns of behavior.

A qualitative impairment in social interaction is manifested in ICD-10 as at least one of following three items: (1) failure to adequately use eye-to-eye gaze, facial expression, body posture and gesture to regulate social interaction; (2) failure to develop peer relationships; and (3) lack of socio-emotional reciprocity.

The next category, qualitative impairments in communication, requires the presence of at least two of the following four items: (1) delay or total lack of spoken language unaccompanied by compensatory attempts, such as gesture or mime; (2) failure to initiate or sustain conversation; (3) stereotyped and repetitive use of language or idiosyncratic use of words or phrases; and (4) abnormalities in pitch, stress, rate, rhythm, and intonation of speech.

Finally, restricted, repetitive, and stereotyped patterns of behavior, interests, and activities must be manifested by at least two of the following five items: (1) preoccupation with stereotyped and restricted patterns of interest; (2) apparently compulsive adherence to specific, nonfunctional, routines or rituals; (3) stereotyped and repetitive motor mannerisms; (4) preoccupation with parts of objects or nonfunctional elements of play material; and (5) distress over changes in small, nonfunctional environmental details. Additionally, unlike DSM-IV, ICD-10 also includes a specific diagnostic code for atypical autism. Atypical autism, as defined by ICD-10, differs from autism in either age of onset or failure to fulfill all three sets of diagnostic criteria.

DSM versus ICD (Table 1.2)

The DSM-IV field trials compared the DSM-III-R criteria with those of ICD-10 (Volkmar et al., 1994). The ICD-10 diagnosis of autism is made on the basis of delayed or deviant communication, social interaction and/or play, qualitative impairment in social interaction, and restricted and stereotyped patterns of behavior or interests. Symptom onset must be prior to age 3. Subjects in the DSM-IV field trial were 454 individuals diagnosed with autism by an experienced clinician, 240 diagnosed with other Pervasive Developmental Disorders, and 283 with conditions other than Pervasive Developmental Disorders. Items from ICD-10, DSM-III and DSM-III-R were compiled into a checklist and for each subject an independent rater decided whether each item did or did not apply, was not applicable, or could not be rated (Volkmar et al., 1994). Based on the response to each item, a clinical diagnosis was determined using the scoring rules for each individual rating system. Thus, the clinician had to have endorsed a sufficient number of ICD-10 criteria (see the above discussion of ICD-10) in order to meet the ICD-10 diagnosis of autism.

Sensitivity, specificity, positive, negative and total predictive values, and agreement with clinician diagnoses were calculated for all three scales. Volkmar et al. (1994) suggested that ICD-10 was superior to both DSM-III and DSM-III-R because it offered a better combination of sensitivity and specificity over the age ranges and developmental levels. One criticism of ICD-10 was that it was too detailed, both in number of items and in length of criteria. Using information from the reliability of individual items, four of the original ICD-10 criteria were eliminated because they had a low frequency of endorsement or duplicated information from other criteria. The field trial resulted in the current DSM-IV definition of autism.

The current DSM-IV-TR (APA, 2000) definition of autism emphasizes that the essential features are impaired development of social interaction, impaired communication, and restricted, repetitive, and stereotyped patterns of behavior. This diagnosis revolves around these three criteria while providing more detailed definitions. The first criterion of the diagnosis is social skills deficits. An individual must exhibit impaired social interaction manifested by at least two of the following behaviors: marked impairment in the use of several nonverbal forms of communication (such as eye contact, facial expression, and gaze), failure to establish developmentally appropriate peer relations, lack of spontaneous seeking of shared interests with others, or lack of social or emotional reciprocity.

The second criterion, qualitative impairment in communication, is endorsed if the individual manifests at least one of the following behaviors: lack of or delay in the development of speech, inability or impairment in initiating or sustaining conversation, stereotyped or repetitive use of language, or lack of imaginative or imitative play. The third criterion, restricted, repetitive, and stereotyped patterns of behavior, is endorsed when at least one of the following behaviors is exhibited: preoccupation with one or more stereotyped patterns of interest, inflexible adherence to specific, nonfunctional routines, stereotyped and repetitive motor behaviors, or preoccupation with parts of objects. In addition to these criteria, the onset of abnormal function must be prior to age 3. Finally, the authors of DSM-IV caution that the clinician or researcher should determine whether the symptoms are better accounted for by either Rett's Disorder or Childhood Disintegrative Disorder. By including specific rule-out diagnoses, DSM-IV forces clinicians to give appropriate consideration to other disorders that share similar symptomatology.

Table 1.2: Comparison of ICD-10[a] and DSM-IV[b] criteria for autism

Domain	ICD-10	DSM-IV
Qualitative impairment in socialization	At least 1 of 3	At least 2 of 4
	(1) Failure to adequately use eye-to-eye gaze, facial expression, body posture and gesture to regulate social interaction	(1) Marked impairment in the use of several nonverbal forms of communication
	(2) Failure to develop peer relationships that involve mutual sharing of interests, activities and emotions	(2) Failure to establish developmentally appropriate peer relations
	(3) Lack of socio-emotional reciprocity as shown by an impaired or deviant response to other people's emotions; or lack of modulation of behaviour according to social context, or a weak integration of social, emotional and communicative behaviours	(3) Lack of social or emotional reciprocity
		(4) Lack of spontaneous seeking of shared interests with others
Qualitative impairment in communication	At least 2 of 4	At least 2 of 4
	(1) A delay in, or total lack of development of social language that is not accompanied by an attempt to compensate through the use of gesture or mime	(1) Marked impairment in the use of several nonverbal forms of communication
	(2) Relative failure to initiate or sustain conversational interchange	(2) Failure to establish developmentally appropriate peer relations
	(3) Stereotyped and repetitive use of language or idiosyncratic use of words or phrases	(3) Lack of spontaneous seeking of shared interests with others
	(4) Abnormalities in pitch, stress, rate, rhythm, and intonation of speech	(4) Lack of social or emotional reciprocity

Table 1.2: *Continued*

Domain	ICD-10	DSM-IV
Restricted, repetitive and stereotyped behavior	At least 2 of 5 (1) Encompassing preoccupation with one or more stereotyped and restricted patterns of interest that are abnormal in content or focus (2) Apparently compulsive adherence to specific, nonfunctional routines or rituals (3) Stereotyped and repetitive motor mannerisms that involve either finger flapping or twisting, or complex whole body movements (4) Preoccupation with parts of objects or nonfunctional elements of play material (5) Distress over changes in small, nonfunctional environmental details	At least 1 of 4 (1) Encompassing preoccupation with one or more stereotyped and restricted patterns of interest that are abnormal either in intensity or focus (2) Apparently inflexible adherence to specific, nonfunctional routines or rituals (3) Stereotyped and repetitive motor mannerisms (4) Persistent preoccupation with parts of objects
Age of onset	Prior to age 3 in at least 1 of 3 areas: (1) Development of selective social attachments or reciprocal social interaction (2) Receptive or expressive language as used in social communication (3) Functional or symbolic play	Prior to age 3 in at least 1 of 3 areas: (1) Social interaction (2) Language as used in social communication (3) Symbolic or imaginative play

[a] From *Multiaxial Classification of Child and Adolescent Psychiatric Disorders: The ICD-10 Classification of Mental and Behavioral Disorders in Children and Adolescents* (p. 199), by World Health Organization, 1996, Geneva: World Health Organization. Reprinted with permission.

[b] From *Diagnostic and Statistical Manual of Mental Disorders, Fourth Edition, Text Revision* (p. 77), by American Psychiatric Association, 2000. Washington, DC: American Psychiatric Association. Copyright 2000 by the American Psychiatric Association. Reprinted with permission.

Autism Spectrum Disorders

The idea of autism existing not as a single entity, but as a spectrum along which there are multiple disorders of varying severity, emerged in the late 1990s and has recently taken hold in the literature and popular culture. At this time, researchers and clinicians began to refer to these conditions as Autism Spectrum Disorders (ASD). For the most part, we will use the term ASD in reference to these disorders for the remainder of this book.

The triad of behaviors believed to underlie Autism Spectrum Disorders is made up of impairments in social interaction, impairments in communication, and narrow, repetitive patterns of behavior (Wing, 1997). Developers of both ICD-10 (WHO, 1996) and DSM-IV (APA, 1994) have attempted to divide Autism Spectrum Disorders into categories of Pervasive Developmental Disorders (PDD), including Autistic Disorder, Asperger's Syndrome (AS) and PDD not otherwise specified (PDD-NOS). However, as already discussed, the attempts at differentiating between these disorders have been, in Wing's (1997) words, "arbitrary . . . difficult to apply and unhelpful in clinical practice" (p. 1761). Both ICD-10 and DSM-IV have attempted to differentiate autism and AS based on developmental history, cognitive functioning, and age of onset. However, research has failed to fully support these factors as clear methods of differential diagnosis (Wing, 1981).

The DSM-IV (APA, 1994) uses the term PDD in place of ASD. The five PDD categories included in DSM-IV-TR are: Autistic Disorder, Rett's Disorder, Childhood Disintegrative Disorder (CDD), Asperger's Syndrome (AS) and Pervasive Developmental Disorder Not Otherwise Specified (PDD-NOS). The authors of DSM-IV stated that Rett's Disorder, CDD, AS, and PDD-NOS were included in order to improve differential diagnosis and increase the specificity used to describe individuals who would have been classified as PDD-NOS in DSM-III-R (APA, 2000). While the focus of this book will remain primarily on autism, it is important that clinicians and students be aware of the other disorders considered to be part of the autism spectrum, because they share not only common defining features, but also similar assessment and treatment methods. In addition, some of the epidemiological, etiological and treatment studies that have been and are being conducted include children with all five disorders.

Rett's Disorder

Rett's Disorder is a relatively new disorder, first described by Andreas Rett (1979). Rett's Disorder was included as an ASD because it shares several fundamental features with autism. Individuals with both disorders exhibit stereotypic motor mannerisms, language abnormalities, and social deficits. In his original description of the disorder, Rett described a loss of ability to respond to affective stimuli (Rett, 1979). Additionally, Hagberg et al. (1983) observed in 35 children a lack of sustained interest in other people and limited social contact, further bolstering Rett's (1979) hypothesis.

Rett's Disorder is a rare developmental condition that is thought to affect primarily females (Van Acker, 1991). It is characterized by normal prenatal and perinatal development. Parents of affected children have reported normal physical and cognitive development for the first 7 to 18 months of life (Gillberg, 1987). Children with Rett's Disorder typically attain early physical, psychomotor, and verbal milestones on time, as opposed to the language delays seen in autism. Following this period of normal development, a deterioration or cessation in the acquisition of developmental milestones occurs. This phenomenon can be manifested in a number of ways, such as losses of previously acquired speech or purposeful hand movements (Van Acker, 1991).

In addition to the onset of a developmental delay, children with Rett's Disorder demonstrate several characteristic symptoms, including a deceleration in the rate of head growth and jerky arm, leg and trunk movements (Hagberg et al., 1983). The ambulation of children with Rett's Disorder is marked by a stiff-legged, broad gait with short steps and swaying shoulder movement. Another characteristic of Rett's Disorder is stereotypic hand movements. These movements include hand clasping, wringing or "hand washing" and hand-to-mouth movements (Leiber, 1985). Features associated with Rett's Disorder can also include apnea, hyperventilation, teeth grinding, facial grimacing, and seizures (Trevanthan & Naidu, 1988). Finally, Rett's Disorder is the only ASD that is associated with a specific genetic etiology. In 1999, Amir and colleagues discovered that Rett's Disorder is the result of a specific mutation on an X-linked gene. Current opinion is that this specific genetic mutation is responsible for more than 75% of classic Rett's Disorder and 50% of those with atypical symptoms (Shahbazian & Zoghbi, 2002).

DSM-IV states that in order to meet criteria for a diagnosis of Rett's Disorder, a child must have apparently normal prenatal and perinatal development, normal psychomotor development for the first 5 months of life, and a normal head circumference at birth. In addition, following the normal period of development, the child must demonstrate each of the following symptoms: deceleration of head growth between 5 and 48 months of age, loss of previously acquired purposeful hand skills between the ages of 5 and 30 months and the subsequent development of stereotypic hand movements, loss of social interaction, poorly coordinated gait or trunk movements, and severely impaired expressive and receptive language with severe psychomotor retardation (Table 1.3).

Similarities between Rett's Disorder and autism have already been outlined, but there are several fundamental distinctions between the two disorders. Researchers who have published epidemiological studies have found a gender difference between autism and Rett's Disorder. Autism is more prevalent in males, whereas Rett's Disorder occurs almost exclusively in females. Another distinction between the two conditions is that Rett's Disorder is associated with physical and psychomotor problems such as decelerated head growth and gait abnormalities. Finally, Rett's Disorder is marked by normal development in the first few years of life, whereas autism is believed to begin in early infancy (Volkmar, Klin, Marans, & Cohen, 1996).

Childhood Disintegrative Disorder

Another disorder on the autism spectrum is Childhood Disintegrative Disorder (CDD). In 1908, Theodor Heller described six children who had undergone a severe regression in a range of behaviors after apparently normal development until the age of 3 (Volkmar & Rutter, 1995). Initially, CDD was included in ICD-9 and ICD-10, but not in DSM-III or DSM-III-R. This exclusion from the DSM was primarily due to the very low incidence of the

Table 1.3: DSM-IV criteria for Rett's Disorder

A.   All of the following:

    (1) Apparently normal prenatal and perinatal development
    (2) Apparently normal psychomotor development through the first 5 months after birth
    (3) Normal head circumference at birth

B.   Onset of all of the following after the period of normal development:

    (1) Deceleration of head growth between ages 5 and 48 months
    (2) Loss of previously acquired purposeful hand skills between ages 5 and 30 months with the subsequent development of stereotyped hand movements (e.g. hand-wringing or hand washing)
    (3) Loss of social engagement early in the course (although often social interaction develops later)
    (4) Appearance of poorly coordinated gait or trunk movements
    (5) Severely impaired expressive and receptive language development with severe psychomotor retardation

---

From *The Diagnostic and Statistical Manual of Mental Disorders, Fourth Edition, Text Revision* (p. 77), by American Psychiatric Association, 2000. Washington, DC: American Psychiatric Association. Copyright 2000 by the American Psychiatric Association. Reprinted with permission.

disorder; fewer than 100 cases had been diagnosed up until 1992 (Volkmar, 1992). However, based on its inclusion in ICD-9 and ICD-10, CDD underwent a review for inclusion in DSM-IV (Volkmar & Rutter, 1995). The researchers who conducted the DSM-IV autism field trial concluded that CDD and autism shared similar symptomatology, but could be meaningfully differentiated from each other. A brief review of CDD's hallmark symptoms and their relationship to autism follows.

Researchers believe that CDD occurs much less frequently than autism (Volkmar, Klin, Marans, & Cohen, 1996). Epidemiological researchers have indicated that CDD may have a prevalence rate of 1 per 100,000 children (Burd, Fisher, & Kerbeshian, 1987), making CDD only one tenth as common as autism (Volkmar, 1992). A clinic-based study conducted over a five-year period found that 0.22% of all children seen in a child psychiatric clinic had CDD (Malhorta & Singh, 1993). Additionally, CDD is believed to be more common in males than females. The male-to-female ratio of CDD is approximately 4:1 (Volkmar, Klin, Marans, & Cohen, 1997). More recent studies have reported an even higher ratio of 5:1 (Malhorta & Gupta, 2002).

CDD is similar to Rett's Disorder in that the first 2 years of development appear to be normal. Following this period of normal development, around the age of 3 or 4, the child undergoes a rapid and abrupt deterioration in adaptive behavior. The age of onset of CDD varies from 2 to 4 years (Volkmar & Cohen, 1989), with reported mean age of onset at 3.16 years (Volkmar & Rutter, 1995) and 3.76 years (Malhorta & Gupta, 2002). After onset of the disorder, children with CDD exhibit speech deterioration or loss, which is so dramatic that it has been likened to the lack of speech development seen in autism (Volkmar et al., 1997). In addition, children with CDD also present with deterioration in self-help skills (such as toileting) and social withdrawal (Volkmar et al., 1997).

Table 1.4: DSM-IV criteria for Childhood Disintegrative Disorder (CDD)

A. Apparently normal development for at least the first 2 years after birth as manifested by the presence of age-appropriate verbal and nonverbal communication, social relationships, play, and adaptive behavior

B. Clinically significant loss of previously acquired skills (before age 10 years) in at least two of the following areas:

  (1) Expressive or receptive language
  (2) Social skills or adaptive behavior
  (3) Bowel or bladder control
  (4) Play
  (5) Motor skills

C. Abnormalities of functioning in at least two of the following areas:

  (1) Qualitative impairment in social interaction (e.g. impairment in nonverbal behaviors, failure to develop peer relationships, lack of social or emotional reciprocity)
  (2) Qualitative impairments in communication (e.g. delay or lack of spoken language, inability to initiate or sustain a conversation, stereotyped and repetitive use of language, lack of varied make-believe play)
  (3) Restricted, repetitive, and stereotyped patterns of behavior, interests, and activities, including motor stereotypies and mannerisms

D. The disturbance is not better accounted for by another specific Pervasive Developmental Disorder or by schizophrenia

From *The Diagnostic and Statistical Manual of Mental Disorders, Fourth Edition, Text Revision* (p. 79), by American Psychiatric Association, 2000. Washington, DC: American Psychiatric Association. Copyright 2000 by the American Psychiatric Association. Reprinted with permission.

In the second component of CDD a child must exhibit qualitative impairment in social interaction or communication and/or restricted, repetitive, and stereotyped patterns of behavior, interests, or activities (Table 1.4). At least two of these categories must be present. Because of this overlap in criteria, DSM-IV-TR cautions that clinicians carefully establish whether a 2-year period of normal development has occurred (APA, 2000). If a clinician is unable to document 2 years of normal development, a diagnosis of autism should be given. In closing, it is important to note that CDD is considered to be more severe than autism and includes a regression of previously acquired skills, a component that is not generally seen in autism (Malhorta & Singh, 1993).

Asperger's Syndrome

Another disorder in the autism spectrum is Asperger's Syndrome (AS). We will cover AS in slightly more detail than the other disorders as it has recently become a source of debate in the research literature and popular media. Hans Asperger first described AS in 1944. Asperger presented the case histories of four children (all male), each with five common clinical features. These five features were: social deficits, insistence on sameness, nonverbal language deficits, stereotypies, and lack of humor. Asperger described these four children as being socially awkward. The autistic quality of insistence on sameness was also present and persisted despite the normal development of cognition and personality. In terms of language, Asperger specified nonverbal language deficits because he saw in these children an absence of facial expression, gestures and eye-to-eye gaze. Also present were a number of stereotyped and repetitive behaviors. The final feature was lack of humor. Asperger noted that these children did not produce amusing remarks, despite exhibiting original thought.

Asperger's Syndrome received relatively little attention in the English literature (Volkmar, Klin, Shultz et al., 1996) until the review published by Lorna Wing in 1981. Wing listed the characteristics of AS as: (1) pedantic, lengthy speech; (2) stereotyped speech; (3) aprosodic speech; (4) impaired nonverbal communication; (5) peculiar social interaction; (6) lack of empathy; (7) repetitive activities; (8) resistance to change; (9) clumsy or stereotyped motor mannerisms; and (10) circumscribed interests. However, without a clear, empirically supported definition, AS as a label has been used in a number of ways. It has been used as a synonym for both "high-functioning autism" and PDD-NOS, as well as in reference to adults with autism and as an independent syndrome (Volkmar, Klin, Shultz et al., 1996).

Asperger's Syndrome was first included in DSM-IV (APA, 1994); therefore it is a very new diagnosis. The DSM-IV provided a description of AS that is similar to the definition of autism. In order to meet criteria for a diagnosis of AS, an individual must exhibit deficits in social interaction and have restricted patterns of interest. A qualitative impairment in social interaction is established by the presence of at least two of the following four symptoms: (1) a marked impairment in use of multiple nonverbal behaviors, such as facial expression or eye-to-eye gaze; (2) a failure to develop peer relationships that are appropriate to the individual's developmental level; (3) a lack of spontaneous seeking to share achievements and interests; and (4) a lack of social or emotional reciprocity.

The second criterion is the existence of restricted, repetitive, and stereotyped patterns of behaviors, as evinced by the presence of at least one of the following four symptoms: (1) an encompassing preoccupation with one or more stereotyped and restricted patterns of interest; (2) an apparently inflexible adherence to specific nonfunctional routines or rituals; (3) the presence of stereotyped and repetitive motor mannerisms; and (4) persistent preoccupation with parts of objects. In addition to these stereotyped behavioral patterns, the behaviors present must cause clinically significant impairment in social or occupational functioning (Table 1.5).

The similarities between the DSM-IV's definitions of AS and autism conclude at this point. The definition of autism also includes a qualitative impairment in communication, such as a lack of or delay in the development of speech, inability or impairment in initiating or sustaining conversation, stereotyped or repetitive use of language, or lack of imaginative or imitative play. However, in DSM-IV the definition of AS specifies that there must be no clinically significant general delay in language. In order to meet criteria for AS, an individual must have language appropriate to his/her developmental level. Additionally, whereas the definition of autism includes an age specifier (symptom onset must begin prior to the age of 3) no such age criterion exists for AS. Another difference between the two

Table 1.5: DSM-IV criteria for Asperger's Syndrome

A. Qualitative impairment in social interaction, as manifested by at least two of the following:

    (1) Marked impairment in the use of multiple nonverbal behaviors such as eye-to-eye gaze, facial expression, body postures, and gestures to regulate social interaction

    (2) Failure to develop peer relations appropriate to developmental level

    (3) A lack of spontaneous seeking to share enjoyment, interests, or achievements with other people (e.g. by a lack of showing, bringing, or pointing out objects of interest)

    (4) Lack of social or emotional reciprocity (give-and-take)

B. Restricted, repetitive, and stereotyped patterns of behavior, interests, and activities, as manifested by at least one of the following:

    (1) Encompassing preoccupation with one or more stereotyped and restricted patterns of interest that is abnormal either in intensity or focus

    (2) Apparently inflexible adherence to specific, nonfunctional routines or rituals

    (3) Stereotyped and repetitive motor mannerism (e.g. hand or finger flapping or twisting, or complex whole-body movements)

    (4) Persistent preoccupation with parts of objects

C. The disturbance causes clinically significant impairment in social, occupational, or other important areas of functioning

D. There is no clinically significant general delay in language (e.g. single words used by age 2 years, communicative phrases used by age 3 years)

E. There is no clinically significant delay in cognitive development or in the development of age-appropriate self-help skills, adaptive behavior (other than in social interaction), and curiosity about the environment in childhood

F. The disturbance is not better accounted for by another specific Pervasive Developmental Disorder or by schizophrenia

disorders is that to meet criteria for AS, there cannot be a clinically significant delay in cognitive development or in the development of age-appropriate self-help skills, adaptive behavior or curiosity about the environment (in children). In other words, criteria for AS cannot be met if an individual's intellectual or adaptive functioning is within the range of ID. Finally, the DSM-IV's description of AS concludes with the statement that in order to meet the diagnosis, the criteria for another specific PDD or schizophrenia cannot also be present.

Relatively recently, a debate has emerged in the literature as to the inclusion of AS within ASD. Some researchers believe that AS is merely another term for high-functioning autism, while others support the argument that AS is separate and distinct from autism. Argument for the connection between autism and AS began with Wing's (1981) initial review of the literature. Wing contended that Asperger's (1944) original report of normal development of language and cognition was incorrect. Wing stated that, with careful questioning, a history of language deficits in infancy became apparent in half of the children in her sample. AS should then be considered a less severe form of autism (Kerbeshian & Burd, 1986; Wing, 1981). Rutter (1985) also reviewed the two disorders and concluded that they were similar. Rutter emphasized that the two disorders shared abnormal communication patterns, unusual attachment to objects, and a lack of empathy for other people (Bowman, 1988; Rutter, 1985).

Szatmari, Bartolucci, and Bremner (1989) compared the history and outcome of children with AS and high-functioning autism. The children in the AS group were diagnosed using Wing's (1981) criteria and those in the high-functioning autism group were diagnosed using DSM-III criteria without strict adherence to the age cutoff. Szatmari and his colleagues (1989) reported that the two groups differed in most measures of social responsiveness, prevalence of language abnormalities, and history of bizarre preoccupations. The groups did not differ in age of onset, IQ, ability to use or understand non-verbal communication, and ease of learning fine motor activities. The authors concluded that while quantitative differences existed between the two groups, no substantive, qualitative differences were found. Thus, the authors stated, "it may be best to think of AS as a mild form of HFA [high-functioning autism]" (p. 717).

Considerable attention has also been paid to the other side of this argument. In Asperger's (1944) original account, he stated that AS could be readily differentiated from Kanner's (1943) autism. What differentiated the two disorders was age of onset, language delay, intellectual functioning, prognosis, and various other clinical features (Asperger, 1944). While many researchers have stated that characteristics of autism become apparent prior to 30 months of age (Eisenberg & Kanner, 1956; Kanner, 1943; Rutter, 1978a), AS was not supposed to be evident in children before the age of 3.

A study by Szatmari, Archer, Fisman, Streiner, and Wilson (1995) investigated the similarities and differences between children with autism and those with AS. For inclusion in the study, all children demonstrated impairments in social interaction, impairments in verbal and nonverbal communication, and repetitive, stereotyped activities. Children in the autism group also displayed evidence of abnormal language and met the autism algorithm requirements of a standardized diagnostic instrument, the Autism Diagnostic Interview (ADI; LeCouteur et al., 1989). Children in the AS group spoke in phrases by 36 months, had no history of abnormal language development and did not need to meet the ADI criterion. Szatmari et al. (1995) found that although the two groups did not differ in measures of nonverbal communication, they did differ on measures of adaptive behavior in communication and socialization and standardized tests of language skills.

In another study, Ozonoff, Rogers, and Pennington (1991) looked at the differences between children with high-functioning autism ($n = 13$) and those with AS ($n = 10$). The children in the AS group all met the ICD-10 (WHO, 1996) criteria for the disorder in that they showed impairment in social interaction and stereotyped or repetitive interests. The final criterion, no history of abnormal language development, was modified. The authors included children with age-appropriate language at the time of the study, as opposed to looking for normal language development. As a result, three of the children in the AS group had obtained an autism diagnosis at an earlier age due to aberrant language development, but now met the Ozonoff et al. (1991) criterion for AS. Ozonoff et al. (1991) based this decision on the lack of empirical research supporting normal language development in children with AS.

The authors of this study reported that the children in the high-functioning autism group had significantly higher scores on a standardized autism instrument, the CARS (Schopler et al., 1980). Thus, the AS group exhibited fewer autistic symptoms than the high-functioning autism group. The AS group also had significantly higher verbal IQ (VIQ) scores than their counterparts. However, this difference may be the product of the selection criteria used to determine the two groups. The AS group, through the criteria used, had superior language skills than the high-functioning autism group. Recognizing this limitation, Ozonoff et al. (1991) reevaluated their results by covarying for VIQ. As a result, many of the group differences, including the significantly greater theory of mind scores obtained by the Asperger's group, became only marginally significant or insignificant. These results establish the possibility that the differences between the two groups were due to language ability. Finally, the authors found that the two groups did not differ in terms of full scale IQ.

Studies in support of AS as a separate disorder and AS as high-functioning autism have both been wrought with a basic methodological problem (Szatmari et al., 1995). As has been illustrated in previous sections, the definition of both autism and AS has been changed frequently and agreed upon rarely. Thus, the criteria used to select participants are unclear or change from study to study. Without a clear understanding of the criteria used for subject selection or continuity between studies, it is nearly impossible to meaningfully compare results. Unfortunately, we see this same problem reappear when researchers attempt to obtain prevalence data.

This discussion illustrates a central focus of current research on AS. Research into the similarities and differences between high-functioning autism and AS is necessary to further our understanding of both disorders. In addition, with the inclusion of AS in DSM-IV (1994), researchers have begun to study whether AS and autism should be assessed and treated in the same manner, or whether they each require specific techniques.

Pervasive Developmental Disorder Not Otherwise Specified

The final ASD is PDD-NOS. The concept of a separate diagnostic subcategory for individuals who do not meet the criteria for a specific disorder yet evince similar characteristics is seen throughout the DSM. Examples include anxiety disorder NOS, cognitive disorder NOS, eating disorder NOS and psychotic disorder NOS, to name a few (APA, 1994). The same is true within the category of PDD, with the inclusion of PDD-NOS.

The diagnosis of PDD-NOS pertains to children with severe and pervasive impairment in social interaction, deficits in nonverbal communication, and/or stereotyped behaviors and interests who do not meet the criteria for a specific PDD (i.e. autism, AS, Rett's Disorder, CDD), schizophrenia, avoidant personality disorder, or schizotypal personality disorder.

Also included in the category of PDD-NOS is "atypical autism." The term "atypical autism" can be used to refer to children who fail to meet criteria for a diagnosis of autism due to a later age of onset, subthreshold symptomatology, and/or atypical symptomatology. More often than not, the category of PDD-NOS is used as a catchall for children whose symptom pattern does not meet the criteria for a specific ASD, yet is significantly different than the symptomatology characteristic of autism or another developmental disorder.

Conclusion

The history of defining autism and related disorders is as complex as the disorders themselves. Given this fact, it is remarkable that Leo Kanner's (1943) original description of the symptoms of 11 children with autism has stood the test of time so well. In the 40 years between Kanner and autism's appearance in DSM-III (APA, 1980), the disorder underwent numerous revisions in diagnostic criteria and definition. In the past 25 years, researchers and clinicians have only begun to understand the scope of ASD, the idiosyncratic differences in both cause and presentation of autism and the related disorders in this spectrum, and the countless factors that influence diagnosis and prognosis.

Through the contributions of individuals such as Michael Rutter (1978) and Edward Ritvo (1978), ASD has risen from an obscure disorder thought to affect a relatively small number of children from upper class, white families, to its current position, which implies ASD occurs in all strata of society. Students and clinicians alike are urged to read these original writings in order to fully appreciate the pioneering work of those who have come before them and to understand the number of questions that remain unanswered. As we will discuss in our review of the prevalence, etiology, assessment, and treatment of ASD, the remaining questions are both numerous and of vital importance.

The remaining chapters of our book will provide a critical appraisal of etiology and prevalence and of the current knowledge regarding the assessment and treatment of ASD in early childhood. Many causes of ASD have been espoused. To date, some promising hypotheses exist, but limited definitive explanations are available. Assessment and treatment are different. Well-established methods for diagnosing ASD and assessing strengths and weaknesses are available, especially with regard to the learning-based interventions that have been developed for young children with ASD. We will attempt to critically review the current state of the art for assessment and treatment of young children with ASD.

Chapter 2

Etiology and Prevalence

History of Etiology

Beginning

The etiology of ASD remains one of the primary controversies in the field of mental health and one of the most controversial topics in the ASD literature. Explanations have spanned psychogenic, genetic, and neurochemical factors. An entire volume could be filled with the numerous debates, ideas, research, and speculation on etiology. Because the primary focus of this text is intervention, we do not have the space here to cover many of these topics. Therefore, only a brief review of the main etiological theories will be provided.

The initial theory regarding the origins of ASD focused on parental pathology. The origins of this hypothesis appeared in Kanner's first publication, in 1943, on infantile ASD (he used the term autism, but in this chapter we use the term ASD to cover all autistic disorders). He made several observations regarding parents of children with ASD. Kanner wrote that very few mothers and fathers of children with ASD were really warmhearted and that most of the parents seemed strongly preoccupied with scientific, literary, or artistic pursuits and were "limited in genuine interest in people" (p. 250). It is important to note that at the time of this writing it was likely that high level professionals and others of wealth were about the only parents with the means to pursue treatment. Nonetheless, Kanner questioned the degree to which the parents' personalities contributed to their children's conditions. He concluded, "we must, then, assume that these children have come into the world with innate inability to form the usual, biologically provided affective contact with people" (p. 250). However, Kanner had only seen a small number of children and these observations were based on casual observation. In addition, psychodynamic theory was predominant at the time, as opposed to biological or learning theories, which undoubtedly contributed to the idea that "deficiencies" of the parents were more than coincidental. As better data collection methods and general theories of behavioral functioning evolved, so did etiological explanations of ASD.

From these statements, however, the first etiological theory of ASD arose. Professionals at the time believed ASD to be an affective disorder resulting from the environment created by the parents. Some professionals, for example, viewed childhood schizophrenia and infantile ASD on a continuum. Kanner's observations merged with the prevailing psychoanalytic theory of the 1950s and 1960s. Thus, ASD, like most psychiatric disorders during this period, was considered to be an emotional disturbance. Concluding his first writing on the topic, Kanner himself called ASD an "inborn autistic disturbances of affective contact" (Kanner, 1943, p. 250).

Psychodynamic Theory

Psychodynamic theories were propagated through the work of Herbert Eveloff (1960) and then later and most notably by Bruno Bettelheim (1967). Eveloff described several case studies, concluding with a theory of etiology that focused on mothers who were cold, impersonal, and ritualistic and fathers who were detached, perfectionistic, intellectual, and did little to protect the children from their mothers. As Eveloff (1960) put it, "These parents are in a sense successfully autistic adults" (p. 90). Bettelheim (1967) also ascribed to this theory. He proposed a rather simple explanation for ASD: mothers who were cold and unloving raised children with social and developmental problems. Bettelheim thus coined the phrase "refrigerator mothers." Putting blame on parents established yet another, and as it turned out, undue burden on the family. Later, parent groups reacted negatively to Bettelheim and his associates.

While Kanner was careful to state that ASD could not be entirely attributed to parent–child relationships, he planted the seed for further psychogenic explanations of ASD. These theories were developed further, with Bettelheim (1967) also noting possessiveness on the part of the mother. The momentum caused by these early events endured until the 1990s. In Chapter 5, we will further discuss the role that Bettelheim played in the early conceptualization of ASD, especially in regard to treatment. By placing the blame for the development of ASD on the parents, Bettelheim eventually met with resentment from parents and professionals alike. With the rise of behaviorism and an emphasis on data-based studies in peer-reviewed journals, as opposed to parent reports or testimonials, the psychodynamic theory of ASD was replaced by genetic, neurobiological, and learning theories, all of which provide empirical research to support their hypotheses.

Current Etiological Theories

Genetic Evidence

Without research to support them, and because their negative view of parents energized families against them, psychodynamic theories eventually gave way to theories proposing genetic and physiological causes (Rimland, 1964). Originally, however, genetic theories were given little credence for at least three reasons (Rutter, 1967). First, children with ASD rarely had parents with ASD. Second, no chromosomal anomaly could be identified as a marker for the disorder. And third, the rate of ASD within sibling pairs was thought to be low (Rutter, 1967). While the first two arguments are now considered accurate, researchers were skeptical of the third argument and began to investigate the nature of sibling concordance. This line of research, which primarily relied on twin studies, proved to be fruitful and markedly changed how the development of ASD is viewed.

One of the first important studies aimed at identifying these genetic links was conducted by Folstein and Rutter (1977). Their small twin study examined 11 pairs of monozygotic (MZ) twins and 10 pairs of dizygotic (DZ) twins. One child in each pair had a diagnosis of ASD. Folstein and Rutter (1977) found a 36% pair wise concordance rate for ASD in the MZ, as opposed to 0% for the DZ twins. The authors noted that, despite the small sample size, the concordance rates for ASD between MZ and DZ twins were significantly different. While no specific biological structures were identified, the contrast in results was revealing when one considers that the incidence for all ASDs and Pervasive Developmental Disorders (PDDs) is believed to be 35 to 60 per 10,000 (Chakrabarti & Fombonne, 2005). These data suggest that close genetic similarities result in ASD rates greater than chance. This research helped to rule out causes that were primarily due to the environment. Other twin studies followed and similar results were reported. Ritvo et al. (1985), for example, studied 23 pairs of MZ and 17 pairs of DZ twins. They observed a 95.7% concordance rate among the MZ twins as opposed to a 23.5% rate among the DZ twins.

These findings were promising. However, methodological problems were present. Results must be viewed cautiously due to possible selection bias and lack of random sampling (Pauls, 1987; Phelps & Grabowski, 1991). The potential value of these data, however, warranted further study to account for the methodological shortfalls of the previous studies. Bailey et al. (1995), for one, confirmed the disparity in concordance rates between MZ and DZ twins. In their British twin study, the concordance rate for ASD among MZ twins was 60%, whereas the concordance rate for DZ twins was only 5%. The authors stated that this pattern of heritability did not support a single-gene Mendelian disorder, but rather an interaction among several genes. Additionally, 90% of the MZ twins were found to be concordant for a mixture of social and cognitive deficits that were similar to ASD, indicating that a broader phenotype might exist. Nonetheless, the replication of these data supported the notion that biological factors were causative and that the next step would be to attempt to isolate the specific mechanisms causing the disorder.

These data helped to debunk psychodynamic explanations of ASD's etiology. However, the goal of isolating specific mechanisms has proven to be much more difficult. In a follow-up to the Folstein and Rutter (1977) study, LeCouteur et al. (1996) also found evidence of a broader phenotype associated with deficits in social skills and cognition that extended into adulthood for MZ twins. Even though the MZ twins shared identical genes, there was a great deal of heterogeneity in the characteristics of ASD present. The authors also found that the concordant MZ twins were no more alike in IQ or symptomatology than randomly assigned matches. The authors believed this indicated a genetic basis for ASD that was not the same in every individual.

Family studies constituted another line of research into potential genetic factors in the etiology of ASD. Such studies looked at the concordance rates of ASD among non-twin siblings and potentially the offspring of individuals with ASD. Many factors could influence the concordance rates found among families (Lauritsen & Ewald, 2001), including the fact that families having a child with ASD may limit the number of additional children due to the difficulties involved in raising a child with a disability and the knowledge that genetic risk factors play a role in the condition (Jones & Szatmari, 1988). Additionally, the lack of studies on the offspring of individuals with ASD limits the conclusions that can be drawn. The latter point is most likely due to the nature of social deficits in ASD limiting the extent of romantic relationships and thus reducing the likelihood that these individuals will have children of their own. Two long-term follow-up studies on individuals with ASD found that none of the individuals being tracked had married or had children (Larsen & Mouridesen, 1997; Rutter, 1970). This finding further added to the complexity of establishing the root cause of the condition.

Several studies have looked at the rate of ASD among siblings. Typically, researchers reported the rate of ASD among siblings to be around 3% (August, Stewart, & Tsai, 1981; Bolton et al., 1994; Piven et al., 1990; Smalley, Asarnow, & Spence, 1988). Other researchers reported the occurrence of ASD in sibling pairs to be as high as 5.9% (Baird & August, 1985), although the sample in this study was rather small ($n = 29$). While these concordance rates may appear minimal, it is important to compare them to the prevalence of ASD in the general population. When compared to a modest estimate of general population prevalence (3/10,000) the sibling prevalence rate is about 100 times greater (Lauritsen & Ewald, 2001). If one were to use a larger estimate of general population prevalence (1/1,000), then the sibling prevalence would be 30 times greater (Lauritsen & Ewald, 2001). Thus, when put in the context of general population numbers, these data are considerably more impressive.

Other researchers have studied the broader phenotype of social and cognitive deficits reported in previous research (Bailey et al., 1995; Folstein & Rutter, 1977; LeCouteur et al., 1996). Bolton et al. (1994) compared the families of individuals with ASD ($n = 99$) to the families of individuals with Down's Syndrome. Six percent of the siblings of children with ASD showed symptoms of a PDD (3% with ASD symptoms and an additional 3% with symptoms of the broader phenotype), whereas none of the siblings in the Down's group had PDD symptoms. These data further illustrated the presence of ASD behaviors in the families of children with ASD, even if the siblings' symptoms did not reach clinical severity necessary for a diagnosis. Continued research into the broader phenotype of autism is obviously required before a full understanding of these factors can be reached.

Genetic research into the etiology of ASD has received increasing attention over the last three or four decades (since1977). Strong evidence exists for a genetic component in the development of ASD, but the nature of this component remains unknown. It does not appear as though a single gene is responsible for the symptoms seen in ASD, as has been noted by numerous studies that show a high concordance of the broader autistic phenotype in siblings. Future researchers will most likely continue to search for specific genes that account for the presentation of ASD. The ultimate goal of genetic research would be to apply gene therapy to reverse the effects of ASD or possibly even prevent it (Tsai, 1999b), although this goal may prove to be overly simplistic in the face of the other etiologic theories still to be discussed. Also, such treatment would assume a primary or perhaps exclusive genetic etiology. If the disorder is multifactorial, such a cure would not be feasible. Research in this area has been expensive and little progress has occurred in recent years. These data are in stark contrast to the poorer funded learning-based research that has produced, if not a cure, then at least substantial improvement in the lives of many individuals with ASD.

Neurobiological Theories

Another line of research has looked for potential neurobiological factors that might underpin the origins of ASD. As Tsai (1999b) pointed out, nearly 75% of individuals with ASD have cognitive functioning within the intellectual disability (ID) range, which indicates that an underlying neurological and/or biological abnormality should be considered as a possible cause. Both neurological and neurochemical etiologies have been researched over the past decades, with the area of neurobiology being given increasing attention in the etiological literature. Neurobiological studies have utilized various forms of brain imaging, including magnetic resonance imagining (MRI), computerized axial tomography (CT) and positron emission tomography (Tsai, 1999b), and have investigated the effectiveness of medications (Lam, Aman, & Arnold, in press). This section will focus on the research being conducted in the area of neurological and neurochemical causes of ASD.

Neurological abnormalities have been reported in 30–50% of children with ASD (DeMyer et al., 1973; Tsai, Stewart, & August, 1981). Examples of some of the neurological abnormalities found in this population include clumsiness, gait disturbances, drooling, tremor, abnormal posture, and emotional facial paralysis (Tsai, 1999b). The most common neurological disorder found in children with ASD is epilepsy, which is believed to occur in 18–42% of individuals with ASD (Kawasaki, Yokota, Shinomiya, Shimizu, & Niwa, 1997). Several types of epilepsy have been reported, including psychomotor (Minshew, 1991; Olsson, Steffenburg, & Gillberg, 1988) and temporal lobe epilepsy (Olsson et al., 1988). The onset of epilepsy in children with ASD appears to be bimodal, with an increase in onset at age 5 and another after the age of 12 (Minshew, Sweeney, Bauman, & Webb, 2005). Although the link between ASD and epilepsy was helpful in disposing of the psychodynamic etiological theories (Minshew et al., 2005), no specific electrical activity unique to ASD has been found (Minshew, 1991; Prior, 1987). Researchers are still unsure of the cause of these neurological abnormalities and the pathways that lead to ASD (Tsai, 1999b). Nevertheless, epilepsy can be a serious problem for children with ASD and its high rate of occurrence in ASD provides evidence of a common genetic basis between the two disorders (Minshew et al., 2005).

Neurobiological research has also been focused on neurochemical abnormalities as an etiological factor in ASD. According to Tsai (1999a), interest in a neurochemical model has stemmed from the lack of identifiable brain pathology in individuals with ASD, indicating that the abnormalities may exist at a chemical level. The largest influence on neurochemical research has come from studies on the effectiveness of psychotropic medications as a treatment for various psychological disorders (Lam et al., in press). Neurochemical studies have focused on neurotransmitters, which are chemicals in the brain that are responsible for carrying signals across the synapses between neurons (Tsai, 1999b).

Serotonin
Several neurotransmitters have been posited to play a role in the expression of ASD. Serotonin is one of the most widely studied neurotransmitters and is believed to be highly involved in neuropsychopharmacology in general (Cooper, Bloom, & Roth, 2003). Serotonin has been implicated in a vast number of human behaviors, including eating, sleeping, sexual activity, and mood regulation (Lam et al., in press). Therefore, it is not surprising that serotonin has been the most studied neurotransmitter in ASD research (Anderson & Hoshino, 2005; Volkmar & Anderson, 1989). The majority of serotonin studies on ASD have focused on the levels of serotonin circulating in the bloodstream (Anderson & Hoshino, 2005). A study by Anderson and Hoshino (1987), for example, found that the group mean blood serotonin level in autistic subjects was 17% to 128% higher than in controls. While Anderson

and Hoshino's (1987) results have been replicated, it is important to note that the serotonin levels in the autistic sample appeared to be normally distributed (Yuwiler, Geller, & Ritvo, 1985). In addition, the mechanism for this possible serotonin elevation remains unclear, as the storage of serotonin in the blood of children with ASD appears to be normal (Anderson, Minderaa, van Bentem, Volkmar, & Cohen, 1984). One also cannot ignore the research into the therapeutic effects of serotonergic drugs, specifically fenfluramine, which, as we will discuss in Chapter 6, have produced a reduction in the symptoms of ASD (Anderson & Hoshino, 2005).

Opioids

Another neurotransmitter group that has received attention in the literature are endogenous opioids. Opioids are naturally produced by the body (i.e. endogenous) and display pharmacological properties similar to morphine (Cooper et al., 2003). Opioids primarily affect the central nervous system, and opiate administration can result in behavioral symptoms such as stereotyped behaviors, insensitivity to pain, and reduced socialization (Lam et al., in press). Because these behaviors are also present in ASD, research has been conducted investigating the possible role of opioids in ASD.

Several researchers have shown elevated endogenous opioid levels in samples of children with ASD (e.g. Gillberg, Terenius, & Lonnerholm, 1985; Ross, Klykylo & Hitzmann, 1985), specifically those with self-injury and stereotypies (Sandman, Barron, Chizcdemet, & Demet, 1991). The theory behind this line of research was that elevated endogenous opioid levels in children with ASD resemble those seen in the perinatal period of normal development (Cammisa & Hobbs, 1993). This elevated endogenous opioid level may interfere with the development of social and emotional systems and interrupt normal childhood attachment. The lack of attachment leads to a social indifference and lack of desire to communicate (Sahley & Panksepp, 1987), which in turn leads to language deficits. This hypothesis also purports to account for the abnormalities in attention processes and sensory modulation also found in ASD, as both these systems are influenced by endogenous opioids (Sandyk & Gillman, 1986).

Research into the neurobiology of ASD is still a relatively young area. A clear biological mechanism of action behind the etiology of ASD has yet to be proposed. Despite agreement about the potential neurochemical factors in ASD, psychotropic medications have become alarmingly common as a form of treatment for children with ASD, as we will further discuss in Chapter 6.

Measles, Mumps, and Rubella Vaccine

Another theory concerning the etiology of ASD has looked at the possibility of an environmental insult after birth. This theory was proposed in the late 1990s based on a research study conducted by Wakefield et al. (1998). They concluded that ASD was related to the administration of the measles, mumps, and rubella (MMR) vaccine. This finding produced a great stir among the popular press, advocates, and practitioners. The media attention given to Wakefield's study has most likely equaled or surpassed that given to any other etiological theory of ASD and rivals that given to just about any other behavioral or mental health disorder we are aware of in the last 50 years. As a result, this study's impact on popular views regarding the cause of ASD has far exceeded its merit. Unfortunately, what is portrayed in the popular media is often premature science based on preliminary findings. Often, what the press focuses on is science that is particularly novel or odd, or the information may be somewhat arbitrarily selected. For clinicians and researchers, however, questions from parents, the press and others regarding the safety of immunizations seem inescapable. Therefore, a brief historical overview follows.

In the United States, the MMR vaccine was licensed for use in 1971 and almost completely replaced the independent measles, mumps, and rubella vaccinations during the 1970s (Dales, Hammer, & Smith, 2001). The composition of the US MMR vaccine has not changed since 1979. Currently, the Centers for Disease Control (CDC) in the United States recommends that all children receive the MMR vaccine (CDC, 2003). Typically, children receive their first dosage between 12 and 15 months of age and the second dosage between 4 and 6 years of age. The CDC reported that the most common side-effect of the MMR vaccine in children is fever, followed by minor rash (CDC, 2003). If side-effects do occur, they are usually evident within 7 to 12 days post-vaccination. Until recently, however, no serious long-term side-effects such as ASD were considered.

In 1998, a British physician, Andrew Wakefield, and colleagues published a study of 12 children with PDD and gastrointestinal disease. The study's purpose was to investigate the relationship between gastrointestinal problems and PDD. The 12 children included 11 boys and 1 girl referred to a pediatric gastroenterology department. All of the children had a history of a PDD and intestinal symptoms, such as diarrhea, abdominal pain, bloating, and food intolerance.

According to parent interview, all children achieved early developmental milestones on time. In 8 of the 12 children, the onset of behavioral problems was linked to their MMR vaccination by either the parents or the child's physician. Five of the children had allergic reactions to the MMR vaccination and 3 of the 5 had convulsions. The average interval of exposure for the 8 children was 6.3 days (range 1–14 days). However, the onset of gastrointestinal symptoms was unclear because the children either were not toilet trained or were unable to communicate symptoms.

Wakefield et al. (1998) felt that their evidence, along with other studies showing intestinal symptoms in children with ASD, "would support the hypothesis that the consequences of an inflamed or dysfunctional intestine may play a part in behavioural changes in some children" (p. 639). Wakefield et al. (1998) cited several studies that proposed that both the measles virus and measles vaccination are risk factors for Crohn's disease.

Wakefield et al.'s theory was that the MMR vaccine led to impaired intestinal functioning. The permeability of the intestines increased, allowing for excessive absorption of gut-derived peptides from foods. These peptides have opioid effects on the central nervous system. As stated in the opioid hypothesis of ASD, opioid excess led to disruption in brain development. This opioid excess is thought to be ultimately responsible for the development of autistic behaviors. This theory directed researchers to look at the number of ASD cases in England after 1988 because in 1988 the British government instituted a vaccination campaign targeted at all children who had never received the MMR vaccine.

Since Wakefield et al.'s first article in 1998 on the causal relationship between ASD and the MMR vaccine, numerous studies have been conducted and found evidence to refute

Wakefield et al.'s claims. One of the first such responses to Wakefield et al. (1998) came from Chen and DeStefano (1998). They called for a clinical or epidemiological study to determine whether the rate of ASD (or any disorder for that matter) in those vaccinated exceeded the rate of ASD in unvaccinated controls. Chen and DeStefano (1998) also pointed out that since the original measles vaccine was introduced in the mid-1960s, hundreds of millions of people had received the vaccine and had not developed gastrointestinal or behavioral problems. The authors also pointed to a selection and recall bias in Wakefield et al.'s study with respect to selection only of children with gastrointestinal problems and parent recall of the onset of behavioral problems.

In another study, Peltola et al. (1998) looked at the incidence of gastrointestinal symptoms in children vaccinated with MMR in Finland. Nearly three million MMR dosages were administered between 1982 and 1996, with children receiving two doses, one at 14–18 months and another at 6 years. Peltola et al. (1998) looked at all children who developed gastrointestinal signs or symptoms lasting at least 24 hours after having received the MMR injection. Data were collected through a reporting system established by Finland's National Board of Health and National Public Health Institute. A total of 31 children developed gastrointestinal symptoms after vaccination, 30 of which occurred after the initial dose. None of the children developed ASD. Peltola et al.'s research is just one example of a large sample study that demonstrated no relationship between MMR vaccine administration and ASD.

In another study, Taylor et al. (1999) investigated 498 cases of ASD, Asperger's Syndrome (AS) and atypical ASD from 1979 to 1992 in eight health districts in the North Thames region in the United Kingdom. ASD diagnoses were confirmed for 293 of the subjects using ICD-10 criteria. The authors analyzed the data by using a time series regression allowing for a "step-up" in birth cohorts from 1987 to 1992, as well as differing exponential trends prior to and after 1987. The "step-up" was intended to account for changes in the trend line after the introduction of the MMR vaccine in 1987. The authors reported a steady increase in the number of cases per birth cohort (i.e. year of birth). The number of cases reached a peak in the early 1990s, followed by a dip below the expected trend. The authors attributed this decline to possible delays in diagnosis. No sudden "step-up" in the number of ASD cases was noted after 1987, nor were there changes in the trend line after the introduction of the MMR vaccination. In addition, the age of diagnosis was independent of whether the child had been vaccinated and there was no evidence of temporal clustering between MMR vaccination and the number of ASD diagnoses.

Dales and colleagues (2001) also explored the possible correlation between MMR vaccination rates and ASD diagnoses in California. Immunization records of children born between 1980 and 1994 enrolled in Californian kindergartens and ASD caseloads of the California Department of Developmental Services were reviewed. The percentage of children 17 to 24 months of age who received MMR vaccinations between 1980 and 1987 was virtually unchanged. In 1988, there was an increase in immunization, followed by another plateau in percentage of children vaccinated. Overall, from 1980 to 1994 there was a 14% increase in the number of children receiving the MMR vaccine before 24 months of age (from 72% in 1980 to 82% in 1994). Analysis of the number of cases of ASD during this same time period showed an increase from 176 cases in 1980 to 1,182 in 1994 (a 572% increase). The authors noted that if it was expected that an increase in MMR vaccinations would yield an increase in ASD cases, then a trend in ASD cases similar to that seen in the prevalence of vaccinations would have been expected. Instead, the number of ASD cases continued to rise beyond what would have been predicted by the increase in the number of vaccinations.

It is possible that the temporal relationship between MMR vaccination and onset of autistic symptoms occurred by chance alone (Dales et al., 2001; Nicholl, Elliman, & Ross, 1998). This hypothesis may be especially true considering the average age of symptom onset in ASD is 18 to 19 months (Siegel, Pliner, Eschler, & Elliot, 1988) and MMR vaccinations are generally administered around 12 to 15 months (Dales et al., 2001).

There were, however, several major methodological flaws in Wakefield et al.'s (1998) study. First, the authors did not discuss the specific diagnoses of the children or how diagnoses were determined. Second, no clear chronological course was determined (the onset of gastrointestinal problems was unknown). Third, the evidence for the link between behavior changes and MMR vaccine came from parent and physician reports. Finally, Wakefield et al. (1998) did not propose a specific mechanism of action behind the relationship between the MMR vaccine and the development of ASD. Instead, Wakefield et al. (1998) reported correlations of insufficient power to be considered a reasonable explanation for the etiology of ASD.

The consensus among leading researchers and medical organizations, including the American Academy of Pediatrics (Halsey & Hyman, 2001), Institute of Medicine (Stratton, Gable, Shetty, & McCormick, 2001), and the British Medicines Commission Agency/Committee on Safety of Medicines (1999), has been that there is no causal relationship between the MMR vaccination and ASD. The CDC strongly warned parents against delaying their children's MMR vaccine or, even worse, not administering the vaccine at all. Finally, in 2004, 10 of the 13 researchers associated with the original study by Wakefield et al. (1998) published an article in the medical journal, *Lancet*, retracting the conclusions made in the original article (Murch et al., 2004).

We have chosen to focus on the MMR vaccine since it has received so much media attention. This proposed cause of ASD is just one in a long line of possible causes which appear to be dead ends. Research of this type should be encouraged. However, a major concern from our perspective is the pattern of rushing to judgment based on initial and often sparse data. Additionally, there often appears to be a willingness to discard older, better-researched explanations for new, less data-based theories. Patience and caution must be exercised in greater measure despite the urging of parents desperate for a cure who want to jump on every new theory or intervention. Particularly troubling are the often well-meaning but exaggerated claims and potentially life-threatening results of new methods or theories. The MMR vaccine research illustrates how a potential health hazard may result from parents deciding not to immunize their children because of one study with exaggerated and unfounded claims which attracted a disproportionate amount of attention from the popular media.

Unfortunately, Wakefield et al.'s (1998) study provides an example of one piece of research, not supported by empirical data, which has been blown out of proportion by the popular media and word of mouth. However, we will see the gastrointestinal etiology of ASD appear again when we look at secretin as a pharmacological treatment in Chapter 6.

Learning Theory

In the chapters that follow, we will shift our focus to the assessment and treatment of ASD. Of the current theoretical treatment orientations, behavioral treatments have received the greatest amount of research attention and researchers have demonstrated much greater effectiveness with behavioral interventions than with other methods. Therefore, an understanding of how learning theory attempts to explain the etiology of autism is warranted.

The first attempt to understand the etiology of ASD from a behavioral perspective came from Ferster in 1961. According to Ferster, ASD was the result of a failure of social stimuli (e.g. attention, praise, etc.) to gain the reinforcing properties required to control behavior. The reason for the lack of reinforcement from social stimuli was considered to be deficient parenting. Ferster and DeMeyer (1961) did, however, demonstrate that children with ASD could learn new behaviors (lever pulling in this case) when food was used as reinforcement. Although, we now know that deficient parenting is not related to the development of ASD, Ferster's work was important in demonstrating the ability of environmental stimuli to control the behavior of children with ASD.

As learning theorists endeavored to further understand ASD, several observations were made. As Lovaas and Smith (1989) pointed out, children with ASD were more heterogeneous than homogeneous as a group. In other words, children with ASD are different in more ways than they are alike. Lovaas and Smith (1989) believed that the vast number of individual differences seen in children with ASD indicated that these children have very little in common with each other, thus refuting the notion of a diagnosable ASD group. The next observation was that many of the behaviors considered to be characteristic of ASD are seen in typical child development (Lovaas & Smith, 1989). For example, stereotypic behaviors are common in typically developing infants (Kravitz & Boehm, 1971) and are thought to be related to cognitive and motor development (Berkson, 1983). Because of these factors and others, learning theorists have proposed their own model of the development of ASD.

The behavioral theory of ASD is composed of four basic tenets, as described by Lovaas and Smith (1989). The first tenet was that the laws of learning theory adequately account for the behaviors seen in ASD and that learning theory provides a foundation for the treatment of ASD. The principles of reinforcement and punishment that are at the core of learning theory have been used with great success in the treatment of ASD, thus bolstering the argument. The second tenet was that the behaviors characteristic of ASD are developmental delays and not a central problem whose correction will result in overall improvement. This notion was quite different than the etiological theories proposed above. For example, neurochemical theories posited that one or a combination of neurochemical abnormalities are responsible for the behaviors seen in ASD. A logical extrapolation of this model is that if the neurochemical abnormalities can be identified and rectified, then the behaviors of ASD should improve or disappear altogether. Behavioral theorists, however, view ASD as a series of separate behavior problems that should be considered a developmental delay due to the presence of these behaviors in typically developing young children (Rutter, 1978b). The third tenet of behavioral theory was that children with ASD could learn in specially constructed environments. In other words, the environments of children with ASD could be manipulated to address the function of specific behaviors. The fourth and final tenet was that an incompatibility existed between the normal environment and the nervous systems of children with ASD in that these children are not successful in the normal environment. This tenet places equal emphasis on the environment and the child, as opposed to considering ASD to be a disease that can be cured. Lovaas and Smith (1989) believed that when modifications are made to the normal environment, children with ASD have the ability to learn and be successful. Therefore, ASD is not a disease in the same way that it is conceptualized in other etiological models.

According to Lovaas and Smith (1989), behaviorally oriented theorists made several important choices in deciding how to study autism. The first was to focus on the separate behaviors that constitute ASD, and not the construct of ASD itself. By focusing on individual behaviors, such as self-injury or expressive language, the behavior therapist is afforded more precise measurement and able to address problems that may not be faced by every child with ASD (Lovaas & Smith, 1989). Additionally, behavior therapy is concentrated on the child's environment in order to identify interventions and not the etiology of the disorder. This approach allows for the manipulation of direct cause-and-effect relationships instead of relying on parental report of early history. As will be seen in the discussion of behavioral treatments in the coming chapters of this volume, these choices have informed the way in which behavior therapists view ASD and the way they approach treating the specific behaviors associated with ASD.

Current Status of Etiological Theories

By providing a broad overview of the different etiological theories it is our hope that the reader will better understand the complexity of this issue. No one "cause" of ASD has been identified and the status of current researchers' opinions is that the cause is likely multifactorial. While several theories have been discounted, researchers continue to produce evidence that supports and refutes the remaining theories. Clinicians and students remain faced with answering one of parents' most pressing questions, "Why does my child have ASD?"

At this time, researchers suggest that genetic influences are the most important risk factor for the development of ASD (Rutter, 2005). We do not wish to imply that genes are the only cause of ASD. Genetics no doubt provide a necessary predisposition for ASD, but the fact that MZ twin concordance is not 100% indicates that other variables are also in play. Multiple etiological pathways are most likely involved in ASD. An example of this theory can be seen in the diversity of disorders that fall under the category of ASDs. On the one hand, we have Rett's Disorder, which has a specific, identifiable genetic abnormality at its core. Yet, children with Rett's Disorder evince many of the same behavioral excesses and deficits as children with Asperger's Syndrome, despite the fact that there is no known genetic etiology for Asperger's Syndrome. Future research will hopefully cut across disciplines and begin to look at combinations of genetic, neurological, neurochemical, and environmental factors and how the interplay between these results in the spectrum of symptoms seen in ASD.

Prevalence of ASD

Introduction

An issue that has received increasing attention over the past few years is the prevalence of ASD. Everyone is in agreement that more children are being identified with ASD today compared to 60 years ago. The question, however, is why has the prevalence of ASD increased, especially in the last 10 years? This issue is a major point for debate among researchers, clinicians, and parents. One position is that the increase in diagnosed cases of ASD is the result of expanding diagnostic criteria and public awareness of the disorder. The second position is that we currently are experiencing an "epidemic" of ASD. Before addressing this debate we will first examine current knowledge regarding the prevalence of ASD.

Kanner appreciated the rarity of ASD when he reported that out of the 20,000 emotionally disturbed children he had assessed in his 30 years of practice, he had only seen approximately 150 children with ASD. The issue of rarity and causality was first formally addressed in an epidemiological study of ASD conducted in the 1960s in England (Lotter, 1966). Lotter investigated the rates of ASD and childhood schizophrenia among children aged 8, 9, and 10 years in the county of Middlesex. Lotter (1966) found a rate of 2.1/10,000 for ASD. An additional 2.4/10,000 children presented with many of the symptoms of ASD but not enough for a complete diagnosis. Thus, we see that even in the 1960s researchers were aware of the broader phenotype of ASD that geneticists are still studying (see previous discussion in Etiology section).

Recent Studies

In 1999, Eric Fombonne published a review of 23 epidemiological studies published from 1966 to 1998. The 23 studies were conducted in 12 countries in predominately urban or mixed (urban and rural) areas (Fombonne, 1999). The populations surveyed ranged from 5,120 to 899,750 children, with a median population of 73,301 subjects. Most of the studies utilized a multi-stage screening process. In the first stage, letters or brief screening instruments were sent to health care professionals, schools and other agencies in order to identify potential cases (Fombonne, 1999). The populations that were screened varied greatly from study to study. Some studies screened extensive populations, such as all school-aged children (Lotter, 1966), while others screened previously identified cases in medical or educational facilities (e.g. Fombonne & du Mazuabrun, 1992; Fombonne, du Mazaubrun, Cans, & Grandjean, 1997; Treffert, 1970).

The second stage of the screening process usually required an intensive ASD assessment (Fombonne, 1999). A wide variety of instruments and methods were used during the assessment phase, including parent interview, record review, direct observation, and a variety of psychological tests commonly used to diagnose ASD (e.g. CARS, ABC, ADI, described in Chapter 3). Additionally, the criteria used for diagnosis also varied by study. In Fombonne's (1999) review of 23 studies, three papers were described that used Kanner's (1943) criteria, one used Rutter's (1978a) criteria, one used Rutter's (1978a) criteria without strict adherence to the age of onset criterion, six studies used DSM-III, two used DSM-III-R, five used ICD-10 with or without author-determined variations, five used some type of ASD rating scale or clinical judgment. One needs only to refer to the previous chapter's discussion on the evolution of the diagnosis of ASD to see that these criteria are not necessarily equivalent.

Fombonne (1999) found that overall prevalence rates ranged from 0.7/10,000 to 21.1/10,000, with a median rate of 5.2/10,000. Fombonne (1999) also reported a significant negative correlation between prevalence rate and sample size. The studies with smaller sample size tended to report larger prevalence rates. Additionally, Fombonne looked at the difference in prevalence rate when studies were divided by time around the median publication year (1988). In other words, studies conducted from 1966 to 1988 were compared with those conducted from 1989 to 1998. The median prevalence rate for the 12 studies in 1966–1988 was 4.3/10,000, whereas the median prevalence rate for the 11 studies in 1989–1998 was 7.2/10,000. Fombonne (1999) stated that this comparison indicates an increased prevalence of ASD in the latter decade, most likely due to more accurate diagnosis of the disorder and the broader diagnostic concept that evolved over that time period. In 2003, Fombonne published an update to his 1999 study that included more recent epidemiological studies. Table 2.1 presents a comprehensive list of studies on the epidemiology of autism.

By looking more closely at several recent epidemiological studies, we can further appreciate the problems that Fombonne (1999) pointed out in his earlier review. In 2001, Magnusson and Saemundsen investigated the prevalence of ASD in Iceland. These researchers sampled two cohorts of children referred for PDDs to government-funded assessment and treatment centers in Iceland. The first cohort comprised children born between 1974 and 1983 (15–24 years old at the time of the study) and the second cohort comprised children born between 1984 and 1993 (5–14 years old at the time of the study). A diagnosis of ASD was made using either the ICD-9 criteria (in the older cohort) or with a combination of the ADI-R and CARS scores (in the younger cohort). The ADI-R diagnoses were based on ICD-10's diagnostic criteria and in order to meet the criteria set for this study, a child had to fulfill diagnostic criteria in at least two of the ADI-R's three domains (i.e. impaired social interaction, impaired communication, or restricted, repetitive, or stereotyped patterns of interests or behavior). CARS scores had to be equal to or greater than 30. Finally, in this second set of criteria, a clinician's diagnosis had to also be in agreement with both the ADI-R and CARS results.

In the population of 42,403 children in the older cohort, 16 were diagnosed with ASD and 2 were diagnosed with atypical ASD. This approach resulted in a prevalence rate of 3.8/10,000 for ASD and 4.2/10,000 when atypical ASD is included. The younger cohort consisted of 43,153 children, 37 of whom were diagnosed with ASD while 20 were diagnosed with atypical ASD. The prevalence rate of ASD in the younger cohort was 8.6/10,000 for ASD and rose to 13.2/10,000 when atypical ASD was included. The authors also pointed out that the confidence intervals for the two cohorts' prevalence rates did not overlap.

While these numbers may be considered evidence of the growing prevalence of individuals identified as having ASD, it is vital that we return to the question of diagnosis. It is important to note that 72% of the older cohort was diagnosed based on ICD-9 criteria, whereas only 11% of the younger cohort was diagnosed using ICD-9 (Magnusson & Saemundsen, 2001). In light of the fact that different diagnostic criteria were being used, it is clear that these two groups are not comparable.

While the comparative aspect of Magnusson and Saemundsen's (2001) study may not have provided a great deal of information, the study did include descriptive information regarding the children's level of intelligence. Using a combination of instruments, such as the Bayley Scales of Infant Development (Bayley, 1993), Leiter International Performance Scale (Levine, 1982), Peabody Picture Vocabulary Test-Revised (Dunn & Dunn, 1981), Wechsler Preschool and Primary Scale of Intelligence (Wechsler, 1989), and Wechsler Intelligence Scale for Children (Wechsler, 1949), intelligence quotients (IQ) and developmental quotients

Table 2.1: Prevalence surveys of autism

No.	Year of publication	Authors	Country	Area	Size of target population	Number of subjects with autism	Diagnostic criteria	Percent with normal IQ	Gender ratio (M:F)	Prevalence rate/10,000	95% CI
1	1966	Lotter	UK	Middlesex	78,000	32	Rating scale	15.6	2.6 (23/9)	4.1	2.7; 5.5
2	1970	Brask	Denmark	Aarhus County	46,500	20	Clinical	–	1.4 (12/7)	4.3	2.4; 6.2
3	1970	Treffert	USA	Wisconsin	899,750	69	Kanner	–	3.06 (52/17)	0.7	0.6; 0.9
4	1976	Wing et al.	UK	Camberwell	25,000	17[a]	24 Items rating scale of Lotter	30	16 (16/1)	4.8[b]	2.1; 7.5
5	1982	Hoshino et al.	Japan	Fukushima-Kea	609,848	142	Kanner's criteria	–	9.9 (129/13)	2.33	1.9; 2.7
6	1983	Bohman et al.	Sweden	County of Västerbotten	69,000	39	Rutter criteria	20.5	1.6 (24/15)	5.6	3.9; 7.4
7	1984	McCarthy et al.	Ireland	East	65,000	28	Kanner	–	1.33 (16/12)	4.3	2.7; 5.9
8	1986	Steinhausen et al.	Germany	West Berlin	279,616	52	Rutter	55.8	2.25 (36/16)	1.9	1.4; 2.4
9	1987	Burd et al.	USA	North Dakota	180,986	59	DSM-III	–	2.7 (43/16)	3.26	2.4; 4.1
10	1987	Matsuishi et al.	Japan	Kurume City	32,834	51	DSM-III	–	4.7 (42/9)	15.5	11.3; 19.8
11	1988	Tanoue et al.	Japan	Southern Ibaraki	95,394	132	DSM-III	–	4.07 (106/26)	13.8	11.5; 16.2
12	1988	Bryson et al.	Canada	Part of Nova-Scotia	20,800	21	New RDC	23.8	2.5 (15/6)	10.1	5.8; 14.4
13	1989	Sugiyama & Abe	Japan	Nagoya	12,263	16	DSM-III	–	–	13.0	6.7; 19.4
14	1989	Cialdella & Mamelle	France	I département (Rhône)	135,180	61	DSM-III like	–	2.3	4.5	3.4; 5.6

No.	Year	Study	Country	Area	Population	N	Diagnostic criteria	%	Ratio	Rate	CI
15	1989	Ritvo et al.	USA	Utah	769,620	241	DSM-III	34	3.73 (190/51)	2.47	2.1; 2.8
16	1991	Gillberg et al.[d]	Sweden	South-West Gothenburg + Bohuslän County	78,106	74	DSM-III-R	18	2.7 (54/20)	9.5	7.3; 11.6
17	1992	Fombonne & du Mazaubrun	France	4 régions 14 départements	274,816	154	Clinical-ICD-10 like	13.3	2.1 (105/49)	4.9	4.1; 5.7
18	1992	Wignyosumarto et al.	Indonesia	Yogyakarita (SE of Jakarta)	5,120	6	CARS	0	2.0 (4/2)	11.7	2.3; 21.1
19	1996	Honda et al.	Japan	Yokohama	8,537	18	ICD-10	50.0	2.6 (13.5)	21.08	11.4; 30.8
20	1997	Fombonne et al.	France	3 départements	325,347	174	Clinical ICD-10-like	12.1	1.81 (112/62)	5.35	4.6; 6.1
21	1997	Webb et al.	UK	South Glamorgan, Wales	73,301	53	DSM-III-R	–	6.57 (46/7)	7.2	5.3; 9.3
22	1997	Arvidsson et al.	Sweden (West coast)	Mölnlycke	1,941	9	ICD-10	22.2	3.5 (7/2)	46.4	16.1; 76.6
23	1998	Sponheim & Skjeldal	Norway	Akershus County	65,688	34	ICD-10	47.1[c]	2.09 (23/11)	5.2	3.4; 6.9
24	1999	Taylor et al.	UK	North Thames	490,000	427	ICD-10	–	–	8.7	7.9; 9.5
25	1999	Kadesjö et al.	Sweden (Central)	Karlstad	826	6	DSM-III-R/ICD-10 Gillberg's criteria (Asperger's Syndrome)	50.0	5.0 (5/1)	72.6	14.7; 130.6
26	2000	Baird et al.	UK	South-East Thames	16,235	50	ICD-10	60	15.7 (47/3)	30.8	22.9; 40.6

continued

Table 2.1: *Continued*

No.	Year of publication	Authors	Country	Area	Size of target population	Number of subjects with autism	Diagnostic criteria	Percent with normal IQ	Gender ratio (M:F)	Prevalence rate/10,000	95% CI
27	2000	Powell et al.	UK	West Midlands	25,377	62	Clinical/ ICD-10/ DSM-IV	–	–	7.8	5.8; 10.5
28	2000	Kielinen et al.	Finland	North (Oulu & Lapland)	152,732	187	ICD-8/ ICD-9/ ICD-10	49.8	4.12 (156/50)	12.2	10.5; 14.0
29	2001	Bertrand et al.	USA	Brick Township, New Jersey	8,896	36	DSM-IV	36.7	2.2 (25/11)	40.5	28.0; 56.0
30	2001	Fombonne et al.	UK	England & Wales	10,438	27	DSM-IV/ICD-10	55.5	8.0 (24/3)	26.1	16.2; 36.0
31	2001	Magnússon & Saemundsen	Iceland	Whole Island	43,153	57	Mostly ICD-10	15.8	4.2 (46/11)	13.2	9.8; 16.6
32	2001	Chakrabarti & Fombonne	UK (Mid-lands)	Staffordshire	15,500	26	ICD10/ DSM-IV	29.2	3.3 (20/6)	16.8	10.3; 23.2

[a] This number corresponds to the sample described in Wang and Gould (1979).

[b] This rate corresponds to the first published paper on this survey and is based on 12 subjects amongst children aged 5 to 14 years.

[c] In this study, mild mental retardation was combined with normal IQ, whereas moderate and severe mental retardation was grouped together.

[d] For the Goteborg surveys by Gillberg et al. (Gillberg, 1984; Steffenburg & Gillburg, 1986; Gillburg et al., 1991) a detailed examination showed that there was overlap between the samples included in three surveys; consequently only that last survey has been included in this table.

Note:

From "Epidemiological Surveys of Autsim and Other Pervasive Developmental Disorders:: An Update," by E. Fombonne, 2003, *Journal of Autsim and Developmental Disorders, 33*, pp. 367 and 368. Copyright 2003 by Springer Publishing. Reprinted with kind permission of Springer Science and Business Media. See reference list in Fombonne (2003) for full reference details of all studies.

(DQ) were determined for each of the children diagnosed with ASD. The authors reported that in the older cohort, 33% had an IQ/DQ above 70 (i.e. normal intelligence), 27% had an IQ/DQ between 50 and 69 (i.e. mild or moderate ID), and 40% had an IQ/DQ below 50 (i.e. severe or profound ID). However, in the younger cohort, only 5% had an IQ/DQ above 70, 49% had an IQ/DQ between 50 and 69, and 46% had an IQ/DQ below 50.

Role of Diagnostic Substitution

In another recent study, Croen, Grether, Hoogstrate, and Selvin (2002) examined the prevalence of ASD in the state of California. Croen et al. (2002) looked at all children born from 1987 to 1994 and enrolled in the California Department of Developmental Services (DDS). The authors identified 5,991 children with a diagnosis of "full syndrome ASD" based on the state's DDS definition of ASD. The number of children with ASD in the study was further reduced from 5,991 to 5,038 based on those holding a birth certificate from the state of California. Diagnoses were provided by a qualified professional, which included psychologists, neurologists, psychiatrists, and pediatricians. The authors noted that the diagnoses were generally based on DSM criteria in place during various phases of the study (i.e. either DSM-III-R or DSM-IV). However, there was no way of determining which set of diagnostic criteria was used for each individual child.

Croen et al. (2002) also attempted to assess the impact of diagnostic substitution on the prevalence of ASD by comparing the prevalence of ASD with the prevalence of ID from unknown etiology. Diagnostic substitution is the idea that when one diagnosis becomes more popular, clinicians begin to make the new diagnosis in place of a previous diagnosis. In this case, Croen et al. (2002) were looking to see whether the rate of ID was declining at the same time as the rate of ASD was increasing. If this were the case, it could provide support for the argument that clinicians were beginning to diagnose ASD instead of ID in more children.

Croen and colleagues (2002) reported that the overall prevalence of ASD among children born between 1987 and 1994 in California was 11.0/10,000. When birth year cohorts were compared, rates ranged from 5.8/10,000 in 1987 to 14.9/10,000 in 1994, a difference that was statistically significant. This pattern of increase was seen across gender, ethnicity, maternal age, and maternal education (Croen et al., 2002). The authors found a 17.6% increase in the rate of ASD for the 1987–1990 birth cohorts, followed by a marked increase in prevalence for the 1990–1992 cohorts and then a leveling off for the 1993 and 1994 birth cohorts (Croen et al., 2002).

Sixty-two percent of the children with ASD did not have a diagnosis of ID on their records, and the prevalence of children with ASD but no ID increased from 3.1/10,000 in 1987 to 9.9/10,000 in 1994. Of additional interest, the age at which the children entered the government's service delivery system decreased with each successive birth year (Croen et al., 2002). This earlier entry into services may be the result of either earlier detection of ASD or government attempts to increase the public's awareness of available services for children with disabilities.

As mentioned, Croen et al. (2002) inspected the prevalence of ID without known etiology as a comparison for diagnostic substitution. Children with ID due to a genetic, metabolic, or other known organic condition were excluded from this group. The authors noted that at the same time the prevalence of ASD was increasing in California, the number of diagnoses of ID with unknown etiology was decreasing at a comparable rate (Croen et al., 2002). The authors credited this trend to improved detection and awareness of ASD. Diagnostic substitution appeared to be in effect in this case, with children who would have previously received services with a diagnosis of ID now receiving diagnoses of ASD (Croen et al., 2002). This finding was not surprising since an ASD diagnosis would result in smaller class sizes, increased one-to-one training and other advantageous resources devoted to a child. Given these pragmatics, the choice between a diagnosis of ASD or ID would appear to be a simple decision for most parents.

Another American epidemiological study was conducted in Atlanta, Georgia in 1996 (Yeargin-Allsopp et al., 2003). In the study's first phase, suspected cases of ASD were identified from a population-based surveillance program for developmental disabilities and public school special education programs. In the second phase, experts reviewed suspected cases in children between 3 and 10 years old in the study year (1996) who displayed behaviors consistent with DSM-IV diagnoses of ASD, PDD not otherwise specified (PDD-NOS) or AS. A total of 289,456 lived in the screening area and 987 children were determined to have ASD, PDD-NOS, or AS. The prevalence rate varied from 34/10,000 in 3-year-old children to 47/10,000 in 8-year-old children. Overall prevalence for the three disorders was reported to be 34/10,000. Rates were found be similar among ethnic groups (White, Black, and Other), and males outnumbered females across ethnicity. The prevalence rate reported by Yeargin-Allsopp et al. (2003) using DSM-IV is nearly three times that found using other diagnostic criteria, such as DSM-III and DSM-III-R (see Fombonne, 1999). However, prevalence rates similar to that found in the Yeargin-Allsopp et al. study have also been reported in other studies using DSM-IV (e.g. Baird et al., 2000; Chakrabarti & Fombonne, 2001; Fombonne, Simmons, Ford, Meltzer, & Goodman, 2003).

Summary

As has been noted, the prevalence of ASD has continued to increase ever since the first report in 1966 by Lotter. In the past few years, an ongoing debate in the literature has emerged as to the nature of this rise in prevalence. Is there, in fact, a current epidemic of ASD? While this argument is sensational and attention grabbing, there is currently no evidence to support the hypothesis. In the etiology section, we discussed one theory said to be related to the increase in prevalence of ASD, the MMR vaccine. Some researchers believed that the increase in the number of children with ASD was associated with the increase in number of children receiving the MMR vaccine. Based on the data, it appears as though no correlation exists between the MMR vaccine and the etiology of ASD (Rutter, 2005).

Researchers on the other side of this debate argue that, yes, the prevalence of ASD appears to have risen in recent years. However, this rise in prevalence is most likely not due to an increase in the number of case, but rather to changes in our diagnostic criteria and methodological differences in studies. Other pragmatic issues, such as better funding of ASD programs relative to educational and psychological services for other groups of young children with developmental disabilities, has further motivated this growth in prevalence since parents appear to be following the resources.

In Chapter 1, we went into some detail on the modifications the diagnosis of ASD has undergone since Kanner's first description in 1943. The description of ASD has continually been broadened with each revision of the DSM. In DSM-III (APA, 1980), the category of PDD was divided into infantile ASD (onset before 30 months of age) and childhood onset Pervasive Developmental Disorder (onset between 30 months and 12 years). In DSM-III-R (APA, 1987), formal diagnostic criteria were provided for ASD and PDD-NOS and the age of onset criterion was completely removed. The DSM-IV (APA, 1994) brought about a major alteration with the introduction of Rett's Disorder, Childhood Disintegrative Disorder (CDD) and AS into the category of PDDs. Additionally, researchers and clinicians were provided with detailed criteria for each disorder.

It is apparent that the change in criteria has affected the rates of ASD reported over the years. Wing and Potter (2002) compared 39 epidemiological studies based on the criteria used for diagnosis and found that the mean rate of ASD in studies using the DSM-IV or ICD-10 criteria was 21.0/10,000. The mean rate of ASD found using DSM-III-R criteria was 8.6/10,000. Wing and Potter (2002) found that the mean rates of ASD were lowest when Kanner's criteria were used and highest when DSM-IV or ICD-10 was employed.

As we have already mentioned, a great deal of variance exists in the methodology of all the epidemiological studies discussed. Not only did the diagnostic criteria change, but so did the populations sampled. Fombonne (1999) found a significant negative correlation between sample size and the rate of ASD, with smaller samples reporting significantly higher rates of ASD. Additional variance exists in the method of case determination and the instruments being used to diagnose.

Conclusion

ASD at present has no known etiology other than it appears to have a biological component, which is mitigated by the child's experiences. Rett's Disorder is one of the few exceptions to this general point, as a genetic abnormality has clearly been identified. There currently is no lack of possible biological explanations for ASD. However, considerable additional research will be required to focus attention on the relevant causes. At this time, these data provide very little in the way of effective interventions for young children with ASD.

Prevalence is increasing. Many popular press stories have emerged about why this is the case. Presently, it appears that a clear and simple answer exists. More children are diagnosed with ASD because the definition of ASD has been broadened. ASD programs tend to provide greater resources than typical ID programs and parents, wisely one could argue, are desperate to obtain these resources for their children. So while it is more sensational for the popular press to report on an "epidemic" of ASD, the reality is that the "epidemic" lies in the way we diagnose and not within the children who are being diagnosed.

Chapter 3

Assessment

Introduction

Developing an accurate picture of symptoms and a correct diagnosis are among the most important goals of assessment. In addition to getting the diagnosis right, it is essential to identify treatment targets with respect to a child's strengths and weaknesses. Functional assessment can also help to establish the factors maintaining problem behaviors. Finally, evaluating treatment outcome is an important component of overall assessment.

In clinical practice, and even in a substantial portion of the research literature, these goals are approached in a rather unsystematic manner. It is not uncommon for evaluations to be based largely on haphazard interviews and observation or via unsystematic application of DSM or ICD-10 criteria. Additionally, for outcome measures, often the core assessment instruments used are intelligence or adaptive behavior measures rather than instruments assessing the essential core symptoms of ASD.

As the field has advanced, however, there has been recognition among professionals that disorder-specific, reliable and valid assessment instruments are essential. Additionally, with the move toward treating ASD symptoms in far younger children, scales that are item and norm "age specific" are being developed. The growth of tests for ASD certainly points to the recognition that their use enhances the assessment process. These tests have taken on the preeminent role, particularly in differential diagnosis, and have become increasingly sophisticated. As there is not enough space in this chapter to discuss all the available instruments, we have chosen to cover only the most researched measures that are specific to young children. These instruments have been developed specifically for autism rather ASD. Therefore, we will revert to using the term autism, rather than ASD, in this chapter.

History of Assessment

Rimland (1964) developed one of the first behavior rating scales for autism. The instrument was based upon the core symptoms defined by Kanner (1943). The *Diagnostic Checklist for Behavior-Disturbed Children* (Diagnostic Checklist) contained 76 multiple-choice items regarding social interaction, speech, reaction to stimuli, intelligence, family information, and psychological development. The parents' responses were scored based on whether items were endorsed, and a total score was derived and a cutoff established. After initial study, parent report suggested that the children's behavior became more individualized and the core symptoms of autism more difficult to detect after the age of 5 (Rimland, 1968). As a result, the Diagnostic Checklist later contained items that applied only to children under the age of 5 years (Rimland, 1971).

Several methodological problems have been noted that have limited the use of the Diagnostic Checklist. First, Rimland failed to provide objective definitions of terms (Masters & Miller, 1970) and he relied solely on parent report. In addition, the interrater reliability of the Diagnostic Checklist was never tested. Finally, clinicians were unable to distinguish between autistic and schizophrenic children using this scale (DeMyer, Churchill, Pontius, & Gilkey, 1971). Use of the scale appears to have declined because of these problems, but it was nevertheless an important first step in establishing standardized assessments of young children with autism.

Another instrument developed for the assessment of autism was the *Behavior Rating Instrument for Autistic and Atypical Children* (BRIAAC; Ruttenberg, Dratman, Frankno, & Wenar, 1966; Ruttenberg, Kalish, Wenar, & Wolf, 1977). This test consisted of eight scales: (1) relationship to adults, (2) communication, (3) drive for mastery, (4) vocalization and expressive speech, (5) sound and speech reception, (6) social responsiveness, (7) body movement, and (8) psychobiological development. The behavioral descriptions in the BRIAAC were all empirically derived from observations of children in a psychoanalytic preschool classroom. Although the authors demonstrated that the BRIAAC could distinguish between normally developing children, children with intellectual disability (ID) and autistic children (Wolf, Wenar, & Ruttenberg, 1972), the BRIAAC did not prove useful for differentiating between children with autism and those with other disorders, such as childhood psychosis and developmental aphasia (Cohen et al., 1978). Therefore, while this scale received more empirical attention than the Diagnostic Checklist, it still had a number of limitations. As a result, the BRIAAC has also fallen out of favor in the assessment of autism.

Another important measure in the early development of the assessment of autism was the *Behavior Observation System* (BOS; Freeman, Ritvo, & Schroth, 1984). The BOS was designed to differentiate between autistic and non-autistic children and to provide a sound basis for the description of autism in research (Freeman et al., 1984). The BOS consisted of 24 items divided into four groups: solitary, relationship to objects, relationship to people, and language. Interrater reliability of the BOS was found to be high (Freeman et al., 1984). However, the BOS did not provide a diagnostic cutoff score and could only successfully discriminate between autism and ID (Freeman et al., 1984). These problems are not particularly crucial if the instrument were to be used as a measure of treatment outcome. However, to date, assessment scales have been developed almost exclusively for differential diagnosis. In this regard, the BOS has proven to be less successful.

These three scales have been briefly mentioned because they provide a sense of the historical evolution of scaling in the field of autism. Most assessment instruments have focused on young children, again due to the substantial focus on early identification and treatment that has existed since the initial recognition of autism as a disorder. We have not provided great detail on these measures since more advanced, better researched and thus more popular scales are currently available. However, these measures did prove to be a valuable first step in the assessment of autism.

Currently, there are several scales that are widely used in the assessment of autism. In this chapter we will discuss the *Autism Behavior Checklist* (ABC), *Childhood Autism*

Rating Scale (CARS), *Autism Diagnostic Interview – Revised* (ADI-R), *Autism Diagnostic Observation Schedule* (ADOS), *Checklist for Autism in Toddlers* (CHAT) and the *Screening Tool for Autism in Two-Year Olds* (STAT). The last two scales, the CHAT and STAT, have perhaps been less well developed than the others. However, these scales deal with very young children and infants, which is the primary focus of this book. Thus, we felt that their inclusion in this chapter would be useful.

Autism Behavior Checklist (ABC)

Development

The ABC was developed as one of the five components of the Autism Screening Instrument for Educational Planning (ASIEP; Krug, Arick, & Almond, 1980a). Krug et al. (1980b) intended the ABC to be a reliable and valid screening instrument that could be used in educational settings to easily and accurately determine appropriate classroom placement. The ABC consisted of behaviors taken from several sources, including the Diagnostic Checklist (Rimland, 1964), Creak's (1961) criteria and Kanner's (1943) criteria. The ASIEP's remaining components were designed to assess interaction, learning, language, and educational performance. The ABC may be used independently of the remaining four components of the ASIEP.

Description

The ABC contains 57 items organized into five symptom groupings: sensory, relating, body and object use, language, and social and self-help skills. Individuals familiar with the child, usually a parent or teacher, complete the ABC. Raters indicate the presence or absence of each behavior, and each item is then weighted on a scale of 1 to 4 and compared with standardized groups arranged by chronological age. A total score of greater than 68 indicates a high probability of autism and scores between 54 and 67 indicate the presence of some behaviors characteristic of autism. If a child receives a total score above 54, further assessment by a trained clinician is recommended.

Psychometrics

Krug, Arick and Almond reported the original psychometrics of the ABC in 1979. They assessed 14 children using 42 independent raters. Interrater reliability, calculated using percent agreement, indicated 95% of raters agreed. Although these appeared to be promising data, there were several flaws in the study (Volkmar, Cicchetti et al., 1988). First of all, agreement was determined by percentage, which does not take into account the presence of agreement due to chance. Second, raters in this study were not blind to diagnosis or purpose of the instrument, which may have biased the raters' reports (Volkmar, Cicchetti et al., 1988). Third, a large number of raters assessed a very small sample of only 14 children (Parks, 1988).

To assess validity, Volkmar, Cicchetti et al. (1988) compared ABC scores to clinical diagnoses (using DSM-III criteria) for 94 individuals with autism and 63 with a developmental disorder other than autism. Teachers served as the primary rater in each case and in 33 cases of autism, a parent independently rated the ABC. While parents and teachers obviously were not blind to diagnosis, they were blind to the purpose of the study (Volkmar, Cicchetti et al., 1988). Using the total ABC score, each individual was categorized as probably autistic (Probable), questionably autistic (Questionable) or unlikely to be autistic (Unlikely). Of the 94 individuals with a clinical diagnosis of autism, ABC scores indicated that 80.9% were in the Probable or Questionable categories. Of the 33 individuals in the non-autistic group, 38.1% were placed in the Probable or Questionable categories based on ABC scores. Interrater reliability for 17 of the ABC's 57 items was found to be fair when later corrected for chance (Volkmar, Cicchetti et al., 1988). Additionally, when parent and teacher reports were compared, the parents reported significantly greater pathology.

When Krug et al. (1979) created the ABC, they subjectively assigned each of the 57 items to the five categories. Since that time, several researchers have conducted factor analyses of the ABC. Volkmar, Cicchetti et al. (1988) assessed the ABC's factor structure in addition to its reliability and concurrent validity. They found three factors accounted for 72% of the variance in ABC scores. Wadden, Bryson, and Rodger (1991) conducted a separate factor analysis with 67 children with autism and 56 with various learning disorders. Results of this factor analysis indicated that three factors produced the most stable structure. The three factors were described as Nonresponsive, Aloof/Repetitive, and Infantile/Aggressive. Both of these studies (Volkmar, Cicchetti et al., 1988; Wadden et al., 1991) concluded that the subscales proposed by Krug et al. (1979) were sufficient. However, in another factor analysis that used a far larger sample ($n = 383$), Mirenda-Linne and Melin (2002) were unable to confirm Wadden et al.'s (1991) structure or provide support for Krug et al.'s (1979) five subscales. Mirenda-Linne and Melin (2002) found that five different factors (Nonresponsive Behavior, Infant-Like Behavior, Aggressive Behavior, Stereotypical Behavior, and Echolalic Speech) accounted for the majority of the variance. The lack of agreement on a factor structure is a significant limitation of the ABC.

Overview

The ABC had several advantages over other ASD rating scales (Volkmar, Cicchetti et al., 1988). Advantages of the ABC are the use of teachers as opposed to parents as raters, simple and straightforward scoring, and the acknowledgement of the effect of age on the disorder with the inclusion of separate profile charts for different age groups (Volkmar, Cicchetti et al., 1988). The psychometric properties of the ABC have been well researched. Initial reports of interrater reliability and split-half reliability were high, but based on observation of only 14 children (Krug et al., 1980b). One test of the ABC's validity found that it correctly predicted inclusion in the autistic group in 100% of individuals and inclusion in the group with trainable (i.e. mild) mental retardation in 95% of individuals (Teal & Wiebe, 1986). The ABC has also been shown to successfully discriminate between children with autism and those with ID, emotional disturbance, and hearing and visual impairments.

The ABC is not without its limitations. Criticisms of the ABC have included a focus on aberrant symptomatology, lack of measurement of prosocial behavior, and the need for a revised cutoff score (Sevin, Matson, Coe, Fee, & Sevin, 1991). It also appears that the ABC has questionable validity when used to classify children with higher intellectual functioning (Volkmar, Cicchetti et al., 1988). As newer instruments have been developed, the ABC has been, to a large degree, replaced by instruments with stronger psychometrics.

Childhood Autism Rating Scale (CARS)

Development

The development of the CARS (Schopler, Reichler, & Renner, 1988) began in 1966 with the production of a scale that incorporated the criteria of Kanner (1943) and Creak (1964), as well as characteristic symptoms of childhood autism (Schopler et al., 1980). The CARS was intended for use in evaluating children referred to North Carolina's statewide autism program, Treatment and Education of Autistic and related Communication handiCapped cHildren (TEACCH; Schopler et al., 1988). The CARS was designed to differentiate between children with autism and those with other developmental disabilities. As early research reported promising results, the CARS quickly became one of the most commonly used diagnostic instruments for the detection of autism (Matson, Smiroldo, & Hastings, 1998; Morgan, 1988; Sturmey & Sevin, 1994; Teal & Wiebe, 1986).

Description

The CARS consists of 15 independently rated subscales (Schopler et al., 1988). The 15 subscales are: (1) Relating to people; (2) Imitation; (3) Emotional response; (4) Body use; (5) Object use; (6) Adaptation to change; (7) Visual response; (8) Listening response; (9) Taste, smell, and touch response and use; (10) Fear or nervousness; (11) Verbal communication; (12) Nonverbal communication; (13) Activity level; (14) Level and consistency of intellectual response; (15) General impressions. Each scale is rated with a score of 1 (normal for child's age), 2 (mildly abnormal), 3 (moderately abnormal), or 4 (severely abnormal). Midpoint scores of 1.5, 2.5, and 3.5 are also possible. Individual subscale scores are compiled in order to create a total CARS score, which can range from 15 to 60. A diagnosis of autism is suggested for individuals who obtain a score of 30 or greater.

Psychometrics

Initial psychometric properties of the CARS were determined using 537 children enrolled in the TEACCH program over a 10-year period (Schopler et al., 1980). Fifty-one percent of the children studied scored above the cutoff score of 30. Schopler et al. (1980) observed the existence of a bimodal distribution among these scores, leading them to develop criteria to differentiate between those with mild to moderate autism and those with severe autism. Children whose score exceeded 36 and who received a rating of 3 or greater on at least five subscales were categorized as being severely autistic.

Internal consistency of the CARS was high, with a coefficient alpha of .94 (Schopler et al., 1988), indicating the degree to which all of the 15-scale scores constituted a unitary phenomenon rather than several individual behaviors. Interrater reliability was established using two raters for 280 cases. The average reliability of .71 indicated good overall agreement between raters. Twelve-month test–retest data were also collected. Schopler et al. (1988) found that the means were not significantly different from the first testing to the second. Criterion-related validity was determined by comparing CARS diagnoses to diagnoses made independently by child psychologists and psychiatrists. Diagnoses correlated at $r = .80$, which indicated that the CARS diagnosis was in agreement with clinical judgments. The CARS has also been shown to have 100% predictive accuracy when distinguishing between children with autism and those with mental retardation; this was superior to both the ABC and Diagnostic Checklist (Teal & Wiebe, 1986).

The validity of the CARS under different settings has also been researched (Schopler et al., 1988). CARS scores of 41 children taken through parent interview were compared to scores derived from direct observation. Mean scores under the two conditions were not significantly different and the correlation of $r = .83$ further indicated good agreement. In addition, diagnoses based on parent interview and direct observation agreed in 90% of the cases. The authors suggested that valid CARS ratings and diagnoses could be achieved through parent interview (Schopler et al., 1988).

Overview

The CARS has long been considered among the best assessment instruments in the field of autism, particularly for diagnosis. With its focus on current behavior, the CARS allows for repeated measurement and comparison of symptom expression and severity over the lifespan (DiLalla & Rogers, 1994). However, the CARS was intended for use by clinicians/researchers who are familiar with autism and thus requires a degree of expertise in order to be used correctly. The psychometrics of the CARS have been well established. Interrater and test–retest reliability are adequate and good agreement exists between CARS and clinical diagnoses. Another unique feature of the CARS is that it has been validated in different conditions, such as parent interview, classroom observation, and chart review (Schopler et al., 1988).

The CARS was developed prior to the creation of DSM-IV (APA, 1994) and thus does not follow the current accepted diagnostic criteria. The CARS also came before the conceptualization of ASD and no provision was made for differentiating between autism and other ASDs, such as Pervasive Developmental Disorder Not Otherwise Specified (PDD-NOS) and Asperger's Syndrome (AS) (Klinger & Renner, 2000). With this in mind, it has been recommended that the CARS not be used as a means of establishing a diagnosis directly, but instead as a screening device or as part of a comprehensive evaluation (Lord, 1997). Having said this, our view is that when making a differential diagnosis, assessment instruments should always be used in combination with observation, DSM or WHO criteria, and other related diagnostic information.

Autism Diagnostic Interview (ADI)

Development

The ADI was developed in the 1980s with the goal of differentiating between PDDs through the use of an investigator-based caregiver interview (Le Couteur et al., 1989). In order to differentiate between the developmental delay seen in ID and the unique symptoms of autism, the ADI focused questioning on the fifth year of the individual's life and was not intended for individuals younger than 5 or with a mental age of less than 2 years. The ADI focused on three areas of behavior in autism: social interaction, communication, and repetitive, stereotyped behaviors. In addition to these three areas, the authors of the ADI included behaviors that, while not related to diagnostic criteria, are important for the development of treatments (i.e. self-injury, aggression, toilet training).

As previously stated, the ADI is investigator-based, as opposed to respondent-based. In a respondent-based interview, the interviewer reads a question word-for-word and the respondent is asked to answer "yes" or "no." The ADI format, however, involves the interviewer soliciting information from the respondent using compulsory probes. The interviewer then codes the information provided (Le Couteur et al., 1989). Therefore, it is vital that the interviewer is highly trained in the area of autism and the diagnostic and characteristic differences between autism and other disorders, in order to accurately code the information obtained during the interview.

Description

The structure of the ADI is the same across all areas. Each area begins with a screening question from which the interviewer is expected to probe further in order to help the caregiver recall details about the child's past and present behavior. Each question is then coded with 0 if the specified behavior is not present, 1 when the behavior is present but not frequent or severe, and 2 if the behavior occurs with significant frequency or severity. The authors of the ADI noted that a code of 0 did not necessarily mean that the child's behavior in that area is completely normal, just that it is not abnormal in the way specified for coding (Le Couteur et al., 1989). The individual items are then placed into a diagnostic algorithm according to the ICD-10 criteria for autism in order to operationalize the diagnosis (Le Couteur et al., 1989).

Psychometrics

Le Couteur and her colleagues (1989) determined the reliability of the ADI by comparing the coding agreement between trained clinicians. Two clinicians independently coded the interviews of 16 mothers of children with autism and 16 mothers of children with ID.

In order to control for possible confounds, comparisons were made between clinicians in the United Kingdom and Canada and all were kept blind to the diagnoses of the children whose mothers were being interviewed. Reliability was calculated using the kappa coefficient, a statistical measure that corrects for chance agreement, for each item in the three areas (social interaction, communication, and repetitive, stereotyped behaviors). Of the 14 items in the social interaction area, 10 had kappa coefficients that exceeded .70. In the area of communication, 9 of the 12 items were above .75 and in repetitive, stereotyped behavior 5 of the 6 items exceeded .75. The reliability of the algorithm was assessed by comparing whether the interviewers/raters agreed on whether or not all four ICD-10 criteria were met (see Chapter 1 for a discussion of ICD-10 criteria for a diagnosis of autism). For the 16 cases with ID and no autism, raters were in 100% agreement that autism was not present. For the 16 cases with autism, raters agreed on the presence of autism in 15 (Le Couteur et al., 1989).

Diagnostic validity was assessed by comparing the children in the autism group with those in the ID group in each of the three ADI categories. The ADI was able to differentiate between autism and ID across all items in the three areas except for one (unusual attachment to objects). In addition, all 16 children in the autism group met the ADI's algorithm requirements for a diagnosis of autism, as opposed to none of the children in the ID group (Le Couteur et al., 1989).

Autism Diagnostic Interview-Revised (ADI-R)

Development

In 1994, Lord, Rutter, and Le Couteur undertook a revision of the ADI. The ADI-R was developed in order to address several concerns with the original version. The first concern was that the ADI was intended for use in children over the age of 5 (Le Couteur et al., 1989). However, most children were being diagnosed with ASD at preschool age (Short & Schopler, 1988), so there was a need for an instrument that could differentiate autism from other PDDs at an earlier age (Lord et al., 1994). The second concern was that the ADI was relatively lengthy and time-consuming to complete, so the ADI-R was reorganized in order to decrease its length and increase time efficiency so that it could be used as a part of a multidisciplinary assessment (Lord et al., 1994).

In order to address these concerns, several revisions were made to the overall organization and individual items of the ADI. Questions about early childhood development and current behavior were combined in each area, so that the ADI-R consists of five main components: (1) opening questions about parents' concerns; (2) early and current communication skills; (3) social development and current play skills; (4) repetitive and restricted behaviors; and (5) behavioral problems. Several new items were included in the areas of socialization and communication to encompass behaviors that were more common in older, higher-functioning individuals with autism, such as unusual interests (Lord et al., 1994). Items were also added to aid in differentiating autism from other ASDs, such as Rett's Disorder and Childhood Disintegrative Disorder (CDD). These new items focused on behaviors such as loss of purposeful hand movements and stereotypic hand wringing. In order to shorten the administration time, Lord et al. (1994) removed items from the ADI that they deemed to be redundant, overlapping, applicable to only a small number of children, or those items that had been found to have limited reliability in the original study (Le Couteur et al., 1989). However, the coding of the individual items remained consistent from the ADI to the ADI-R.

In addition to these changes, the ADI-R extended the diagnostic algorithm to include the DSM-IV (APA, 1994) criteria for autism. Another change was the creation of three separate versions of the ADI-R algorithms (lifetime, current behavior, and children under the age of 4). Lord et al. (1994) focused the reliability study of the ADI-R on children under the age of 4. Their sample consisted of 10 children with autism and 10 with ID or language impairment, with mental ages ranging from 21 to 74 months. Mothers were interviewed by clinicians with extensive training and the interviewers required 60 to 90 minutes to complete each interview. Four graduate students who also had extensive training in administering and scoring the ADI-R independently coded the tape-recorded interviews.

Psychometrics

Lord et al. (1994) reported that the interrater reliability of all the items in the socialization and communication domains was good. The kappa correlation coefficients for these items were between .62 and .89, which was comparable to that found on the original version. Interrater reliability of the restricted, repetitive behavior items was slightly lower, but still adequate (Lord et al., 1994).

Discriminant validity of the ADI-R was also very good. Lord et al. (1994) reported that the items relating to behaviors in children who were 4 to 5 years old were the most discriminant. Additionally, significant differences between diagnostic groups were reported for the socialization and communication algorithms. Some items in the repetitive behavior algorithm were unable to discriminate between groups, which the authors credited to the low prevalence of these behaviors in the young sample. These items were removed unless they had good discriminant validity from the original version.

Overview of ADI/ADI-R

Several researchers have asserted that the ADI-R is the current gold standard for the diagnosis of autism (Klinger & Renner, 2000; Lord & Corsello, 2005). The ADI-R has well-established psychometric properties and a diagnostic algorithm that has been revised to stay up to date with DSM-IV (APA, 1994) criteria for Autistic Disorder. However, while the ADI-R includes items intended to aid in the differential diagnosis of ASD, these items are not coded and diagnoses such as PDD-NOS and AS cannot be derived based on the results of the ADI-R. Another potential limitation to the use of the ADI-R is its lengthy administration time, which can be over two hours. Administration of the ADI-R also requires competent interview skills and experience with ASD. Finally, there is the concern that the ADI-R relies entirely on parental report, which can be influenced by the parent's desire for a diagnosis (Klinger & Renner, 2000). However, as we will discuss next, another instrument, the ADOS, was developed as an observational companion to the ADI and thus the combination of the two instruments may be useful in clinical decision-making.

Autism Diagnostic Observation Schedule (ADOS)

Development

Lord and colleagues developed the ADOS in 1989. The authors intended to create an instrument that could discriminate autism from ID and normal functioning, as well as assist in ongoing research regarding the nature of social and communication impairments in ASD. In this chapter we have already discussed several instruments, such as CARS and ABC, which provide an opportunity for clinicians to observe behavior in the natural or laboratory environment. The ADOS differed from these instruments in that it provided a standardized set of scenarios in which clinicians could interact with the individuals they assessed (Lord et al., 1989). The interactive nature of the ADOS is certainly one of its most characteristic features. Another difference between the ADOS and the previously discussed instruments is that the ADOS's focus is limited to social and communicative behaviors and does not attempt to assess the motor behaviors, sensory abnormalities, or restrictive or repetitive interests characteristic of autism (Lord et al., 1989).

The ADOS was designed to provide clinicians and researchers with a set of predetermined, standardized situations in which to encourage social interaction and communication. In this way, the designers of this scale likened the ADOS more to psychoeducational and developmental tests, as opposed to informant-based assessment instruments. In addition, the ADOS was designed to be used by highly skilled examiners and not by untrained paraprofessionals carrying out initial screening to determine the need for further assessment by a trained clinician. With this in mind, Lord et al. (1989) developed the ADOS using a combination of accepted diagnostic criteria (i.e. ICD-10 and DSM-IV), research, and their own clinical experiences.

Description

The ADOS consists of eight standardized tasks that can be presented in any order. The first task consists of a puzzle or pegboard construction in which the examiner retains the pieces and the child must obtain the pieces required for completion. The purpose of this task is to observe the way the child requests help. The second task is intended to investigate symbolic (make-believe) and reciprocal play. In this task, the child is presented with figures that are novel and familiar. The examiner attempts to participate in the child's imaginative play and observes whether the child makes efforts to include the examiner. The third task, joint drawing, assesses turn taking. In the fourth task, the child is asked to demonstrate how he or she performs a simple task, such as brushing his/her hair. In the fifth task, the child is asked to describe the activities occurring in a poster. The sixth task assesses the child's ability to tell a story following the sequence provided by pictures in a text-less storybook. Task seven entails the examiner engaging the child in a conversation about topics from previous points during the assessment (e.g. talking about the drawing that was completed earlier). Finally, the eighth task examines the child's ability to describe both social and emotional situations. Lord et al. (1989) state that the entire ADOS can be completed within 20 or 30 minutes.

Throughout the observation period, the examiner rates the child's performance on each individual task. Immediately after completing the observation schedule, the examiner provides general ratings in the areas of reciprocal social interaction, communication, nonspecific abnormal behaviors (e.g. anxiety, attention, overactivity) and stereotyped/repetitive behaviors (Lord et al., 1989). The items in these areas are rated on a 3-point scale, where $0 =$ within normal limits, $1 =$ infrequent or possible abnormality, and $2 =$ definite abnormality. As with the ADI-R (Lord et al., 1994), the scores on the ADOS are put into a diagnostic algorithm based on ICD-10 criteria for autism.

Psychometrics

Lord et al. (1989) examined the reliability of the ADOS with a sample of 20 children and adolescents with autism and 20 with mental retardation. All of the participants had full-scale IQ scores between 50 and 80 and were between 6 and 18 years old. Participants were matched based on chronological age and verbal IQ. In addition, all of the children in the autism group were individually assessed by the authors to ensure that they met DSM-III-R criteria for a diagnosis of autism, and 15 of the 20 children in the group also had CARS scores above the cutoff of 30 (Schopler et al., 1988).

Blind raters viewed videotaped ADOS assessments. Interestingly, interrater reliability was conducted with both raters serving as the examiners for the child for half of the assessment period but scoring the entire session independently. Each of the children were reassessed 3 to 9 months later using alternate sets of materials. Weighted kappa coefficients for interrater reliability were between .61 and .92 for the individual items and between .58 and .87 for the general items (Lord et al., 1989). Test–retest reliability was adequate for all individual and general items, with no significant difference in test–retest reliability between groups.

In the same study, Lord et al. (1989) also assessed the concurrent criterion-related and discriminant validity of the ADOS. The sample consisted of four groups, with 20 children in each. Diagnostic groups consisted of children with: autism/mild ID, ID, autism/normal IQ, and normal development. The authors reported that half of the ADOS's general rating items were able to differentiate between all four groups (Lord et al., 1989). Several of the general rating items (e.g. unusual use of eye contact, amount of social overtures) were able to differentiate between the children with autism and those without autism, but not between the two autistic groups. In addition, none of the items in the nonspecific abnormal behaviors area showed significant group differences.

Discriminant validity of the algorithm was also assessed and deemed by Lord et al. (1989) to be good. When combined, both the social and communication criteria differentiated successfully between the children with and without autism. However, when considered separately, the social and communication algorithms misclassified several of the children with autism and normal IQ, which the authors hypothesized could have been due to the high verbal abilities of these children.

Additional Versions

In addition to the original ADOS (Lord et al., 1989), several variations have been created over time and will be addressed briefly. In 1995, DiLavore, Lord and Rutter developed the Pre-Linguistic Autism Diagnostic Observation Schedule (PL-ADOS). DiLavore et al. (1995) were concerned that the ADOS's conversational delivery style, focus on verbal abilities and attentional demands placed on the children (i.e. sitting at a table for 30 minutes) made the ADOS inappropriate for young children and those with little or no verbal communication skills. Therefore, the purpose of the PL-ADOS was to create an observational assessment for infant and toddlers and nonverbal children. The PL-ADOS was designed to be delivered during the course of natural play activities. The child is allowed to move around the room and the examiner engages the child in a set of 12 activities in order to observe the quality and quantity of social interaction and play. The authors found that the PL-ADOS could successfully discriminate between children with and without autism (DiLavore et al., 1995), but inappropriately classified children with autism and some expressive language (Lord et al., 2000).

The third version of the ADOS, the ADOS-Generic (ADOS-G), was developed in order to assess children without the appropriate verbal communication required for the ADOS but who had some verbal abilities and were misclassified with the PL-ADOS (Lord et al., 2000). The ADOS-G format differed in that it provided four different modules (activity sets), with only one being administered based on the individual's verbal ability. Module 1 was based on the PL-ADOS and is used for children who are nonverbal or express single words or phrases. Module 2 is for children who are able to speak in phrases but do not exhibit fluent speech. Module 3 is for children and adolescents with fluent speech and Module 4 is intended for adolescents or adults with fluent speech (Lord et al., 2000).

Reliability and validity of the ADOS-G modules were assessed using children and adolescents with autism (confirmed using the ADI-R), PDD-NOS, and non-spectrum disorders (e.g. ID, language disorders, anxiety disorders). Items from Modules 1 and 2 had high interrater reliability (kappa coefficients greater than .60) and exact agreement over 80%. Modules 3 and 4 had relatively lower interrater reliability (Lord et al., 2000). Additionally, interrater reliability for items relating to restricted/stereotyped behaviors was adequate. Test–retest reliability for socialization and communication areas was excellent and test–retest reliability for the repetitive/stereotyped behaviors domain was good (Lord et al., 2000). Validity analyses across modules indicated that the ADOS-G could effectively discriminate between autism and non-spectrum disorders. However, the ADOS-G was less effective at differentiating between autism and PDD-NOS.

Overview

The ADOS stands out among the most commonly used assessment instruments for autism, as it is the only one based on standardized observation and social and communicative behaviors. Many clinicians will agree that having the opportunity to observe behavior is useful in compiling the information necessary to establish a diagnosis. The ADOS enables clinicians to observe a wide variety of social and communicative behavior. In addition, the ADOS and its versions, especially the ADOS-G, have well-established psychometric properties. The presence of distinct versions based on language ability is also unique to the ADOS series. However, the authors have yet to clearly delineate the exact circumstances in which one version should be chosen above the others.

While the strengths of the ADOS are easily recognizable, several limitations to its use are also evident. The first potential limitation is that the examiner must receive substantial training and supervision in order to become qualified to administer the instrument. Unlike the ABC, which can be completed by less-qualified professionals when children are being screened to see if there is a need for further assessment, the ADOS requires a certain degree of preexisting knowledge about ASD and experience with children. In addition, the fact that the ADOS relies on the interaction between the clinician/examiner and the child leaves open the possibility that the examiner may be cueing or indirectly prompting specific types of behavior from the child (Lord et al., 1989). Finally, the authors of all three versions of the ADOS have commented on the problems this instrument has with assessing repetitive/stereotyped behaviors. The presence of at least one of these behaviors is necessary for an individual to meet DSM-IV (APA, 1994) criteria for a diagnosis of Autistic Disorder. Therefore, clinicians and researchers who choose to use the ADOS as part of an evaluation should be careful to obtain additional information and observations regarding repetitive and stereotyped behaviors.

Instruments for Early Identification of Autism

With the development of standardized interviews and methods for determining the age at which parents first become concerned about their children's abnormal development, researchers and clinicians have begun to recognize a gap between parents' first concern and the age at which children are actually being assessed. Generally, parents report that they first become concerned about their child's development and behavior around the child's first birthday (De Giacomo & Fombonne, 1998; Rogers & DiLalla, 1990). However, the child is usually not assessed by a pediatrician or psychologist until the age of 20 to 27 months (De Giacomo & Fombonne, 1998).

Coupled with the importance attached to early intervention services (Filipek et al., 1999; Rogers, 1998), this time gap has created a need for instruments that can identify autism in younger children. Two such instruments have recently been developed. The first is the Checklist for Autism in Toddlers (CHAT), which was created in 1992 by Baron-Cohen, Allen, and Gillberg. The second is the Screening Tool for Autism in Two-Year-Olds (STAT; Stone, Coonrod, & Ousley, 2000). Due to the limited amount of research conducted on these two instruments, they will only be discussed briefly.

Checklist for Autism in Toddlers (CHAT)

The CHAT was developed to address the need for early identification by screening entire populations of 18-month-old children (Baron-Cohen et al., 1992). The CHAT differs from other instruments we have discussed in that it is intended for use by parents and pediatricians during regular 18-month check-ups, regardless of whether the parent presents with developmental or behavioral concerns. The three areas assessed by the CHAT are: pretend/imaginative play, protodeclarative pointing (pointing at objects to gain other people's attention) and gaze monitoring. There are two sections in the CHAT; the first consists of nine yes/no questions answered by the parent or primary caregiver and the second consists of five yes/no questions answered by the pediatrician based on in-office observations.

In the original study (Baron-Cohen et al., 1992), the CHAT was administered to 50 randomly selected children at their 18-month pediatric appointment. The items passed by the largest portion of the children were retained and then administered to 41 siblings of children with autism (Baron-Cohen et al., 1992). Four of these children were deemed to be at high risk for autism. When these children were assessed independently at the age of 30 months, they all received a diagnosis of autism.

In order to test the use of the CHAT as a population screen, Baron-Cohen, Cox, Baird, Swettenham and Nightingale (1996) screened 16,235 18-month-old children in England and found 10 prospective cases of autism. Over the next six years, Baird et al. (2000) followed up and continued to screen this sample. They identified 38 children who were at high risk for autism (i.e. failed all five key protodeclarative pointing items) and 369 children who were at medium risk for autism (i.e. failed two protodeclarative pointing items but did not meet criteria for the high-risk group). When only the high-risk group was considered, the sensitivity of the CHAT (i.e. ability to correctly identify autism) was low. However, when the medium-risk group was included, the CHAT's sensitivity increased. With both groups, the CHAT had excellent specificity (i.e. ability to correctly identify normal children).

In another study conducted using the CHAT, Scambler, Rogers, and Wehner (2001) administered the CHAT to the parents and clinicians of 44 slightly older children (aged 2 and 3 years) with significant development delays. Scambler et al. (2001) compared the CHAT to well-established clinical diagnoses (based on the ADOS-G, ADI-R, and DSM-IV criteria) and found that the CHAT had high sensitivity and specificity. When considering the CHAT, it is important to note that there are currently no published reliability data and that the CHAT's ability to differentiate between autism and other childhood disorders and ID has also yet to be determined.

Screening Tool for Autism in Two-Year-Olds (STAT)

In order to address the problems seen in the CHAT, Stone et al. (2000) developed the STAT. The STAT was intended to provide a brief, interactive measure for identifying children between the age of 2 and 3 years in need of further assessment, as well as to differentiate autism from other developmental disorders. The STAT consists of a 20-minute interaction between the examiner and the child with 12 items that assess the child's play, imitation, requesting, and attention-directing skills (Stone et al., 2000). Each item is scored as a pass or a fail. In the first study published on the STAT, Stone et al. (2000) assessed 40 children (7 with autism diagnoses, 33 with other developmental disorders) in order to determine a scoring algorithm, and another 33 children (12 with autism diagnoses, 21 with other developmental disorders). All children were between 27 and 35 months old. Stone et al. (2000) developed a scoring algorithm based on differential STAT scores based on clinical diagnosis. The algorithm resulted in 1.00 sensitivity and .91 specificity. This algorithm was then applied to the validation sample and sensitivity was determined to be .83 (high) and specificity was also high (.86).

Stone et al. (2004) went on to assess the reliability of the STAT with 29 children with autism, PDD-NOS, and developmental delay. Interrater reliability for placement in a risk category (high versus low risk) was 1.00, which indicates perfect agreement. Test–retest reliability was calculated using a subset of the interrater reliability sample an average of 20 days later. Test–retest reliability for placement in a risk category was determined to be excellent (.90).

Stone et al. (2004) also investigated the concurrent validity between the STAT and another observation-based assessment, the ADOS-G (Lord et al., 2000). Fifty children with autism, 17 with PDD-NOS, and 39 with non-spectrum disorders were compared based on STAT category (high versus low autism risk) and ADOS-G classification (autism versus no autism). However, because the STAT was designed to screen for autism only (not ASD in general), the 24 children who received a PDD-NOS classification on the ADOS-G were removed from the analysis. Results of the comparison between STAT category and ADOS-G classification resulted in a Cohen's kappa of .95. Two false positives on the STAT were noted (i.e. in the high-risk STAT category but classified as not having autism by the ADOS-G). Stone et al. (2004) looked at the 24 children classified with PDD-NOS on the ADOS-G and found that 64% of them were categorized as low risk on the STAT and 36% as high risk. This observation led Stone et al. (2004) to state that the STAT may be inappropriate for assessing milder forms of autism.

Overview of Early Identification Instruments

The development of screening instruments for young children, such as the CHAT and STAT, provides an interesting and much-needed direction for future research into the assessment of ASD. Although early identification of ASD is important, it must be balanced against the need for accurate diagnosis. While many parents become concerned about their children's development between the first and second year of life (De Giacomo & Fombonne, 1998; Rogers & DiLalla, 1990), many less severe abnormalities may not be present that early. The CHAT currently has a relatively low sensitivity, which even its authors note reduces its applicability as a population screener (Charman & Baird, 2002). The STAT also has limitations, especially its inability to detect less severe forms of autism (Stone et al., 2004).

Conclusions

The trend in diagnosing autism has been somewhat different from that seen in the mental health field and is more in line with the assessment of ID and developmental disabilities in general. Mental health professionals in clinical practice have relied primarily on unstructured clinical interviews and often loose interpretations of DSM or ICD criteria. Rarely are any psychometrically sound instruments employed for diagnosis. With respect to evaluating treatment outcome, often no follow-up occurs and when it does, typically informal or haphazard questioning of the client, staff, or caregivers forms the basis for additional treatment recommendations. Among researchers in the general mental health literature, the picture is better but far from optimal. Typically, there is some effort to incorporate a disorder-specific scale or scales (e.g. a depression measure for depression, ADHD scales for attention deficit hyperactivity disorder, etc.) along with interviews and DSM or ICD criteria. Outcome measures are mixed and often based on staff, parent, or client report, but in many instances also include a test specific to the disorder.

By contrast, in the ID and more general developmental disabilities literature, testing forms the core of assessment for differential diagnoses, with interviews serving an adjunctive role. Professionals would not consider clinical interview as an acceptable alternative to intellectual and adaptive behavior testing for establishing whether a child had ID. Autism scales appear to follow this course for establishing the diagnosis. We believe additional refinement of existing scales and the development of additional scales that are age specific are likely, particularly with regard to diagnosis. The biggest efforts are likely to be in the areas of accurately identifying autism at younger and younger ages. Given the emphasis on early identification and treatment, such a goal is very desirable. Advances in this area need to occur rapidly. However, current claims of accurate diagnosis at 1 or 2 years of age are premature and overblown in our view. Some patience from parents and professionals and additional research are needed.

It is also unfortunate that scales are not more inclusive of other ASDs. To date, scales have focused almost exclusively on autism. Measures that can aid in better differential diagnosis between autism and PDD-NOS, Rett's Disorder, CDD, Asperger's Syndrome and related conditions are urgently needed.

We are more critical of assessments of treatment "outcome" as it applies to ASD. Typically, measures of IQ, adaptive behavior and the presence of self-injury and aggression appear to be what researchers are using to claim improvement or cure of ASD. While all of these problems are important, they are not specific to ASD and they tell us little about whether the core condition of ASD has improved. Measures that are specific to core symptoms of ASD that are tailored to specific age groups and settings are needed. Without such instruments, claims of improvement must be tempered (see a review of comprehensive treatments in Chapter 5). Finally, measures of short- and long-term side-effects need to be developed and utilized when medications are used (see Chapter 6).

ASD probably has better developed assessment strategies than most areas diagnosed and treated by psychologists, psychiatrists, or educators. Additionally, while areas of research in these fields tend to wax and wane, ASD appears to be an area that has consistently received research attention. We believe that these efforts have been fruitful and look forward to watching the progress that will be made in the future.

Chapter 4

Interventions by Class of Behavior

Behavioral Treatments

Operant conditioning has been a uniquely American development while the Russians gave us classical conditioning and the British were instrumental in promoting a broader learning-based interpretation including social learning, operant and cognitive components. The British also gave us the first learning-based applied journal, *Behaviour Research and Therapy*. Although this journal was not a primary outlet for studies on autism, it did help produce a momentum that resulted in the development of many journals that do now publish behavioral (learning-based) studies, many of which deal with ASD.

The bulk of the treatment research on autism and related conditions in the Pervasive Developmental Disorder (PDD) spectrum have come from the United States and thus the operant point of view is dominant in the psychological treatment literature. Key were the early theoretical works of Thorndike, Guthrie, and Tulman, who established a learning/laboratory model to develop laws and rules that could be applied to produce efficient learning. However, the biggest breakthrough came with B. F. Skinner and his students, who gave the field quantifiable laws of learning based in part on the findings of these earlier researchers and including concepts such as reinforcement, punishment, shaping, fading, chaining, and similar "laws of learning." These concepts were then rapidly applied to human problems once they had been established with rats and pigeons in the university setting. Thus, in the 1950s and 1960s, intervention rules and methods developed much more rapidly than at any prior time. These basic premises have proven to be very sound and continue to be practiced today. However, the number of researchers and clinicians involved in the use of operant-based methods continues to grow at an exponential rate. The vast majority of this literature involves the development and refinement of procedures used to treat specific problem behaviors, such as self-injury or speech, and more recently packaged treatments aimed at helping the whole person. These treatments have been developed and used almost exclusively with very young children, since early identification and treatment are considered essential in promoting the best possible outcome in ASD.

Early Developments in Operant Conditioning

The initial hallmark papers for applied application of operant methods and principles were by Skinner, Soloman and Lindsley, and Lindsley and Skinner (as cited in Rutherford, 2003), who employed these principles with 15 males with schizophrenia. The task of pushing a plunger to receive a preferred reinforcer, which was used here, theoretically was similar to attempts to lever-train rats in the Skinner box. Thus, the first attempt to form a conceptual bridge for learning principles from animal to human behavior was made, although with mixed success. Lindsley (1959) conducted perhaps one of the most cited of these early studies in which methods were used to modify the verbal behavior of psychotic patients. Rutherford (2003) provides an excellent overview of these initial applied efforts. In conjunction with these promising studies, Skinner and his student Lindsley established the Harvard Medical School Behavior Research Laboratory at Metropolitan State Hospital at Waltham, Massachusetts. The center was in operation from 1953 to 1965. The aforementioned Lindsley paper, testing mostly chronic schizophrenics, was a product of the laboratory.

Verbal behavior and its modification had been a major theme of Skinner's career. (For those who are interested, see Skinner's debates with the linguist Chomsky; i.e. Chomsky, 1967; MacCorquodale, 1970). For example, hebephrenic schizophrenics, a rare juvenile form of the disorder where patients make up their own language, were viewed conceptually as reinforcing their own strange speech. Similarly, these researchers believed that individuals with schizophrenia in general could have speech and thoughts altered in positive ways by operantly modifying speech patterns. These topics were the overarching goal of these early studies.

Later, practical problems in individuals with intellectual disability (ID) were approached. Ellis (1961) treated those with ID and incontinence. Using learning-based methods, they toilet-trained adults residing at the Pinecrest Developmental Center in Pineville, Louisiana. Since persons with ID, severe psychopathology, or PDD were considered largely as "untreatable" prior to 1955, these studies opened an entire field of possible study. Thus, research of this nature established the idea that all persons had considerable learning potential.

These researchers and their teams can be credited with many of the early developments and thus the current state of behaviorally based interventions in ASD. A student of Skinner's, Nathan Azrin, indirectly had a great impact on ASD research. Azrin set up an applied laboratory at Anna State Hospital in Anna, Illinois. He and his associates developed operant-based treatments for many ID problems, which are often seen in ASD. Azrin had worked as a post-doctoral researcher at the Behavioral Research Laboratory. Thus, in no small part, Azrin's work at Anna was an evolutionary spin-off from the Harvard applied laboratory. Allyon, who worked with Azrin, had also visited the Behavioral Research Laboratory (Rutherford, 2003). Allyon and Azrin teamed up to demonstrate the utility of the token economy for long-term psychiatric patients, many of whom also had ID (Allyon & Azrin, 1965; 1968). In later research, behaviors common in autistic children such as self-injury and stereotypies were studied, as were common problems for small children, such as toilet training (Azrin & Foxx, 1971; 1974). The later training was done using repetition, which in some ways was a precursor to the intensive 40-hour per week training of ASD reported on by Lovaas, Smith, and others, which will be described in detail later in this book.

First Applied Studies in ASD

C. B. Ferster (1961) wrote one of the first published papers that viewed autism within a behavioral framework, which he entitled "Positive reinforcement and behavioral deficits of autistic children." Ferster described infantile autism as a relatively rare form of schizophrenia. (This conceptualization may partially explain why it was studied so early in the operant research.) Verbal behavior was a topic of intense interest and the oddities of verbal behavior were a factor in attracting these behavioral research papers. Conceptualizing autism as schizophrenia provided a rationale for study with these children. Ferster's view was that autistic behavior was learned in the same way as other behaviors and that every child is born with a potential for normal development. Through a specific learning history, a child could develop an autistic repertoire (Margolies, 1977).

Lovaas and associates have more recently expressed these sentiments. Because of this view and the fact that most of the treatment research, as previously mentioned, has been conducted in the United States, operant learning as a theoretical model has appeared frequently in the literature. In 1961, Ferster and DeMyer were among the first to attempt to increase the behavioral repertoire of a child with autism using reinforcement schedules. They had the autistic children press a key for edible rewards. Ferster and DeMyer (1961) concluded that the behavior of children with autism could come under the control of reinforcement schedules in the same way one would expect in typically developing humans and animals. The reader can easily see the similarities to the Skinner and Lindsley notion of bridging the basic research to applied problems. Studies such as this (Ferster & DeMyer, 1961; Hingtgen & Churchill, 1969) demonstrated that learning theory principles could be applied to control overt behavior of autistic children (Margolies, 1977).

Ferster and associates may have been the first, but many other studies directed toward practical problems of children with ASD followed in rapid succession. Mudford (2004) estimates that at least 700 research reports on the use of behavior modification have been published in a span of about 40 years. Matson, Benevediz, Compton, Paclawskyj, and Baglio (1996) provide a review of 251 of these studies published between 1980 and 1994, for those who wish to get a flavor of the broad range of topics that have been addressed. In short, major improvements in young children with ASD have been noted in areas such as aberrant behavior, social skills, language, daily living, and academic skills. For example, Wolf, Risley, and Mees (1964) treated tantrums in a $3^1/_2$-year-old boy using time-out. Additionally, he was taught to verbally label pictures by prompting and reinforcement versus simply repeating what others say (echolalia), a common autistic feature. Parent training was also used and involved teaching the parents to use the researcher's training strategies to increase the child's appropriate speech skills. Mudford (2004) also notes that Hewett (1965) developed a treatment for a mute, uncontrollable 4-year-old boy so that he could initiate sounds, words, then short functional sentences in a training sequence similar to the speech curriculum that Lovaas (2003) used later for children with ASD.

Overview of Treatment Review

This chapter and the next focus on psychological interventions that are data- or evidence-based methods of treatment for children with ASD. The National Academy of Sciences (NAS) created a working group to evaluate evidence-based practices for young children with ASD (National Research Council, 2001). Treatments were divided into two categories: individually based interventions and comprehensive treatment models. This latter group, covered in Chapter 5, are used with groups of children, treating multiple behaviors, usually for 20 to 40 hours per week.

In this chapter we look at individual interventions. Typically, literature reviews in this area are arranged either by treatment technique, or by type of problem behaviors and positive living skills training. We have chosen the latter model, since from a practical perspective, the parent, researcher, or clinician typically begins by identifying a skill set they wish to address for the child with ASD. We have also listed the topics in the order they are often dealt with for the child. We start with aberrant behavior, since these "problem" behaviors often impede the development of other prosocial skills. This topic is followed by the pivotal skill sets of social behavior and communication, and the chapter concludes with a discussion of the development of self-help skills.

Aberrant Behavior

Problem behaviors typically observed in children with ASD include stereotypy, self-injury, and aggression (Schreibman, 1988). This subset of behaviors is referred to as aberrant behavior (it is out of the norm), problem behaviors, challenging behaviors and so on. Not all children with ASD have these difficulties and, in some instances, they are not frequent or intense. However, for the subset of children with ASD who evince these aberrant behaviors in a major way, these behaviors are a very serious impediment to their safety and the safety of others. Additionally, this set of behaviors impedes the development of more socially appropriate responses. The parent or clinician simply cannot teach prosocial behaviors with this set of behaviors present. Since these behaviors interfere with the learning process in profound ways, they must be successfully dealt with in the early stages of training and teaching (Newman, Needleman, Reinecke, & Robek, 2002). In a sense, aberrant behaviors are the most pivotal of the pivotal behaviors since they overwhelm the training experience. Once aberrant behaviors have been successfully treated, prosocial skill-building, such as self-help, social and communication skills, can take center stage.

This topic of aberrant behavior takes up far more space and attention than any other skill area for persons with ASD, or any other developmental disabilities. These behaviors are the most difficult to treat, they create the greatest harm to the individual and they cause the greatest problems and disruptions to other learners. One severely self-injurious or aggressive child can disrupt an entire classroom and use up more teacher/trainer resources than all the other children combined. The same can be said for the home environment, making it difficult for parents to give their other children adequate attention. Obviously, these behaviors put children with ASD and those around them at risk for injury.

Initially, operant methods were developed that emphasized suppressing these target behaviors via direct intervention. Typical procedures involved reinforcing incompatible behaviors and often at the same time using punishment procedures, such as briefly restraining the person physically from engaging in the destructive behavior (Favell, McGimsey, & Jones, 1978). Other methods sometimes involved using a manual guidance procedure, such as overcorrection (Foxx & Azrin, 1973). In most instances, the psychologist/mental health professional's role was viewed as "suppressing" or getting rid of the problem behavior. Comprehensive strategies looking at the whole person or entire environment were rarely considered.

The trend has been to move away as much as possible from aversive methods and programs that focus exclusively on one aberrant target behavior. Some people have even claimed that aversive methods are never necessary (Lavigna & Donnellan, 1986; Meyers & Evans, 1989). The data do not support these claims at present; the studies they report have tended to be weak and their rationale suspect. In fact, we argue that while great strides have been made in the quality of treatment for children with ASD, much remains to be learned as a whole and with respect to what types of behavior decelerators/punishers are needed. No magic bullet cures exist at this point, although many clinicians, advocates, and researchers in this area have made such claims, typically with no data other than testimonials to support their assertions.

The stress on using positive supports rather than restraint or other aversive measures appears to have grown out of views of political correctness rather than what the science tells us. For example, Foxx (2005) presents an excellent review entitled "Severe aggression and self-destructive behavior: The myth of the nonaversive treatment of severe behavior." He points out that aversive measures may be necessary primarily with adults who have well-entrenched, intensive problems. However, he builds a strong case against those who argue that positive procedures alone are as effective as or more effective than traditional positive procedure and aversive combinations. We also argue, as have many professionals, that in cases such as self-injury, pica, and aggression, the child with ASD has the right to the treatment most likely to work. A "positive" but ineffective treatment for children with serious behavior problems exposes the child with ASD and others to greater risk of harm, because the aberrant behavior persists at unacceptable rates. We find this hard to justify on moral grounds if more effective but less politically correct procedures are available.

Unfortunately, much has been lost in the semantics. Is there, for example, such a thing as a "positive" intervention? For anything to be reinforcing (e.g. attention, snack foods), a deprivation state must exist and the item must be withheld. The reinforcers would then be given contingently only when a particular socially acceptable behavior occurs, or a socially unacceptable behavior does not occur. On some level, this procedure might be viewed as aversive. Similarly, hugging a tactilely defensive child with ASD to try to acclimate the person to touching might be viewed as aversive by the child. The issue is really a very complicated one. We are not aware of any researchers or clinicians who are trying to intentionally harm children. Procedures such as the contingent slaps Lovaas used with autistic children are generally considered inappropriate today, given current technology of positive behavioral interventions. We agree with that assessment. Time-out or verbal reprimands, such as saying no or physically redirecting the person to an appropriate activity, would constitute what professionals now refer to as aversives. We do not consider these interventions as too extreme or inappropriate.

The semantics of the two camps can also add to the confusion. Foxx (2005) rightly points out that how "severe problem" is defined differs greatly across professional/parent groups. Often, those in the nonaversive camp are referring not to severe forms of self-injury or aggression, but to mild noncompliance. Conversely, the advocates for a broader choice of treatments are often referring to self-injury that can result in mutilation or death, or aggression that can result in serious injuries to self and others and major property destruction. Foxx (2005) contends that it is a myth that severe behavior problems have convincingly been demonstrated to be effectively treated with positive methods alone in reliable, peer-reviewed journals. He also notes that the Association for Behavior Analysis (ABA) is the world's leading behavior analytic organization and that they published a task force report on the right to effective behavioral treatment which supports the use of aversive behavioral procedures where indicated (Van Houten et al., 1988). The ABA continues to maintain this position, as do the National Institutes of Health (NIH) who convened a Consensus Development Conference on the topic (NIH, 1989), with many of the nation's leading experts on the treatment of aberrant behavior in attendance.

The potential for abuse with any procedure is always present. Pharmacology in particular as well as aversives, present the potential for misuse and resultant physical harm to the person with ASD. Thus, patient/parent consent, the use of qualified professionals and outside review of treatments, such as Individualized Education Plan (IEP) team reviews, are essential. When aversive methods are incorporated in a plan, it is recommended that they only be one of a number of treatment elements and that the least intrusive procedure possible be used for the severe behavior problem targeted (Matson et al., 1996). As mentioned, overcorrection and contingent restraint are aversive methods that have been used. Table 4.1 presents some examples of aversive treatment methods that have been successful in this population.

Of course, the most positive learning environment possible that will still produce relevant skill gains is the goal. As a rule, the younger the child and the less severe the self-injury, aggression, pica, or other serious aberrant behavior, the less likely any aversives will be needed. Many children will have no aberrant behavior, thus no aversives will be required, other than perhaps having to say no or verbally redirect the child to a task. We have mentioned that researchers are working to develop methods that will minimize the need for aversives while still producing positive behavior change. Additionally, these restrictive methods would be used rarely with the young child with ASD in any event. The possible substitute interventions that have been the most discussed and researched, at least in some cases, are functional assessment (FA) and, to lesser extent, positive behavior procedures, such as social skills and communication training.

Nonaversive behavioral treatments have largely been described as environmental manipulation, positive reinforcement, or FA and the treatments that ensue (Matson,

Table 4.1: Examples of aversive methods used in the treatment of ASD

Method	Example study
Time-out	Husted, Hall, & Agin (1971)
	McKeegan, Estill, & Campbell (1984)
Overcorrection	Maag, Rutherford, Wolchik, & Parks (1986)
	Mohr & Sharpley (1985)
Response cost	Falcomata, Roane, & Hovanetz (2004)
	Pelios, MacDuff, & Axelrod (2003)
Extinction	Ricciardi & Luiselli (2003)
Sensory extinction	Maag, Rutherford, & Wolchik (1986)
	Rincover (1978)
Verbal reprimand	Charlop-Christy & Haymes (1996)

Laud, & Matson, 2004; O'Brien & Repp, 1990). Little has been done in the way of research strategies for environmental manipulation. However, positive reinforcement strategies and FA have been receiving a good deal of attention in the literature. Therefore, a review of these methods follows.

Positive Reinforcement Strategies

Five reinforcement behavior reduction programs are typically discussed in the treatment literature. These methods are differential reinforcement of incompatible behaviors (DRI), differential reinforcement of alternate behaviors (DRA), differential reinforcement of other behaviors (DRO), differential reinforcement of low rate behavior (DRL), and noncontingent reinforcement (NCR).

The problems most often treated with reinforcement procedures are self-injury, stereotypies, aggression, and other problem behaviors (O'Brien & Repp, 1990). O'Brien and Repp reported that the most frequently used reinforcers are social, edibles, money, and vibratory stimulation. O'Brien and Repp (1990) concluded that schools and residential facilities were the primary sites for such treatment, which was carried out almost exclusively by professionals (versus parents). These procedures have received less attention as sole treatments for aberrant behavior in recent years. One reason is the recognition that the reinforcer provided may not be powerful enough, particularly when the aberrant behavior is well entrenched, to offset the reinforcing properties associated with the maladaptive routine or the reinforcing aspects of the aberrant behavior itself. As a result, much greater focus has been placed on evaluation of the behavior's function via FA.

Another procedure in the reinforcement domain that has received some attention is NCR. This procedure differs from methods such as DRO in that the stimulus change is programmed independently of the occurrence of the aberrant behavior, as opposed to reinforcement based on the absence of the behavior. NCR involves reinforcement presentation on a schedule that is not contingent on the target maladaptive behavior. Obvious practical advantages of NCR include being able to provide reinforcement at convenient intervals for the caregiver. However, a major disadvantage is that typically decreases in aberrant behavior are slow (Thompson & Iwata, 2005). Additionally, the use of this method in applied settings has not received a great deal of research attention. The technique does not seem to be catching on at this time as a means of treating maladaptive behavior. The same cannot be said of FA, which has become an extremely popular approach in research and practice, and has been promoted by the courts, particularly in the US Justice Department in their litigation against state developmental centers.

Functional Assessment

The operant model conceptualizes events such as *antecedents* (precursors), the *behaviors* themselves and *consequences* (what happens immediately after the occurrence of the target behavior). These conditions are sometimes referred to as the ABCs of behaviorism. Focusing on antecedents and consequences via systematic analysis, researchers and clinicians attempt to determine what events are causing and maintaining these target behaviors. To date, functional assessment (FA), which is a structured means of assisting in such a determination, has been used almost exclusively with aberrant behaviors such as the ones mentioned previously in this chapter. In one of the early reports on FA, Iwata, Dorsey, Slifer, Bauman, and Richmond (1982) presented an antecedent-based methodology for people with severe ID and self-injurious behaviors. They were successful in identifying environmental events that caused the aberrant behavior in many cases. This methodology has become quite popular among those in the scientific community. Gradually, clinicians have begun to warm to these methods as well. The functional analysis approach provides a proactive, positively oriented assessment that can be linked to intervention. FA can also be introduced in an ongoing fashion to refine or modify treatment plans as contingencies change for the child over time.

FA can be conducted in one of four ways or by using some combination of these methods. The approach popularized by proponents of the Association of Behavior Analysis (ABA) is experimental functional analysis (EFA). Typically, the person with self-injury or aggression is tested under contrived (analogue) conditions. These conditions consist of presenting one specific condition prior to treatment and following an event for a given time interval, then shifting to another set of conditions (e.g. attention for self-injury, then a tangible award). This approach is popular among researchers and has resulted in a substantial number of articles (Sturmey, 1996). Typically, hypothesized reasons for the target behavior to occur are that the aberrant response results in *attention*, a *tangible* item such as food or a toy the child likes, or *escape* from an undesirable setting such as a classroom with academic demand, or the child prefers to be *alone* since the behavior is reinforcing in and of itself. This latter factor is particularly salient for children with ASD, since "self-stimulating" behaviors such as hand flapping are common.

At the time of this writing, many researchers, particularly those in the ABA camp, see the EFA as the gold standard for FA. Several practical concerns have surfaced regarding EFA procedures, however. First, the typical EFA requires multiple sessions and upwards of two to four hours to conduct an assessment on one aberrant behavior with one child. Also, two or three masters or doctoral level staff are required to carry out the assessment. Second, in a tangible condition, for example, the child with ASD would be given a reward each time he engaged in the target behavior. The child is therefore in a position to have the reason for self-injury strengthened. Third, if a tangible reinforcer had not been a maintaining variable, a sufficient number of trials could "shape" the aberrant behavior into a consequence. Fourth, physiological arousal resulting from increasing the self-injury, aggression, or other aberrant behaviors may continue at rates along those of baseline once the session has been terminated and the child with ASD has been reintroduced into the natural environment. Fifth, the likelihood of self or staff injury is present. A session would be terminated if the child's problem behavior gets out of control. However, admitting the behavior is out of control is also admitting that an increased potential for injury has been produced. Terminating the session does not necessarily mean the dangerous behavior will immediately stop. Sixth, by systematically manipulating environmental events under artificial conditions, the ecological validity of the assessment is compromised. Just because the behavior occurs in a particular way in an analogue situation does not mean the behavior will occur in the same way in the natural environment. The seventh and final concern about EFA is that the aberrant behavior may be maintained by idiosyncratic events that may or may not be manipulated in the experimental assessment. The complex nature of the assessment may make it difficult to replicate the conditions that maintain the aberrant behavior in the natural environment (Hall, in press; Matson, 2004).

To address the shortcomings inherent in EFA, a second type of FA, checklists for functional assessment (CFA), was developed. This approach is perhaps the most promising area of FA since it does not pose many of the ethical and logistic issues associated with EFA. CFA has been developed as a means of dealing with these problems by providing an assessment that can be done in half an hour by one masters level professional with a knowledgeable informant such as a parent, direct staff person, teacher, or other caregiver. This assessment is based on the last week or two of the child's behavior in their normal operating environment. CFAs do not require direct contact with the client, which avoids many of the problems with EFA noted above. Advocates of EFA have been skeptical that these CFAs would not produce results as reliable and valid as an EFA. If the informant's memory fails, if they do not fully understand the question or they do not know or have not observed the behavior that is being asked about, the data on the CFA may be of little value.

The first CFA developed, the Motivation Assessment Scale (MAS), contained a set of questions designed to address common conditions such as attention that maintains aberrant behavior. The MAS did not prove to be very reliable or valid (Newton & Sturmey, 1991; Zarcone, Rodgers, Iwata, Rourke, & Dorsey, 1991). However, the MAS was an important first step in establishing the variables maintaining self-injury in children with ASD (Durand & Crimmins, 1988). Additionally, the scale set the general conceptual model for how CFAs should be done.

A newer scale, the Questions About Behavior Function (QABF), built on the functions established through EFA research (Iwata et al., 1982) and the MAS checklist format pioneered by Durand and Carr (1991). The QABF has 25 items with five subscales of 5 items each. The subscales are escape, attention, nonsocial, tangible, and pain-related. The idea is to provide a means to collect FA data more rapidly using less technically trained assessors. The subscales of the QABF have been confirmed by factor analysis (Matson & Vollmer, 1995; Paclawskyj, Matson, Rush, Smalls, & Vollmer, 2001). Additionally, interrater and test–retest reliability have also been established. These initial data were sufficiently encouraging to promote additional research and widespread clinical application internationally.

To date, the largest and most robust study of an FA method was performed using the QABF (Matson, Bamburg, Cherry, & Paclawskyj, 1999). The authors tested the validity of the QABF in a sample of 398 adults with ID, whereas in the typical EFA experiment only two to four people were studied. Additionally, we know that the functions of aberrant behavior are never clear and easy to identify in adults where the person has years to devise strategies to obtain desired outcomes with their maladaptive behavior. The function of their behavior is thus often multi-functioned, unclear and difficult to identify. The fact that this study used adults with long-standing self-injury, stereotypies, or aggression added substantially to the robustness of the results. Individuals were placed in Group 1 ($n = 118$) if they evinced self-injury; Group 2 ($n = 83$) comprised individuals with aggression, and Group 3 ($n = 197$) those with stereotypies. Persons with more than one of these problems were excluded to avoid ambiguous group assignments and to maintain groups where only one dependent variable would be treated at a time. Thus it was possible to reduce possible interpretation errors relating to effects of the independent variables. Clear environmental

Table 4.2: Prominent QABF antecedents and severity scores for each group

	Group 1 SIB	Group 2 Aggression	Group 3 Stereotypies
Percent of group identified with clear antecedent	83%	74%	93.30%
Prominent antecedents	Nonsocial (45%)	Attention (38.7%)	Nonsocial (93.3%)
	Escape (36%)	Escape (35.3%)	
Severity scores for prominent antecedents (means)	Nonsocial (M = 6.36)	Attention (M = 4.89)	Nonsocial (M = 11.66)
	Escape (M = 8.22)	Escape (M = 6.16)	

M = mean. SIB = self-injurious behavior.
From "A validity study on the Questions About Behavior Function (QABF) scale: Predicting treatment success for self-injury, aggression and stereotypies," by J. L. Matson, J. W. Bamburg, K. E. Cherry, & T. R. Paclawskyj, 1999, *Research in Developmental Disabilities, 20*, p.168. Copyright 1999 by Elsevier Publishing. Reprinted with permission.

causes were noted in 83% of the self-injury group, 74% of the aggression group, and 93.3% of the stereotypies group. Data are broken down by function in Table 4.2.

In the second part of the study, 180 individuals from the initial 398 were selected. Thirty of the adults with ID and self-injury, 30 with aggression, and 30 with stereotypies had treatment plans developed based on environmental functions identified using the QABF. Each of the three groups also had 30 matched controls whose treatments were not derived by functional analysis. For QABF-derived plans based on attention, training of appropriate communication was stressed. For a nonsocial function, environment enrichment and social skills training were used. All of these procedures could be used in some form tailored to the individual for attention-related problem behaviors. Controls received a standard treatment protocol of interrupting the aberrant behavior, blocking the behavior with a caregiver's hand or arm to stop harm to self or others, and redirecting the person verbally to appropriate tasks. These procedures are standard in many schools, developmental centers, and community living arrangements. Treatment was administered for 6 months. In all three conditions, improvements were much greater (significantly on statistical examination) compared to the controls. Thus, with an FA that could be done in minutes and with minimal tailoring of the treatment, a positively oriented intervention that produced excellent treatment effects could be produced. We consider these data compelling.

More recently, researchers have found that results from the QABF are fairly similar to those found in the more labor-intensive EFA. Paclawskyj et al. (2001) administered the QABF to 13 persons with ID evincing self-injury, tantrums, or stereotypy. For 10 of 13 participants, the problem behaviors were motivated by either escape or sensory conse-quences, with attention the cause in one case. The EFA data and QABF data identified the same primary motivating factor in 56.3% of the cases.

In another confirmatory study of the QABF, Nicholson, Konstantinidi, and Furniss (in press) tested 28 males and 12 females between 10 and 26 years of age (average age 17.6) who lived in four residential schools and colleges for people with ASD and/or ID in the north of England. The QABF was completed for 118 problem behaviors, including self-injury, stereotypies, swearing, screaming, throwing property, aggression, and property destruction. The study was geared toward evaluating the psychometric properties of the scale. In their summary comments the authors state that their data largely replicate previous findings of acceptable internal consistency, and factor analysis confirms the factor structure with subscales of the QABF from previous research. They also conclude that while being far from perfect as a means of identifying functions of behavior (we concur), the QABF represents a considerable advancement over other comparable CFAs. They also note that where the person tested had multiple problem behaviors, it became more difficult to tease out the functions. We believe this result is likely to occur with any FA method. Finally, we concur with their conclusion that where resources allow, a QABF should be used in combination with other methods, such as structured descriptive analysis or experimental analysis. When time and other resources do not permit employing these techniques, the intervention should use brief renewals of treatment conditions to baseline or other methods that might help confirm the QABF conclusions (Aikman, Garbutt, & Furniss, 2003).

Hall (in press) has also studied this problem with four adults with ID. He used the third type of FA, descriptive assessment. Using this method, the rater checks off antecedent behaviors and consequences in real time, in the natural environment as the behavior occurs. A major weakness of this procedure, particularly with low rate, high intensity behaviors, is that they may not occur during observations. EFA was also conducted using the methodology of Iwata et al. (1994). Hall (in press) conducted the EFA in a quiet room on the facility grounds. For one participant, four test conditions and a control condition were used, while for the other three participants, three experimental conditions and one control condition were used.

The attention condition required a support staff person to sit in a room with his or her back to the participant, who had access to preferred rewards such as chocolate, magazines, and toilet tissue. An incident of the aberrant behavior was followed by the staff person turning round and saying, "don't do that" followed by statements of concern. During the demand (escape) condition, the support staff asked the participant to match socks and fold clothes, complete a puzzle or mop the floor. A staff person sat beside the participant, giving frequent physical and verbal prompts while the participant worked. An incident of the aberrant behavior terminated the task for 30 seconds, allowing the participant to escape the task and the demands associated with it for that interval. For the tangible condition, chocolate and magazines were removed from the room. The staff person sat next to the participant and interacted with him every 30 seconds. If a problem behavior occurred, preferred items were presented to the participant for 30 seconds. The alone condition was presented to one male and the only female participant. The staff person left the room and did not return until the condition was completed. Occurrences of the problem behavior were ignored. The play condition had the tangible reinforcers present, and the staff person interacted with the participant every 30 seconds. No demands were made and occurrence of the problem behaviors was ignored. The experimental conditions just described were presented in random order. Conditions lasted 10 minutes each, with a 2-minute break between each condition.

Three to four blocks of the four to five conditions were conducted for each participant over a 3-week period. Each participant was exposed to each condition three or four times.

The final FA in the study was the administration of the 25-item QABF. As noted, this measure is much less labor intensive than the other three. The assessment was completed by having a support staff rate each item from 0 (never occurs) to 3 (always occurs). Hall (in press) found that QABF and EFA data were in agreement in three of four cases, whereas EFA and descriptive assessment were only in agreement in one of four. He reported that 10 hours was required to do the descriptive assessment, 2 hours for the EFA (it would also take a considerable amount of time to train the support staff) and 15 minutes to do the QABF. Given the potential dangers associated with the EFA and the positive data that has emerged with the QABF, it would appear to be the FA of choice, particularly for children with ASD, since the problem behaviors will be of recent origin and thus easier to identify than in the adults described in these studies. Should these procedures fail, more extensive, intensive and intrusive methods could be considered.

Two other forms of FA, interviews and scatter plot, have also been developed. These methods have seen limited research and application, but they are nonetheless worth noting since they may prove to be of value in some situations. Of the FA interviews, the best known is probably the system of O'Neill, Horner, Abin, Storey, and Sprague (1991). O'Neill et al.'s (1991) FA interview and methods aim to identify the possible variables affecting an individual's behavior and focus attention on the variables that appear to be the most influential. Once these settings or events are identified, further observation and systematic study can be implemented. The FA interview is usually conducted with the clinician serving as the interviewer and one or two people who have daily contact with the child (e.g. parents, teachers, etc.) providing the information. O'Neill and his colleagues (1991) stated that an FA interview has three primary objectives: (1) to describe the challenging behaviors; (2) to identify the environmental factors that are influencing the person's challenging behaviors; and (3) to identify the consequences that maintain the behaviors. O'Neill et al. (1991) provided a framework for meeting these objectives that included describing all of the behaviors that are undesirable (not just the most problematic behaviors), operationally defining the challenging behaviors and searching for behavioral chains (different behaviors that occur in a predictable sequence). Environmental variables, such as medications, sleep cycles, daily routines and activities, and staffing patterns, are also considered, as are the time of day, physical location, and activities during which the challenging behaviors occur. O'Neill et al. (1991) also identified the function of the behavior (e.g. obtaining tangible items or social attention) and the alternative methods by which the individual is able to obtain the same end (e.g. alternative methods currently in the individual's repertoire for obtaining the tangible item). At the conclusion of the interview, the clinician should evaluate the information obtained to decide whether the behaviors, environmental variables and functions have been sufficiently defined through the interview process. O'Neill et al. (1991) recommended that the interview data be used as a supplement to the direct observation methods previously discussed.

This technique has some clear advantages and some disadvantages when compared to other methods of FA. Open-ended questions, for example, provide the opportunity to obtain more tailored answers. Clinically, these data can be useful in developing interventions for the child with ASD. On the negative side, these open-ended questions result in nonstandardized responses. Because of the lack of uniformity, norms cannot be developed and testing the reliability and validity of the assessment method becomes quite difficult. These psychometric studies have not been done. Therefore, whether this approach can accurately and consistently identify functions of aberrant behavior remains unanswered.

Scatter Plot

The scatter plot is a simple method that serves as an adjunct to other procedures when refining the FA. A matrix or grid formed with time intervals up the vertical axis and successive days across the horizontal axis is used. A square is filled in when a problem behavior occurs, thus pinpointing a particular time on a particular day when the problem behavior was present, as presented in Figure 4.1. Often, a pattern emerges, with target behaviors clustering at given points in time, say when the child gets up, and at lunch. Further analysis of those times in the day may produce, for example, demands to get dressed, brush one's teeth, etc. in the morning, while at lunch the child may be distracted by noise and the activities of others. Little formal research is available on this procedure, but it is accepted among clinicians and researchers and is often used in clinical settings because it is not particularly labor intensive and can provide interesting information on patterns of responding.

Functional Assessment: Conclusion

Two points are of note regarding the linking of FA to treatment. First, it is believed that behaviors are linked, occurring in response chains. Thus, intervention can be targeted to the earliest and thus least maladaptive event in the chain, which typically allows for a more positively oriented treatment. For example, a child with ASD may start to lose eye contact with a task, then start to make humming noises, then start to hand flap and then start

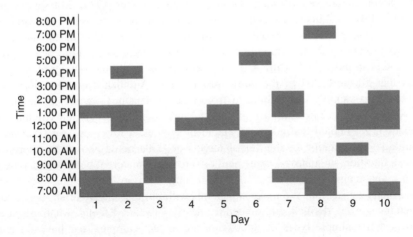

Figure 4.1: Example scatter plot.

to hit herself (i.e. self-injury). Given that these events consistently occur in the sequence noted, the treatment would be focused on eye contact versus waiting until self-injury occurs. Therefore, treatment might be a verbal prompt to make eye contact with a task, rather than brief physical restraint or in some medically oriented settings, resorting to a psychotropic drug as treatment.

The second aspect of FA is to alert the caregiver as to what is maintaining the self-injury. If, for example, escape from the classroom activity is the cause of the aberrant behavior, different more positive tasks might be implemented, richer reinforcement schedules might be introduced and sound, light, movement, or other environmental factors might be introduced to make the environment more pleasant. Taking this approach may eliminate or dramatically decrease the need to see escape as a compliance issue that requires time-out or some other more intrusive intervention.

To date, there are no foolproof FA methods, nor is such an eventuality likely in the foreseeable future. However, these methods and the research growing around them are encouraging. This method may become one of the most popular adjuncts to treatment in the future. Time commitments and expertise needed to establish antecedents and consequences can be prohibitive with EFA. The most promising method at present appears to be using the QABF in combination with a scatter plot and/or other real time data from naturalistic settings. In the most complex cases, all means of FA might be tried. These methods, if adopted, will likely be used in conjunction with skill-building models such as social skills training.

Social Skills Training

Social skills deficits and excesses have been an area receiving considerable attention for some time. Hersen and Bellack were the first authors to popularize this intervention approach in the broad clinical literature, primarily with chronic schizophrenics and later with adults evincing unipolar depression (Bellack, Turner, Hersen, & Luber, 1984). Mueser and Bellack (1989) defined social skills as a specific set of behavioral components that are used, among other things, to express one's thoughts, feelings, and desires. One of the most critical methods of promoting these components is speech content. An example of inappropriate speech content in individuals with ASD is preoccupation with and talking about personal concerns that are unrelated to the conversation topic. Another major social problem is that the child may simply isolate himself from others (Matson, Compton, & Sevin, 1991). Problems also occur in rate and pace of speech, voice tone and pitch and volume. Mueser and Bellack (1989) noted that a simple statement such as "I love you" can, depending on the qualitative presentation of the verbal targets or skills noted above, be interpreted as affection, a question, an annoyed agreement or sarcasm. Nonverbal behaviors can be added to the mix and include distance between the people who are interacting, eye contact or gaze, and facial expression. We make two points with our comments. First, these problems have been recognized, defined, and treated for nearly 30 years. Second, what appear at first blush to be fairly simple types of interaction are in fact complex and have far-reaching implications.

History of Social Skills Training

The study of social skills in children became popular in the 1980s (Matson & Ollendick, 1989). Inappropriate social skills have been related to a variety of problems, such as depression (Matson et al., 1980), hyperactivity (Milich & Landau, 1982) and conduct problems (Gardner & Cole, 1987). ASD is generally believed to be related to social interpersonal problems since social skills are defining characteristics of ID and ASD (Schreibman, 1988). For autism, Matson et al. (1991) found that these children were more stubborn, more likely to get upset if they had to wait, more likely to continue to try to get others to do as they wished and less likely to engage in helping behaviors, such as doing nice things for others or helping a friend who is hurt, when compared to same-age peers. Similarly, the absence of appropriate social skills can impede language and intellectual development and result in severe isolation, which is another important factor in developing social relationships (Sasso, Garrison-Harrell, & Rogers, 1994). The majority of children with ASD also evince ID. For persons experiencing comorbid conditions of ASD and ID, limitations in social skills are frequently greater than if only one disorder is present (Kraijer, 2000; Njardvik, Matson, & Cherry, 1999). Less difference is noted between other forms of adaptive behavior when ASD is not present (de Bildt et al., 2005). The more severe the ID and/or ASD, the larger the problems with social skills (Gilham, Carter, Volkmar, & Sparrow, 2000; Liss et al., 2001).

The literature on communication has become quite massive. Thus, we can only provide some example studies of what is available. McConnell (2002) groups these training methods into child-specific interventions, collateral skills programs, and peer-mediated interventions. The child-specific and peer-mediated models have received by far the most attention and thus the bulk of the review will focus on these methods.

Child-Specific Interventions

The procedures that have been developed in this area are largely borrowed from the general child and ID literature. Typically, these procedures involve the identification of specific social behaviors, such as eye contact, facial expression, and speech content. Kazdin, Matson, and Esveldt-Dawson (1984) provide a model for child treatment using these methods based on Bellack and Hersen, as described a bit later. Mueser and Bellack (1989) define this type of training as a highly structured intervention where new behaviors are taught through performance. They equate training to teaching motor or musical skills. This thinking was a major departure from earlier "psychotherapies" that dealt with interpersonal skills. Client-centered therapy, psychodynamic approaches, Gestalt therapy and the like conceptualized interpersonal interaction as self-actualization and self-exploration. Calling these constructs transitory skills or behaviors that could be broken down into components and trained as a skills set is uniquely learning-theory oriented. This thinking was a major breakthrough for emotionally disabled individuals, and those with ID or ASD since these persons did not display the verbal give-and-take needed to engage in talk therapy. Further, following a teaching/training model using specific techniques employed in a defined order with observable defined behaviors went a long way in demystifying the interpersonal relationship.

Training then proceeds in a gradual, hierarchical fashion from easy to difficult social behaviors. Treatment goals and training strategies are adjusted according to performance. Extended practice and overlearning are encouraged. Thus, when the person is in a stressful situation, which is usually one where the person has not evinced the skill before or has failed to adequately perform the skill in the past, the residual skill they are able to display is often sufficient to turn a failure experience into a success.

Matson, Kazdin, and Esveldt-Dawson (1980) presented a model for treating handi-capped children with moderate ID and social skills difficulties. The two African American boys, aged 11 and 12 years, were diagnosed with conduct disorder and a history of stealing, running away, and physically attacking others. They were treated on seven target behaviors: physical gestures, facial mannerisms, eye contact, number of words spoken, voice intonation, verbal content, and overall social skills.

Training was one-to-one with the therapist and child. Six scenes were presented per session from one to three times, depending on the accuracy of the child's responses. Following the presentation of a scene, which consisted of a brief social vignette, the child was routinely exposed to the natural environment. The therapist then provided feedback on each target behavior. When target behaviors were performed incorrectly, the scene was re-presented with the trainer modeling the responses in the correct way to the child. After all the scene presentations, which could range from six to eight presentations per training session, the child was assessed a final time with no instruction. The data from this trial were recorded on a graph to determine the child's progress during independent trials. Two training sessions were conducted daily, Monday through Friday. Same age-matched non-handicapped peers were also tested on each targeted social behavior. Mean times, plus and minus one standard deviation, were plotted. The idea here was to provide a real world normative test of what constituted acceptable behavior on all the target behaviors. Performance at or above these lines was viewed as a successful outcome. These data and those of the non-handicapped peers are presented in Figures 4.2 and 4.3.

Initially, generalization scenes were ones where no training or practice was provided. Rather, the scenes were presented and the child's performance was noted. The requisite skills did not improve until treatment was provided. Follow-up sessions at 4 and 6 weeks showed that the skills were maintained at high levels. Figures 4.4 and 4.5 illustrate these generalization scenes.

The techniques and methods of child-specific intervention were developed primarily by clinical psychologists in inpatient and outpatient settings. Through studies such as the Kazdin et al. (1984) experiment, techniques initially developed for chronic schizophrenics and depressed adults were modified for use with children who evince a developmental disability (Bellack et al., 1984; Hersen, Eisler, & Miller, 1973). Since then, special educators have made clever and useful modifications to these strategies to make them more applicable to parents and teachers. Strain and associates have been particularly active in this area. They have been instrumental in doing research to identify targets for social skills curriculums in school settings for children with ASD (Strain, 1983). They used naturally developing preschoolers to help train the peer social interactions of socially withdrawn, handicapped preschoolers (Strain, 1977; Strain, Shores, & Timm, 1977). Caregivers are encouraged to provide positive interactions between preschoolers with ASD (Strain & Danko, 1995). Positive imitations, appropriate play, and other cooperative social behaviors have emerged as

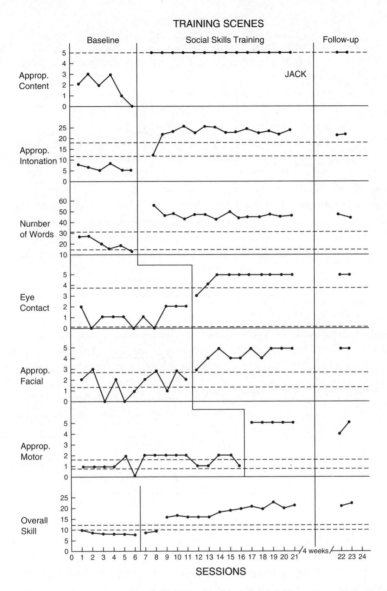

Figure 4.2: Training scene for Target Child 1 (Jack). Multiple baseline analysis of the effects of training on specific target behaviors and overall rating of social skill for Jack. The horizontal lines depict the range delineated by the mean plus and minus one standard deviation for the validation sample. Due to equipment failure on day 7, audiotaped data for the first three behaviors were not recorded. (From "Training interpersonal skills among mentally retarded and socially dysfunctional children," by J. L. Matson, A. E. Kazdin, & K. Esveldt-Dawson, 1980, *Behaviour Research and Therapy, 18*, p. 422. Copyright 1990 by Elsevier Publishing. Reprinted with permission.)

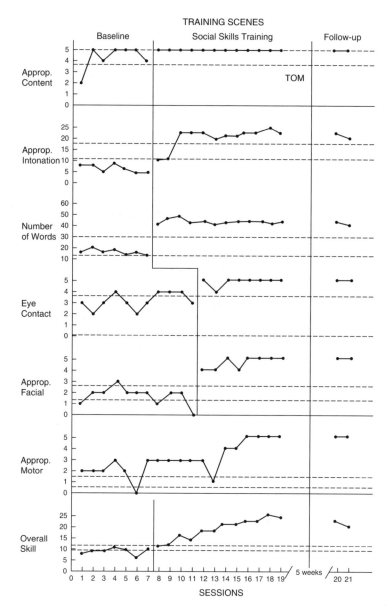

Figure 4.3: Training scene for Target Child 2 (Tom). Multiple baseline analysis of the effects of training on specific target behaviors and overall rating of social skill for Tom. The horizontal lines depict the range delineated by the mean plus and minus one standard deviation for the validation sample. (From "Training interpersonal skills among mentally retarded and socially dysfunctional children," by J. L. Matson, A. E. Kazdin, & K. Esveldt-Dawson, 1990, *Behaviour Research and Therapy, 18*, p. 423. Copyright 1990 by Elsevier Publishing. Reprinted with permission.)

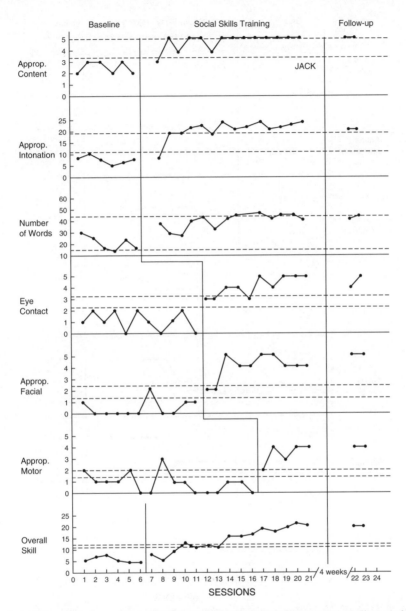

Figure 4.4: Generalization scenes for Target Child 1 (Jack). Multiple baseline analysis of the effects of training on specific target behaviors and overall rating of social skill for Jack. The horizontal lines depict the range delineated by the mean plus and minus one standard deviation for the validation sample. (From "Training interpersonal skills among mentally retarded and socially dysfunctional children," by J. L. Matson, A. E. Kazdin, & K. Esveldt-Dawson, 1990, *Behaviour Research and Therapy, 18*, p. 424. Copyright 1990 by Elsevier Publishing. Reprinted with permission.)

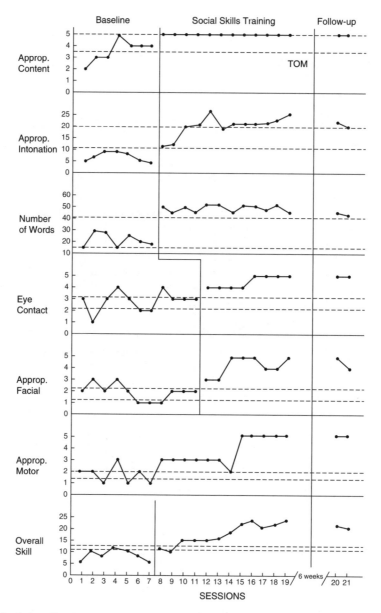

Figure 4.5: Generalization scenes for Target Child 2 (Tom). Multiple baseline analysis of the effects of training on specific target behaviors and overall rating of social skill for Tom. The horizontal lines depict the range delineated by the mean plus and minus one standard deviation for the validation sample. (From "Training interpersonal skills among mentally retarded and socially dysfunctional children," by J. L. Matson, A. E. Kazdin, & K. Esveldt-Dawson, 1990, *Behaviour Research and Therapy, 18,* p. 424. Copyright 1990 by Elsevier Publishing. Reprinted with permission.)

key in improving how handicapped children are viewed. Incorporating a variety of activities, peers, environments, curriculums, and caregivers into training has been an excellent way to enhance the likelihood that children with ASD can learn to perform these skills in real world environments while decreasing the major costs associated with such training.

Peer-mediated interventions often involve what are referred to as typical peers. These children are in effect therapists. A typical child and a child with ASD are paired during an activity such as recess. However, simply pairing the two children does not ensure meaningful interactions (Pierce & Schreibman, 1995). Thus, supports to typical peers (e.g. training as a therapist) are recommended to sustain the use of new interaction strategies (Sainato, Goldstein, & Strain, 1992). However, as we have noted, the typical child may not wish to give up their free time or they may wish to be paired with a child with ASD for only a brief time period. These desires and wishes must be adhered to in a sensitive fashion to ensure the rights of both children. Also, these programs are unlikely to be feasible with very young children such as the ones this book addresses. Typical children of this age are unlikely to be able to perform the requisite treatment strategies accurately.

Additional refinement of these strategies has continued at a good pace. Mahoney and Perales (2003) in summarizing efforts, particularly pertaining to parent social skills interactions, identify several "teaching objectives" they refer to as "pivotal intervention objectives." Some of these behaviors appear straightforward and easy enough to measure, such as imitations, vocalizations, cooperation, and conversation. However, we would caution the reader that other "pivotal intervention objectives" being mentioned in some curriculums, such as problem-solving, feelings of control, interest and trust/attachment, are more troublesome. These concepts are broad, vague, open to multiple interpretations and thus may need to be broken down into more readily observable and measurable units. They do not really pass the test of clinical relevance although the values espoused are fine conceptually.

In addition to involving those who interact with children with ASD regularly, such as parents, teachers, and peers, self-management has also been tested. Approximately 80% of children with ASD have ID. Additionally, our emphasis here is on young children (typically 2–6 years of age), making this procedure applicable to a much smaller percentage of children than the other methods we have reviewed. Nonetheless, some reports of success with young children have been noted.

Self-management involves training the child with ASD (who is typically over the age of 4), to self-monitor or evaluate his or her behavior and act on these observations to perform more socially acceptable behavior. Specific skills are taught using methods such as those described earlier in this section or by directly reinforcing and shaping the response in the natural environment. An additional layer of training is added. These extra procedures consist of using checklists, pictures, or other external prompts to help the child track desired behaviors. When the target response is detected by the child, he or she employs the skills learned in the training settings.

In one example using this training model, Shearer, Kohler, Buchan, and McCullough (1996) taught three 5-year-old children with ASD social skills by exposing them to adult-mediated training while playing with typically developing peers. Children monitored their level of engagement with other children and frequency of social interactions. Using a similar format, Strain, Kohler, Storey, and Danko (1994) also applied training to the home environment after positive effects were achieved in the school setting.

We applaud the attempts to extend treatment to naturalistic environments and to involve children in training as much as possible. However, while these attempts appear promising, some reservations should be mentioned. First, self-monitoring is often not successful with adults of normal intelligence. Motivation, failure to fully understand the procedures, and difficulty in attending to self-monitoring when attention can wander to other tasks (e.g. what will I say during a conversation) is likely with young children. These factors and others make this procedure difficult to apply in complex learning situations over time. Add to these factors the fact that the young children we are referring to in this book have ASD and in the majority of cases ID as well, and the notion of a positive outcome is minimized further. We would therefore caution that self-management is likely to be ancillary to more structured, externally driven interventions with young ASD children.

Collateral Skills Programs

McConnell (2002) describes collateral skills programs as ones where social interactions can be increased as a function of training different skills, such as academic pursuits or play. He notes that the literature using these methods is small. We would argue that such procedures are likely to be of limited value in early intervention models for children with ASD, since this technique presupposes that the children possess the relevant social skills but choose not to use them due to insufficient opportunity or motivation (e.g. it is not reinforced frequently enough in the environment). These assumptions are likely to be more frequently the case when dealing with older children or adults with ASD since they would have had more time to develop and practice such skills. Secondly, social skills are likely to be so essential that for most early intervention programs, these skills are likely to be front and center among the most important skills to train. Thus, leaving them to chance as a collateral positive effect of other forms of training is likely to be unacceptable.

One possible exception to the latter point noted above is communication and speech training. Koegel, Camarata, Valdez-Menchaca, and Koegel (1998), for example, found that preschoolers with ASD could be taught question asking, which then generalized across settings and objects, and increased social interactions. Obviously, to have a social exchange persons with ASD need to acquire building block skills of communicating/socializing in the same way that a person would first need to learn to read before he could pursue in-depth study of history or literature.

Peer-Mediated Interventions

This set of procedures involves employing other children in a classroom, or other naturalistic environment, as a co-trainer or co-participant with the child who has ASD. The literature typically gives considerable weight to the positive aspects of such interventions, which we will do as well. However, it is important to note that these "other children" must willingly participate and should be allowed to continue to participate in such activities by their own choosing. We have seen numerous examples where children have been coerced into involvement and remaining involved in such programs when, in fact, they would prefer not to do so. Ethical concerns exist here that must be addressed whenever children are being asked or required to participate in peer-mediated interventions. Professionals or parents, as advocates, should be equally concerned about the rights and well-being of all children involved and must be careful not to push their value system upon others.

With the concern noted above addressed, there are many potential positive elements associated with the peer-mediated approach. Peer-mediated interventions have been reported to be effective in enhancing interactions between children with ASD and their peers (Goldstein & Ferrell, 1987) and in increasing social interaction rates (Lee & Odom, 1996), and it has been shown that older elementary age children can implement learning-based procedures to increase the social interactions of their young siblings (Coe, Matson, Craigie, & Gossen, 1991). Peer-mediated interventions have a number of potential benefits for all the children involved in the training. The child who provides the modeling receives reinforcement for the skills he or she has already acquired, as well as strengthening those skills through repetition. At the same time, the child is able to see the benefits of these skills first hand when practiced by others.

The area of social skills training varies somewhat from the training methods used for other domains of behavior studied in children with ASD. Other areas tend to rely largely on traditional operant conditioning methods. These procedures incorporate a range of methods that could be described as social learning or cognitive behavior therapy. Techniques such as modeling, social reinforcement, and self-monitoring are commonly described. Typically, these procedures have not been described as often in the packaged programs discussed previously as operant methods. However, the potential these methods have for promoting skill acquisition and maintenance in real life situations would seem to suggest that they deserve further attention in the future, perhaps with other skill areas, such as aberrant behavior and communication.

Communication Training

Children with ASD are known to have verbal skill deficits from 2–3 years of age that persist even after later linguistic skills develop. These children are particularly deficient in their adherence to conversational rules (Adams & Bishop, 1989). The child with ASD is described as unable to understand the meaning of social signals and the mental status of others (Sigman & Kasari, 1994). Thus, much of the intervention, as with social skills, is seen as training, teaching, or instruction that is aimed at remediation of what are viewed as poorly learned social exchanges. Thus, early intervention for communication is recommended (Aldred, Pollard, & Adams, 2001).

The positive effects of treatment may cover a range of skills, such as comprehension, production and use of language forms such as phonology, syntax and morphology, content such as semantics, and use of language (Goldstein, 2002). A review of the literature suggests that communication research can be broken down into acquisition of skills and a second category that we describe as social content of communication. This latter category includes initiations, pauses, content of conversations and other communications. They are often problematic for the child with ASD who may know how to verbalize but has marked problems communicating appropriately in the overall social context. However, there is no great differentiation in skill training methods based on the specific behavior or behaviors that are trained.

Children with ASD frequently have difficulty organizing their environment, responding to salient factors in their environment and in processing auditory information (Grandin, 1995; Schopler, Mesibov, & Hearsey, 1995). For these and related reasons, children with ASD often receive visual and structured activities to support these efforts to enhance communication (Hodgdon, 1995). In most training programs, language and related communication skills are trained with techniques such as those noted above, as well as in conjunction with many of the same behavioral techniques used for aberrant behavior, social skills, and other desirable behaviors. Typical instructional methods include simple commands (e.g. touch your nose), pointing to specified objects (e.g. touch your hand), the imitation of instructions, obtaining reinforcers by pointing at them, naming objects and pictures, naming actions, using correct grammar, and the training of other communication skills (Sundberg & Michael, 2001). Learning-based methods have proven to be more effective than psychoanalysis, holding therapy, swimming with dolphins, weighted jackets, sensory integration, facilitatitive communication, and a number of other "unusual" treatments. These behavioral methods have been with us for some time and have a sound theoretical as well as empirical foundation (Michael, 1984; Skinner, 1957).

Goldstein (2002) has categorized the major methods that are employed to train communication. He divides these into five broad categories, which will be briefly discussed, and into which the research to date has fallen. He groups the studies into: (1) communication interventions incorporating sign language; (2) discrete trial training; (3) interventions implemented in the natural milieu; (4) communication to replace challenging (aberrant) behaviors; and (5) interventions to promote social and scripted interactions.

We will only review three of these categories. Interventions to promote social and scripted interventions will not be reviewed since we have included these topics in the previous section. That approach was taken because of the sizable literature on social skills and because we consider it to be of sufficient import to be a topic in its own right. Additionally, "communication" to replace challenging behaviors has been omitted. Carr and Durand (1985) had hypothesized that challenging behavior could serve a communicative function. Unfortunately, for a period of time many clinicians and researchers were conceptualizing all aberrant behavior as a byproduct of poor communication. Conceptualized broadly enough, such a hypothesis is likely true. However, the work that produced the FA literature led to the recognition of a broader range of possible environmental functioning. These functions include: *escape* from demands, *attention* seeking, *nonsocial* where the behavior was stimulating or reinforcing in and of itself (e.g. stereotypies, self-injury), motivation to receive a *tangible* reinforcer (typically food), or *physical*. The latter function might occur when the child is uncomfortable (wheelchair bound and had not been positioned or had an opportunity to stretch out of the chair in a reasonable period of time), has an illness, or in physical pain. Thus, we refer you to the FA section of the aberrant behavior review earlier in this chapter for a more detailed analysis of these issues.

Sign language and the broader category of augmentative communication has a huge literature outside of the area of ASD, and has received some attention from within it as well. Typically for those who are learning impaired, three camps have emerged. These groups include the oralists who strongly oppose the use of sign language, noting that it limits communication to the small subset of persons who know sign language. Those who support sign language argue that it provides a level of precision in expression not likely to be equaled in oral speech for children with ASD. A third group is described as total communication. These professionals espouse the notion that mixing and matching communication methods should be encouraged to produce optimal communication skills. This latter approach entails the combination of oral and sign language training. In view of estimates that about 50% of persons with ASD have insufficient speech to meet their daily needs (Wing & Atwood, 1987), one can see the importance of the issues just addressed. Furthermore, many children with ASD also have marked receptive language problems that further compound communication problems (Miranda & Mathy-Laikko, 1989).

While considerable clinical description in the form of case studies is available in the ASD literature, controlled experimental studies are few. However, given the relatively short time period in which learning-based research has been appearing for persons with ASD, it may be even more surprising that we have as large a literature as we do.

Several researchers have compared the effects of teaching expressive vocabulary using the three forms of communication training. Brady and Smouse (1978) compared oral, total, and completely nonverbal training and found that total communication training produced a significantly greater number of words learned. In another study, Barrera and Sulzer-Azaroff (1983) compared oral and total communication training in three children with ASD who displayed echolalia. The presence of echolalia in children with ASD can be viewed as a positive prognostic indicator due to the existence of both verbal and imitative abilities. However, echolalia is also a serious language impairment frequently seen in ASD (Rutter, 1968). In the Barrera and Sulzer-Azaroff (1983) study, the three children with ASD were taught expressive vocal labeling using an oral language procedure consisting of only vocal cueing and a total communication procedure, in which the cues were provided using vocal and American Sign Language gestures simultaneously. For all three children in the study, performance under the total communication training was consistently superior to performance during oral communication training (Barrera & Sulzer-Azaroff, 1983). Additional studies have almost uniformly produced more complete learning of vocabulary than speech training alone for many children with ASD (Barrera, Lobatos-Barrera, & Sulzer-Azaroff, 1980; Layton, 1988; Yoder & Layton, 1988). Interestingly, those with the greatest communication repertoires benefit most. Thus, total communication training appears to be a good means of speech training for children with ASD.

Discrete trial training is claimed as the backbone intervention method for the UCLA Young Autism Project (YAP). For children receiving training, this method would seem most appropriate since it simply would involve changing the target behavior but maintaining the same training method, a more efficient and less confusing formula for child, trainer, and parent. Goldstein (2002) identifies 12 language studies using discrete trial training. In most of the studies, authors taught single-word or brief phrases as responses. Typically, these studies used differential reinforcement, modeling, fading, and other basic operant procedures. More recent studies have been designed to teach more and more complex tasks. For example, Buffington, Krantz, McClannahan, and Poulson (1998) paired gestures with verbal responses. One can look at the fairly substantial discrete trial literature in general and apply most of the procedures equally well to a variety of skills the parent, teacher, or therapist wishes to teach to the child with ASD, including a range of verbal and nonverbal communication skills.

Interventions implemented in the natural milieu are gaining in popularity due to concerns about generalization of skills to natural settings. Additionally, legal advocates discuss "rights" issues associated with access to normal classrooms. A limitation of such models for children with ASD involves the general lack of precision of treatment since typically there will not be one-to-one ratios of trainer to child. As a result, some well-documented interventions might not be applicable for this population. Additionally, the children are easily distracted and a general classroom can add more distractions. Finally, due to aggressive, self-injurious, and other serious problem behaviors, general classrooms or many typical family activities may simply be impractical.

With these reservations in mind, there are still many opportunities for training of communication and other skills for many children with ASD in the natural environment. Incidental teaching is one such method (Hart & Risley, 1975). The child initiates or attempts to communicate and the opportunity is reinforced. Environmental conditions can be modified to increase the likelihood of an initiation (e.g. preferred toys, edibles, etc. can be made available periodically in the environment). A key element is that events occur naturally (e.g. edibles at lunch or snack times) to further enhance generalization. These procedures assume that the child has the skill but is not sufficiently motivated to perform it in the natural environment or does not know the context(s) in which the skill should be displayed. Where the skill has not been acquired, modeling and then reinforcement of approximations of the skill are often employed. Typical skills taught are eye contact, attention, motor initiations (Hwang & Hughes, 2000), spontaneous verbal statements (Charlop & Walsh, 1986), and answering questions (McGee, Krantz, & McClannahan, 1985). We will briefly review two studies that exemplify the procedures used for this type of training. The first is by Koegel, O'Dell, and Koegel (1987) and the second is by Matson, Sevin, Box, Francis, and Sevin (1993).

The Koegels have been important innovators in the treatment of young children with ASD. Among their many contributions has been their work in language. An example of the work they have done in the Natural Language Teaching Paradigm (NLTP) they have employed over several years for two children they describe as having extremely poor histories of language development. The children were 4 and 5 years of age when the study began. NLTP consisted of changing the teaching parameters to make them more consistent with those found in a natural language speaking situation. These modifications included using stimulus items selected by the child rather than the trainer, instead of presenting stimuli serially until the skill was acquired. Items pooled varied from trial to trial based on the child's interests. To further enhance the naturalistic aspects of skill training, the trainer played with a toy and modeled a response versus instead of just asking the child to give a particular verbal response. This latter step would be repeated if it did not elicit a response. The criterion for reinforcement was also made less explicit. Thus, not only would the particular verbal response established as the treatment criterion be reinforced, but successive approximations to the response would be reinforced as well. By changing the criteria, the probability of the child producing a reinforceable response markedly increased. Finally, an effort was made to decrease edible reinforcers and substitute praise and opportunities to play with the trainer.

The procedure was effective, although over a fairly lengthy period of time (Figures 4.6, 4.7 and 4.8). Some, but certainly not all, of the effect may be due to developmental change.

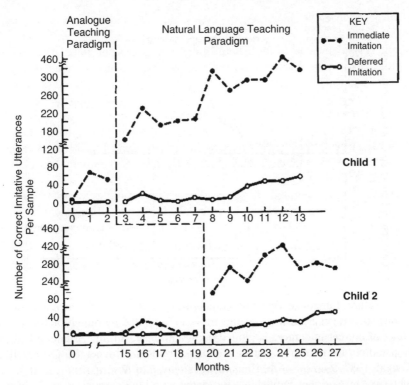

Figure 4.6: Natural Language Teaching Paradigm imitation data. In-clinic treatment results plotted according to the multiple baseline analysis. The number of correct utterances per sample is plotted on the ordinate. In-clinic probes are plotted by month on the abscissa. Solid dots represent imitative utterances that were immediate and the hollow dots represent imitative utterances that were deferred. (From "A natural language teaching paradigm for nonverbal autistic children," by R. L. Koegel, M. C. O'Dell, & L. K. Koegel, 1987, *Journal of Autism and Developmental Disorders, 17*, p. 194. Copyright 1987 by Springer Publishing. Reprinted with kind permission of Springer Science and Business Media.)

The procedure was nonintrusive and involved the child with ASD in decision-making about desired stimuli, another important aspect of the study.

Matson et al. (1993) focused on another problem area in communication training, self-initiated speech. Researchers have typically used modeling, positive reinforcement, and graduated time delay. Graduated time delay is a shaping method where a verbal stimulus is paired with a nonverbal discriminative stimulus. For example, the trainer may present an apple and say "apple." Gradually, the trainer's verbal prompt is faded out by longer and longer time delays between presentation of the apple and the verbal communication of the trainer. Researchers have demonstrated that gains using this procedure can be maintained over several months (Ingenmey & Van Houten, 1991; Matson, Sevin, Fridley, & Love, 1990).

In the Matson et al. (1993) study, three boys with ASD aged 4 and 5 years were treated. Parents compiled a list of words or phrases they considered important for their children

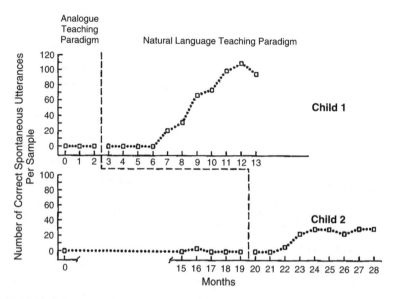

Figure 4.7: Natural Language Teaching Paradigm monthly in-clinic generalization data. Spontaneous speech generalization results. Probes are plotted by month on the abscissa and number of correct utterances is plotted on the ordinate. (From "A natural language teaching paradigm for nonverbal autistic children," by R. L. Koegel, M. C. O'Dell, & L. K. Koegel, 1987, *Journal of Autism and Developmental Disorders, 17*, p. 194. Copyright 1987 by Springer Publishing. Reprinted with kind permission of Springer Science and Business Media.)

to be able to say unprompted. Typical targets were to say hello, excuse me, thank you, play with me, and help me. The children had not previously used these phrases. A correct answer for each child was the word or phrase within 10 seconds of the presentation of a nonverbal cue (the trainer entering the room for hello) and prior to the trainer giving a verbal prompt. Initially, the delay interval was 2 seconds between the presentation of the stimulus and the verbally modeled correct response. The interval was increased to 4 seconds after two consecutive sessions where self-initiated or correct imitations occurred for at least 80% of the trials. Using these criteria, the delay was increased in 2-second intervals to 10 seconds. Reinforcers were as naturalistic as possible. For example, 30 seconds of play accompanied the phrase "play with me." Acquisition was established as three consecutive sessions of self-initiated verbalizations. Generalization probes were also used. These probes consisted of two novel therapists and one novel setting, where the same target responses were measured. One child was followed up at 2 months. The other two boys with ASD were followed up at 10 months. The graphs for all three children show good acquisition and retention of target behaviors (Figures 4.9, 4.10 and 4.11).

The methods described in those two studies have consistently been among the most employed in the communication literature. For example, Taylor et al. (in press) observed their three boys with ASD aged 4, 10 and 12 verbally interact with peers. They then created

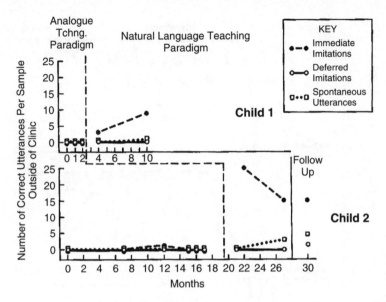

Figure 4.8: Natural Language Teaching Paradigm monthly out-of-clinic generalization data. Results of generalization probes outside of the clinic setting. The number of correct utterances are plotted on the ordinate and months are shown on the abscissa. Solid dots represent the children's immediate imitative utterances, hollow dots represent deferred imitative utterances, and squares show the children's spontaneous utterances.
(From "A natural language teaching paradigm for nonverbal autistic children," by R. L. Koegel, M. C. O'Dell, & L. K. Koegel, 1987, *Journal of Autism and Developmental Disorders, 17*, p. 195. Copyright 1987 by Springer Publishing. Reprinted with kind permission of Springer Science and Business Media.)

therapist/child interactions likely to elicit the target behavior (e.g. "I want a pretzel" or "I want popcorn" while observing the trainer eating these items). These and other studies demonstrate several consistent themes in language/communication training, including the use of naturalistic reinforcers (e.g. popcorn) presented in naturalistic or near natural settings, using approximations of targets, observing child interactions or asking parents to establish relevant, socially valid behaviors to train, emphasizing modeling of appropriate behaviors and practicing the responses.

Critical Appraisal of Individual Skills Interventions

We have given a brief overview of the primary problem behavior areas that have received the most attention: aberrant behavior, social skills, and communication. The greatest amount of research and quite possibly the greatest advances have been in the areas of aberrant behavior. This topic is the top priority, since for children who evince self-injury, aggression, and related behavior problems, it overwhelms all other problems, goals, and resources devoted

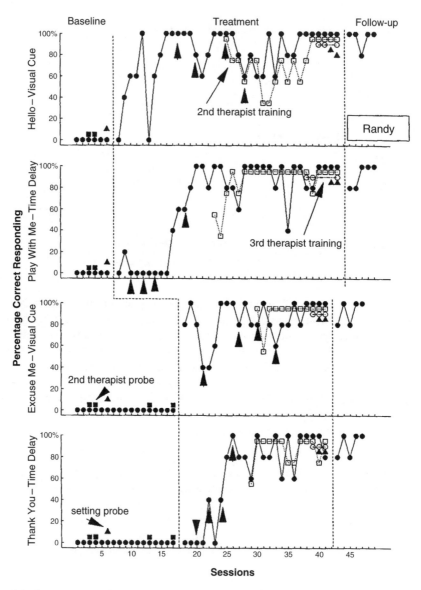

Figure 4.9: Comparison of language acquisition of Child 1 (Randy). Percentage of correct self-initiated verbalizations during baseline, treatment, and follow-up sessions for Randy. Duration of the delay interval (e.g. 4 s, 6 s) and the phase of visual cue fading (e.g. Step 3, Step 4) employed in each session are noted by an arrow at each progression. (From "An evaluation and comparison of two methods for increasing self-initiated verbalizations in autistic children," by J. L. Matson et al., 1993, *Journal of Applied Behavior Analysis, 26*, p. 392. Copyright 1993 by Society for the Experimental Analysis of Behavior, Inc. Reprinted with permission.)

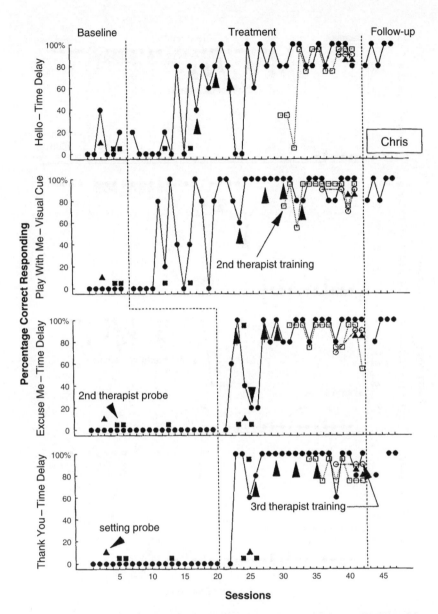

Figure 4.10: Comparison of language acquisition of Child 2 (Chris). Percentage of correct self-initiated verbalizations during baseline, treatment, and follow-up sessions for Chris. Duration of the delay interval (e.g. 4 s, 6 s) and the phase of visual cue fading (e.g. Step 3, Step 4) employed in each session are noted by an arrow at each progression. (From "An evaluation and comparison of two methods for increasing self-initiated verbalizations in autistic children," by J. L. Matson et al., 1993, *Journal of Applied Behavior Analysis, 26,* p. 393. Copyright 1993 by Society for the Experimental Analysis of Behavior, Inc. Reprinted with permission.)

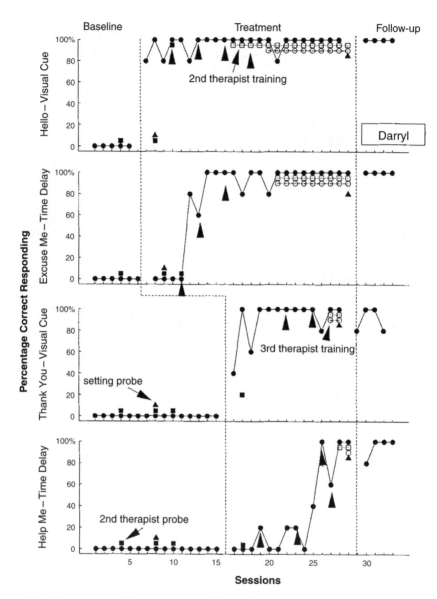

Figure 4.11: Comparison of language acquisition of Child 3 (Darryl). Percentage of correct self-initiated verbalizations during baseline, treatment, and follow-up sessions for Darryl. Duration of the delay interval (e.g. 4 s, 6 s) and the phase of visual cue fading (e.g. Step 3, Step 4) employed in each session are noted by an arrow at each progression. (From "An evaluation and comparison of two methods for increasing self-initiated verbalizations in autistic children," by J. L. Matson et al., 1993, *Journal of Applied Behavior Analysis, 26*, p. 396. Copyright 1993 by Society for the Experimental Analysis of Behavior, Inc. Reprinted with permission.)

to training. The therapist will not be successful in teaching communication if the child fails to comply, engages in a temper tantrum, hits and kicks others, and so on. Thus, methods that establish a compliant/cooperative relationship between the trainer and the child with ASD must occur to some degree before any other problem areas can be effectively addressed. Effective procedures are available for the most part. However, one concern is the intensive resources and highly trained staff that are needed to carry out successful training. Both resources are in short supply. People with patience and dedication who also are willing to spend the time developing the technical expertise to learn the requisite skills are not all that common. Pair that with the reality that most jobs of this sort do not result in high pay and the issue is compounded further. For future reference, we would encourage even greater utilization of parent trainers when possible.

We are disappointed by the overselling of some intervention strategies. As a field, we will not return to the early days of behavior therapy where contingent shock was used to promote socialization (Lovaas, Schaeffer, & Simmons, 1965) or where contingent thigh slaps were a part of intervention strategies (Lovaas, 1987). However, some in our field have promoted the myth that all severe behavior problems can be effectively treated without aversive consequences of any kind (Foxx, 2005). This movement has been more successful with governments and politicians than in court cases, where a much greater scrutiny of the facts is likely to occur and the opinions of experts as determined by academic degrees and published research on the topic being discussed are given priority (Royko, 1986). Some use of limit setting, brief time-out, verbal reprimands and the like in conjunction with functional analysis and skill-building is best practice at this time. Young children such as those described in our book are unlikely to need the more restrictive methods that may be required for adults such as time-out rooms or contingent restraint. However, at this point to suggest that no limit-setting procedures are required (e.g. no, don't do that, redirection, withholding reinforcers, etc.) is simply not feasible and a gross misreading of the available literature.

Another caution we would have is not to depart too greatly from established interventions. Frequently, as a new procedure becomes available, it is often seen as a replacement for all interventions that preceded it. New methods and procedures should be adopted with caution and as an adjunct to existing methods. Over time and with proper comparisons via publication of peer-reviewed journal articles, new methods may supplant, partially supplant or augment existing strategies. These decisions to change intervention strategies should be made based on multiple studies, by different researchers in different locals. Having said that, the approach of wholesale treatment substitution with new, minimally supported methods is epidemic in the ASD field, particularly with respect to young children. Testimonials are not an acceptable method for establishing treatment credibility. This latter approach led to the popularization of many of the ineffective, unsubstantiated therapies that are discussed throughout the book.

Chapter 5

Comprehensive Treatment Models

Evolution of Training Models

Autism was first defined in 1943. Therefore, the history of intervention is rather short relative to many classic problems treated by mental health and educational experts. As discussed in Chapter 1, Kanner (1943) first described the disorder but he offered little information regarding treatment. He surmised that problems in parent training might be a contributing factor in the development of the condition. Additionally, Kanner put forward some elements of psychodynamic thought, such as the lack of a nurturing mother. However, he did not develop a treatment model and use it on large groups of children; that development came when Dr Bruno Bettelheim arrived on the scene.

Bettelheim was a professor at the University of Chicago Medical School. He called his psychodynamically driven program the Orthogenic School. He became something of a national celebrity with TV shows about his career and national publications such as *Time* and the *New York Times* reporting on the major "advancements" he was making in the treatment of children with autism. This media hype was something of an alternate universe to the views in the professional community, since little empirical treatment research was being published to support his program. All this media attention does demonstrate, however, that Bettelheim was a charismatic figure. Additionally, there is no doubt that he popularized etiology and treatment for autism. However, most of his "data" involved testimonials, which we criticized previously as a poor means of establishing the validity of treatment. No research has confirmed the effectiveness of the Orthogenic School, even today when so much autism research is being published.

Born in Vienna in 1903 and interned in the infamous Dachau and Buchenwald concentration camps in 1938 and 1939, Bettelheim immigrated to the United States in the late 1940s. He based his psychodynamic treatment model on the Israeli Kibbutzim, the congregate living arrangement used to rear children in that country. His rags-to-riches story was inspiring to many and furthered interest in his training program. Bettelheim went to great lengths to insure that the school buildings were colorful, and filled with artwork and beautiful furniture. He claimed that the source of autism in children lay in their "refrigerator mothers," defined as cold, unfeeling parents who drove their children into mental isolation. These theories were accepted internationally by the general public for one or two decades. As can be imagined, this model produced tremendous guilt on the part of the parents, who currently are very hostile to Bettelheim and his theories.

Operant psychology and the introduction of chlorpromazine (Thorazine) in 1957 not only led to the use of new learning methods and synthetic drugs to treat mental health and developmental disorders, but reoriented psychiatry and psychology from a psychodynamic towards a learning-based/biological model. This change in emphasis also refocused discussions about etiology to biological and learning factors (as opposed to psychodynamic factors). A substantial number of researchers showed that individuals with ASD, schizophrenia or intellectual disability (ID), and other heretofore hard-to-treat groups, could make rapid improvements with learning-based treatments. The package methods we cover here, which are based on the techniques described in Chapter 4, will be reviewed in detail.

By the early 1960s, Bettelheim was being challenged by parents and researchers for what they considered the hurtful nature of his theories to families. They also claimed that, based on the data, his explanations of cause and treatment were unfounded. Bernard Rimland (1964) in his book *Infantile Autism: The Syndrome and Its Implications for a Neural Theory of Behavior*, went to lengths to debunk the notion that autistic children were the product of uncaring parents. A sufficient database was rapidly developing to stress biological and learning-based causes and interventions. The popular press lagged far behind in terms of recognizing that Bettleheim's claims of treatment success were not based on data. Nonetheless, by the time of Bettelheim's suicide at age 86 in 1992, he had become largely discredited among parents and practitioners in autism field. Former patients came forward with allegations of child abuse and reported exaggerated claims of success by those associated with the Orthogenic School. Some professionals still defend Bettelheim's methods, noting that he used corporal punishment, but should not have, yet stressing that many positive outcomes did result from his school. His supporters are a small minority, primarily composed of some psychologists and psychiatrists and other mental health professionals. In the overarching view, however, psychodynamic formulations of autism appear quaint by today's treatment standards and Bettelheim's exaggerations hastened the disintegration of this theoretical model. Behavioral/educational and, to a lesser extent, pharmacological treatment models are the primary evidence-based approaches used today. Other methods also show some promise, but less research is available. Certainly far more than half of all the treatment studies, perhaps as much as 80%, use behavioral procedures, some within and some outside the traditional school setting. Thus, we will review comprehensive learning-based models in detail, given the great amount of attention and success they have enjoyed in the treatment of young children with ASD.

Behavioral/Educational Treatment Packages

The names most closely associated with pioneering treatments for ASD are probably Ivar Lovaas and Eric Schopler. Their approaches are considerably different, but both appear to have yielded a good deal of success. However, the two camps have been competitors, thus little cross-fertilization has occurred. Perhaps due to the fact that effective interventions have been around for such a short time, no direct comparison of these two models has been conducted. Such analysis in the future might prove quite interesting. However, claims of superiority of one intervention strategy over the other will await future research. Additionally, superiority may be dictated based on the particular needs of a given family or child.

Using procedures similar to those described in Chapter 4, Lovaas was one of the first to empirically establish the learning potential of young children with ASD. His research built upon the work of Ferster and DeMyer (1961) and many other learning-based researchers. Schopler and associates have used a more traditional educational model with behavioral components, emphasizing classroom programs and parent training. Lovaas and Schopler have done two things that have made them, in our view, the most visible, and at the same time controversial researchers in the ASD field. First, they have been persistent and stayed at it for a long time. For example, Lovaas' first studies appeared in the 1960s and he is still publishing on the topic. Of the other early researchers noted above, he is the only one who continued to publish over decades. Schopler and the TEACCH group, as noted, are the other main pioneers and have been doggedly consistent over a long period of time.

A second reason for the overall success of these camps is that most researchers tend to tackle a particular problem within the child's repertoire. The area treated might be self-injury (DeLeon, Neidert, Anders, & Rodriguez-Catter, 2001), verbal behavior (Matson et al., 1993), academics (Egel, 1981), social skills (Pierce & Schreibman, 1995), enhanced affection (Gena, Krantz, McClannahan, & Poulson, 1996), vocal and gestural communication (Keen, 2005), or visual discrimination (Graff & Green, 2004). Lovaas and Schopler, on the other hand, packaged many of these research findings together to provide an overall pedagogy, dealing with a broad range of skills to treat the overarching disorder of ASD.

University of California Young Autism Project (UCLA-YAP)

A reason for Lovaas' visibility is his claims of success, which include suggesting a cure for ASD in some cases. Lovaas (1987) and McEachin, Smith, and Lovaas (1993) presented data that suggested that some children improved to the point of successfully passing regular education classes, achieved average scores on IQ tests, language, emotional and social factors, and maintained these improvements over years. His results have been dramatic, but have sparked debate about the degree of improvement, whether the program is too "intensive" for some parents and children, critiques of the methodology and so on. Smith, Groen, and Wynn (2000) described a partial replication of "cure" with 28 young children evincing PDD-NOS or ASD. Participants were followed up after 2 years, at which time the treatment group still showed significant gains in IQ, visual-spatial skills, language, and academic ability relative to controls. They also found that gains were greater for the least impaired children (e.g. PDD-NOS versus ASD). Similarly, Eikeseth, Smith, Jahr, and Eldevik (2002) tested UCLA-YAP versus eclectic therapy over a one-year period. Children were treated in a school setting and showed much larger gains on standardized testing with the UCLA-YAP method. Therefore, cure or total recovery was not completely replicated. However, significant gains in many substantive areas were obtained and maintained over time.

Emphasis in the UCLA-YAP treatment model is placed on generalizing gains across naturalistic environments such as home and school while incorporating parents, teachers and peers in training (Lovaas & Smith, 1989). Additionally, Lovaas and Smith have described a one-to-one training program that is implemented for 20–40 hours a week for upwards of a year. As a result of these efforts, claims of major improvements in the ASD children's overall functioning have been made. Getting away from a piecemeal approach and providing a comprehensive and intensive treatment environment was an interesting and important new approach, although, as often happens in the ASD field, controversy has followed (Bryson, Rogers, & Fombonne, 2003). Additionally, less intensive, more specific treatments such as those mentioned in the previous chapter may be sufficient for many children with ASD.

One of the most recent statements on the status of the UCLA-YAP model for treating young children with ASD is a book chapter entitled "Early and intensive behavioral interventions in autism" by Lovaas and Smith (2003). Lovaas and associates have based their treatment program on an operant conditioning model using training sessions arranged in brief one-on-one discrete-trial training (Sheinkopf & Siegel, 1998). Lovaas and associates have consistently rejected the notion that ASD is a disorder with a biological etiology as proposed by the London group of Rutter and Wing, for example. Rather, they take a strict behavioral analytic approach (as noted in Chapter 2). Emphasis is on treating overt behavior. Children who have an ASD diagnosis are those who are toward the end of the spectrum of children who display multiple maladaptive behaviors according to Lovaas and Smith (2003). Thus, the intervention goal is to reduce behaviors that occur in excess and to overcome behavioral deficits or delays. Some of the behavioral targets they mention are tantrums, aggression, communication, cognitive skills, caregiver interactions, peer and toy play, attention to tasks, and self-care. While not conceptualized as a disorder, many behaviors listed as symptoms by the London group and DSM might also be treated such as echolalia (communication), fixation on routine, and social skills deficits and excesses.

One of the hallmarks of the UCLA-YAP developed by Lovaas and associates, as noted, is one-on-one training for 40 hours per week. Some debate has occurred among researchers about whether this intensive 40-hour per week training is necessary, or if less time- and cost-intensive methods might be as effective or nearly as effective. For example, Anderson, Avery, DiPietro, Edwards, and Christian (1987) found that an average of 20 hours per week of one-on-one training for 1 year resulted in marked improvements for over half of the children treated. Lovaas (1987) notes also that in the under-5 age group, receiving 20 hours per week enabled some children with autism to show gains in IQ. Forty hours per week of one-on-one training is thus considered too intense by some, particularly those who support a primarily home/school model such as TEACCH rather than the clinic model of Lovaas and associates. Lovaas and Smith (2003) appeared to have addressed some of these concerns by limiting the hours of treatment to less than 40 for children aged 3 or younger, or as a fading procedure for children finishing the program, or for children in whom 40 hours of training per week is contraindicated. The model is fairly new, but results are encouraging. Additional "tweaking" of the treatment model is likely to occur for some time, however. We also predict the development of several variations on the overall model to meet the specific needs of particular parents and children.

The UCLA-YAP outpatient parent-training model is a dominant early intervention training program for ASD. The UCLA-YAP model is based on a broad range of behaviorally based studies shown by many researchers to be effective with ASD (Matson et al., 1996). Perhaps this is one reason it is popular nationally and internationally (Bibby, Eikeseth, Martin, Mudford, & Reeves, 2001). Courts have ordered this procedure and training centers have sprung up in many locations. Perhaps for these reasons the UCLA-YAP model has also come under the most intense criticism; much is at stake in resources, children's futures, and professional reputations. Gresham and MacMillan (1997a, 1997b) have been among those who have raised many serious criticisms of UCLA-YAP, including the issue of cure and whether the children had, in fact, improved. Others have chimed in on the notion of a cure for ASD. The American Academy of Child and Adolescent Psychiatry (AACAP), for example, formed a panel of psychiatrists/experts and concluded that PDD, of which ASD is a subtype, has a relatively poor prognosis (AACAP, 1999).

Methodological issues in UCLA-YAP were also addressed by Gresham and MacMillan (1997a, 1997b), such as lack of random assignment, and whether severity of ASD symptoms was milder for experimental group children relative to controls or the general population of children with ASD. Others support the notion that data were flawed but conclude that results were modest, not spectacular as Lovaas and associates claimed (Howlin, 1997; Jordan & Jones, 1999). Bibby et al. (2001), for example, used parent training in the home rather than the clinic model of UCLA-YAP, which has also been reported. They analyzed data from 66 children served by 25 different consultants over a mean of 31.6 months and concluded that no child over 72 months attained normal functioning. The general tone of their report was that results did not replicate data previously reported by Lovaas and associates, but they do acknowledge that in their real world environment, variations on prescribed treatment could and did occur. Thus, in effect it was not a replication, only a partial replication of the UCLA-YAP.

Conversely the UCLA-YAP also has its strong supporters; and there are many. The popularity of the approach, spread largely by word of mouth among parents, is considerable. Eikeseth (2001) noted that Lovaas and colleagues made a convincing case for long-term gains, although he was also an author on the Bibby et al. (2001) paper. Eikeseth et al. (2001) treated 13 children with the UCLA-YAP program who were older than 4 years. They averaged 28 hours of one-to-one training over 1 year. The children were reported to have significantly benefited, although a cure was not claimed. Additionally, the courts have weighed in, pointing out that they consider the UCLA-YAP treatment valid and prefer it to many other models. Various judges have ordered school districts in the United States to pay for this particular treatment for young children with ASD. Again, controversy has risen because of the prohibitive costs if several children in the same school district are receiving this training.

UCLA-YAP Conclusions

Stepping back from the details of the controversies, what can be concluded? First, that while gains may not always occur, they are apparent in a substantial number of children, although cure may as a goal not always be reached. Second, treatment of this sort is very expensive and extremely demanding for the child, parents, and trainers who are involved. Parents must consider carefully whether the benefits outweigh the tremendous commitment in money and time. Many parents have decided that the UCLA-YAP model is worth the investment. Stated another way, this program is likely to be for some but not all families. Third, behavioral methods used in a package this extensive make it difficult to determine the active components of effective treatment. However, we do know that when used separately in controlled environments, the procedures employed in UCLA-YAP have, for the most part, been useful and effective for children with a range of ASD symptoms/target behaviors.

Fourth, the intensity of the debate is remarkable relative to the broad psychological literature in general. We attribute this to the extreme interest in the topic shown by parents, researchers, and professionals, and by the passion professionals and parents have toward particular theoretical/treatment approaches. While this intensity is not entirely a bad thing, we hope people can step back to some degree so that they may see the forest as well as individual trees. Some of the infighting between camps has been counterproductive. Fifth, with skilled researcher clinicians such as Lovaas and Smith, it is possible to see quite different results in a controlled clinic versus home setting where the trainer is less skilled. Matson and Ollendick, in a study dating to 1977, found that children toilet-trained by parents who had read behaviorally based materials fared far worse than children whose parents received supervision with psychologists using the same information.

More recently, Symes and Hastings (in press) noted that there have been few published studies on therapist behavior in the context of early intensive behavioral interventions with ASD children. They tested discrete-trial training (see Green, Brennan, & Fein, 2002) since it is one of the behaviorally based strategies proven to be most effective in skill training of children with ASD in early intensive behavioral intervention programs. All but 2 of their 19 therapists were female. They ranged in age from 19 to 51 and provided training at the children's homes in the United Kingdom. Therapists were interviewed with the aim of identifying facilitating factors and barriers that therapists believed impacted service delivery. Therapists reported that after treatment children were likeable, compliant, competent, motivated, and more independent.

Symes and Hastings (in press) also found that therapists trained in theory and management skills via behavioral training methods were more likely to carry them out effectively. Matson and Ollendick (1977) reported similar findings with young children (2 years of age) evincing normal patterns of development. Scott (1996) and Symes and Hastings (in press) make the point that establishing a conceptual overview of a theory helps therapists understand what they are doing. We point out that it is impossible to account for every possible eventuality of treatment. Thus, therapists also know how to adjust training when it does not go as planned, since they have a fund of alternative skills and strategies to fall back on when one strategy does not work. As important, they are able to identify at a reasonably early stage when a program is not going well so that adjustments can be made.

Stymes and Hastings (in press) also noted that the nature of skill target sets is very important. Many times therapists design the most technically sound program from a theoretical point of view, but they may not take into account the level of resources needed to deliver the training. An interaction may be designed where a more passive style of intervention is possible (e.g. a child already has the skill, uses it in the wrong context, but is simply reinforced when the context is more appropriate, rather than constructing an entirely new set of skills).

Treatment fidelity, then, is a major issue for clinicians. Most children with ASD will not be treated in intensive clinic programs, but in home and school environments, due to cost, commitment of resources, generalization, and other issues. Thus, parents and teachers who, on the whole, have much less formal didactic training and experience in the broad range of challenging behaviors and skill-building required for early intervention for children with ASD, will provide most of the training. Specific, structured strategies to insure that accurate performance of the plan occurs are required. One way of doing this has been via behavior drills. These drills are composed of sheets of paper with a list of the most critical elements of the training plan printed on them. At variable intervals, a "master" trainer will observe training and check off whether each component of training was carried out correctly or incorrectly. Later, the "master" trainer sits down with the therapist and goes over all parts of the behavior drill check sheet. Steps or components of the drill carried out correctly are praised and steps carried out incorrectly are discussed, with the "master" therapist reviewing what to do differently on the next training trial with the child. In this manner, trainers receive continuous feedback on how they are doing, aspects of the intervention plan that need to be adjusted, and where the training should proceed as currently performed. These refresher courses are one example of the need to develop and implement technologies that will aid in consistently accurate treatment. A "train and hope for the best" strategy is unlikely to prove sufficient.

While the UCLA-YAP is the earliest comprehensive model of training and best known of the behavior analytic models, it is not alone (Anderson & Romanczyk, 1999; Green, 1996). More recently, variations of the UCLA-YAP have appeared. All the models, however, are learning based, stress the importance of structure in the environment, emphasize positive reinforcement and skill-building and the treatment of a number of behavioral domains rather than more circumscribed target behaviors, as is seen in the bulk of the scientific literature. In defense of the latter research, however, it should be argued that the goals of intervention differ. In the more specific target behavior literature, which may focus exclusively on self-injury or communication for example, effective treatment strategies are being worked out and developed. The treatment models such as the UCLA-YAP largely rely upon the specific treatments developed in these specific studies but add the component of using multiple treatments with multiple target behaviors with the objective of treating the whole person. Both methods of research are valuable. It seems fair to conclude that these interventions build upon one another. Most of this literature has been with children and the general trend has been to intervene at younger and younger ages for more hours using greater amounts of one-to-one training.

Other comprehensive programs that are behaviorally based and which provide a comprehensive service model are also available. The New England Center for Children is one such program. More programs are comprehensive in scope and evidence based in orientation. The vast majority of programs are like the New England Center for Children one in that they discuss the contributions of individual techniques and researchers rather than discussing the methods as a single comprehensive model. The Lovaas studies have received more publicity, but have been replicated in more tightly controlled studies (Metz, Mulick, & Butter, 2005). And, a vast literature of behavioral studies has been incorporated into the packaged models. As noted, we concur with Metz et al. (2005) that the single greatest achievement of the UCLA-YAP is the demonstration of the efficacy of these researched procedures over an extended time period. In a sense, they took the transistors, plastics, screen, and other components that had been invented (specific behavioral methods) and put them together to make a nice TV.

The process has been evolutionary. As Green (2001) notes, the notion of an evidence-based model for the development of individual procedures grew from the interventions developed in the 1960s by Bijou, Wolf, Risley, and others. These points summarized by Green are worth noting. Among the early developments which have proven to be major points in the establishment of valid and reliable treatments were: (1) the integration of developmental milestones with operant learning methods; (2) an emphasis on positive reinforcement in appropriate skill-building; (3) functional analysis of problem behaviors; (4) individualization of goals and treatment methods; (5) emphasis on parent training; and (6) pointing out the value of planning for generalization in training strategies. Of course, these points have been refined in the ensuing years, and those refinements and new developments continue. From the outset, there has been a recognition that early identification and training are essential.

Pivotal Response Training

Although highly intensive programs involving 20–40 hours per week of one-to-one training may produce the greatest gains in a controlled setting, for a variety of reasons they will only be possible for a small subset of children with ASD. Situations will arise where both parents must work and, therefore, the necessary time is just not available. Similarly, families with several small children must be careful not to become so involved with the child with ASD that the other children receive very minimal parenting. Also, parents may live in areas that are far from service centers, making daily commutes impractical. Another issue is that parents may simply not be willing to invest the amount of effort and time needed to carry out such a program, even if they could manage the time commitment. Additionally, many children may have milder symptoms of ASD and do not require such intensive care, and might benefit more from attending regular day programs and elementary schools. For these and many other reasons outpatient care with some additional supports in the school and perhaps the home environment are much more likely to be the norm. These programs are available through many universities and medical schools.

Typical of this model, Koegel, Koegel, and Brookman (2003) provide an excellent overview of how to coordinate services in an outpatient program. They discuss the role of the clinician, parent, and school. Obviously, one of the most important goals is insuring that the children and their parents and teachers can carry out the desired behaviors in real life settings. The authors, through the University of California Santa Barbara (UCSB), run an Autism Research and Training Clinic. They note that the goal of their program is to provide comprehensive treatment in key areas to promote independence and self-education. Parents coordinate daily activities and the treatment is provided in regular school settings. This latter point can be very important in promoting generalization. Target behaviors are selected, parents are trained in learning-based treatment strategies and children receive training at school and home. Koegel et al. (2003) claimed 80% criteria for correct use of the treatment procedures within about 25 hours of parent training.

Koegel et al. (2003) emphasized that for children with ASD, motivation and child initiations are particularly important. Given the many needs these children have, treatment can be overwhelming. Thus, the notion of prioritizing skills in a hierarchy from most to least important is quite useful. In some cases, it will be possible to have similar priorities for several children. The idea of grouping children with similar skills and deficits, such as children with ASD, can result in more efficient service delivery. Nonetheless, everyone is unique in their challenges and needs. Thus, some fine-tuning specific to each child is also needed.

Motivation is defined in this model as responding to the environment, an area where children with ASD routinely have difficulty. Skill sets that are stressed include focus on enhancing the relationship between social communication and consequent reinforcement.

Other more specific skill targets are response latency, correct responses, response attempts, and positive affect. The latter skills are considered building blocks in language, cognitive and social development. Koegel et al. (2003) rightly pointed out that the training methods they used were extensions of earlier techniques described in the applied behavior analysis literature and which we have alluded to earlier in this chapter. Our view is that taking such an approach strengthens rather than detracts from their methods. Along these lines, Koegel et al. (2003) also noted that motivation is increased when a child is provided with choices, task variation, interspersal of maintenance tasks, reinforcement of response attempts, and when natural and direct reinforcement are used.

Self-initiations are the second overarching goal of their program. Koegel et al. (2003) suggested that similar variables are used relative to the motivation training goals just named in that similar teaching procedures are used. They defined self-initiation as beginning a new verbal or nonverbal social interaction. The authors noted that social interactions occur less often in children with ASD than in normally developing children. Along these same lines, Sevin, Matson, Coe, Fee, and Sevin (1991) found that self-injury, aggression, intellectual functioning and a host of other variables did not distinguish children with ASD from those with ID. The primary distinguishing features were greater problems in the areas of social skills and communication. These deficit areas have been recognized as problematic for some time and behaviorally based methods have been developed and are available (Matson et al., 1993; Taras, Matson, & Leary, 1988).

Children with ASD have limited social and verbal repertoires. Additionally, the model of Koegel et al. (2003) emphasized that even when language is present, it is often negative and consists of protests and demands. They suggested that improvement in self-initiations of communication and social behavior can result in concomitant changes in academic, social and communication domains, while decreasing aggression, self-stimulation, self-injury and tantrums. These claims appear to be backed up by the functional analysis literature. When the functions of these types of maladaptive behaviors are studied, they are often attempts to gain attention, escape activities or obtain tangibles, such as food (Applegate, Matson, & Cherry, 1999; Matson et al., 1999, 2005).

This model marks quite a change from earlier philosophies, such as the Orthogenic School of Bettelheim. Koegel et al. (2003) emphasized parent education and "empowerment." As they pointed out, parents are the most important stable influence for the child over time. Their parent education model used practice with feedback. Parents worked with their child and were provided with specific information on training procedures. The Koegels and associates noted that parent education had other positive effects on the family, such as the possibility of blending training into daily routines and using training methods and targets that match the family's values (Koegel, Bimbala, & Schreibman, 1996; Moes, 1995). Koegel et al. (1996) suggested that parent training had effects outside of the gains made by the child with ASD in specific skill areas. These collateral effects included the more positive overall nature of parent–child interactions, as well as parent reports of increased happiness, decreased stress levels, and more pleasant communication with their child (Koegel et al., 1996).

These authors referred to their packaged programs as Pivotal Response Training. The Koegels claimed that instead of changing one behavior at a time, thousands or tens of thousands of behaviors are changed at once, creating a pivotal event. The pivotal areas of ASD intervention, according to Koegel, Koegel and McNerney (2001) are: (1) improved motivation; (2) increased response to social cues in the environment; (3) self-management and independent recruitment of reinforcement; and (4) self-initiations of social interactions. Koegel et al. (2001) stressed that by providing training and instruction in these four pivotal areas, multiple behaviors can be influenced at one time. Our view is that rarely is one behavior changed at a time. Self-injury, for example, might be decreased while competing positive behaviors, such as communicating needs, are acquired. However, it is unlikely that "thousands" of behaviors are changed at once. Having said this, the parent-training model that has been around for many years and is being adopted for children with ASD is a good idea. The value of working out all the wrinkles to apply these techniques with young children with ASD is commendable. Also, it seems safe to say that many more life skills are being trained at once with Pivotal Response Training and the UCLA-YAP program than with the training programs for a few behaviors commonly reported in the literature. As noted, this piecemeal approach is more typical in the general behavioral treatment literature. The approach is intensive and requires a high level of commitment by the parents, teachers and clinicians. However, the intensity of the Pivotal Response Training method is nothing like that of the UCLA-YAP described earlier.

Overview of Behavioral Models

Treatment research has evolved by targeting specific domains of behavior that are typically problematic for children with ASD. Severe problem behaviors such as self-injury, aggression (aberrant behaviors) and minimal speech (language) have been among the areas of greatest attention. Other topics are social, daily living and academic skills. As noted, these data and procedures have been followed and put together in packages to create training modules such as the UCLA-YAP and UCSB Autism Research and Training Clinic. We will briefly review the data from research on these topics. Often treatments such as UCSB may be too intensive for some. Thus, a strategy to deal with one or two behaviors may be involved. The procedures to be reviewed can be used alone or in a "packaged" comprehensive training model. Along with the many positive points relative to early intervention it should be cautioned that few data exist to demonstrate the long-term value of these interventions 5 or 10 years in the future. Some have argued that there is no long-term benefit and that the children gradually regress to the mean skill level for those with similar handicaps. This position is primarily espoused by those who adhere to biological models of development (Guralnick, 1998; Herrnstein & Murray, 1994; Scarr, 1992). While this argument per se may be faulty, these authors have a good point in that genetic/biological variables are likely to be important mitigating factors. Thus, while short term gains with these interventions may be impressive, the long-term effects of these interventions with respect to how much progress results and in what areas are still open to question.

TEACCH

The Treatment and Education of Autistic Children and related Communication handicapped CHildren division (TEACCH) is a method for educating children with ASD in the classroom. The focus of the program is on teaching the child to function as a person with autism, as opposed to total recovery. This model is developmental, emphasizing strengths in visual-spatial understanding, object manipulation and structured routines (Bryson et al., 2003). TEACCH began in 1966 through the Department of Psychiatry of the University of North Carolina School of Medicine. The program, which is statewide and to our knowledge the only comprehensive large-scale program of its kind, provides services for toddlers to adults with ASD and their families. Content areas include diagnosis, individualized treatment planning, special education services, social skills training, vocational training, school consultation, parent training and parent group activities.

Seven principles guide the services provided by TEACCH. These principles are to: (1) improve the ability of the person with ASD to adapt to their environment by educationally oriented skill training and by modifying the person's environment to accommodate deficits; (2) involve parents as co-therapists so that skill developments and improvements will generalize to the home; (3) individualize educational programs through ongoing assessment; (4) employ a tightly structured environment; (5) emphasize skill acquisition; (6) follow a cognitive behavior therapy treatment model; and (7) employ cross-disciplinary training such that therapists cover topics traditionally used by psychologists, educators, speech pathologists and other professionals (Schopler, 1989; 1994).

In addition to the services provided on a statewide level, TEACCH also provides professional training opportunities at their six regional centers. They offer one-day workshops, teacher training courses and a yearly conference whose subject matter has since 1974 been published as a yearly book series entitled *Current Issues in Autism*. Additionally, the TEACCH group has published data-based articles and training materials on the topic of ASD. An example of these books is *The TEACCH Approach to Autism Spectrum Disorders* (Mesibov, Shea, & Schopler, 2005). The philosophy of parent involvement supports their program, whose guiding motto was a rejection of Bettelheim's blame of the parents. TEACCH embraces the notion that parents are essential for providing critical instruction to their children with ASD.

Indicating how service provision has changed, the most visible programmatic models are now all quite parent-centered. Thus, a hallmark of the TEACCH program is home training. Parents are taught to serve as co-therapists. These home programs are called extended diagnostic services and are considered an economical means of increasing treatment (Schopler, 1987). Related to this point, parents can serve as a source of continuity over time as the child moves from grade to grade and thus classroom to classroom. Additionally, the parents can assist in interfacing with various agencies in providing continuity in training techniques that are used in a "lifetime" service model.

Most of the research on TEACCH involves specific components of the program, rather than an analysis of the overall program. For example, Schopler, Brehm, Kinsbourne, and Reichler (1971) found that improvement in performance followed classroom instruction using the TEACCH model. Similarly, Marcus, Lansing, Andrews, and Schopler (1978) noted increased compliance and parent teaching skills when training was home-based. Along the same lines, Short (1984) found that parents significantly improved their teaching skills and consequently their child's appropriate behavior.

Perhaps one of the more important of the TEACCH studies was conducted by Ozonoff and Cathcart (1998), since it was carried out at a different site from the studies mentioned above, thus providing an external (to the program) evaluation of the methods. Ozonoff and Cathcart (1998) studied 22 children with ASD recruited from Salt Lake City, Utah. Importantly, and not all that common in program studies, random assignment to either the experimental or control group was performed. Children were 2 to 6 years of age and matched on severity of symptoms of ASD across the experimental and control groups. This latter point is also critical but not routinely addressed in these programmatic research studies. Children in the experimental group received TEACCH-based home programming from trained graduate students from the Department of Psychology at the University of Utah. The typical home program lasted 10 weeks and consisted of a weekly hour long parent–therapist clinic visit. During this visit, one therapist worked with the child, modeling treatment while a second therapist discussed the training with the parent behind a one-way mirror in real time. Treatment in the experimental group was individualized for each child but included structured teaching using visual strengths to enhance skills in language and initiation (the developmental approach of TEACCH alluded to earlier in this discussion), a picture schedule to help the child anticipate future events, use of gestures, pictures, signs or words to enhance communication, and training in prevocational activities to aid in school entry, such as learning numbers, colors, shapes, writing and drawing. Therapists went to the child's home to directly observe parental teaching at least one time. Children in the control group did not receive any home treatment. Ozonoff and Cathcart (1998) found that the experimental group, which basically had an additional intervention to the day programs all 22 children received, improved more than the other children.

A major strength of the TEACCH program studies we have reviewed is the focus on mulitimodal treatment package across naturalistic settings. However, the treatments were not explained in sufficient detail to know exactly what the essential treatment elements were, nor was treatment integrity measured to insure accurate, consistent application of methods. For parents or other paraprofessionals who have limited training experience, this latter issue is of particular concern. In our opinion, the biggest strengths of the model in general appears to be the one-to-one instruction and parent training in natural settings and over extended time periods. Additionally, in the North Carolina example, the program is statewide. This latter point is quite impressive since it is the only state in the United States where ASD services are coordinated on such a large scale. Many benefits obviously are available for the largest possible number of children when such widespread methodology is used.

The Ozonoff and Cathcart (1998) paper shows that these researchers were able to demonstrate significant short-term gains in several areas by preschoolers with ASD. Similarly, the data of Schopler and associates show piecemeal validation of TEACCH teaching strategies. The consensus at present is that TEACCH has not yet published data from their comprehensive preschool treatment model (Rogers, 1998). We believe this is essential in further codifying the validity of the model, what elements are most essential and in what areas greatest gains are made. We look forward to seeing the publication of these results in the future.

UCLA-YAP and TEACCH are among those with some research to support them and certainly the best known among the general public. Often, programs receive sporadic attention in the literature but do not rival UCLA-YAP and TEACCH in particular in the attention they have received. Parent groups also deserve credit here. Both of these programs have been successful in gaining parent support, and in turn parent groups have done well to gain political and local support and thus resources for these programs. This aspect of clinical service provision is often given short shrift by researchers, but it is essential if broad support for these programs in real world settings is to be achieved.

Summary of Comprehensive Treatment Models

Since several widely disseminated programs for children with ASD are now available it should come as no surprise that clinicians, parents and researchers are trying to determine if one of these approaches would be the best alternative for their child. The internet is replete with testimonials from parents and practitioners about their experience and their evaluation of the best program. We do encourage the reading of such documents and feel some insights about the nuts and bolts of programmatic trends can be determined from these readings. However, we are highly skeptical about using such information to decide what is the "best" program. It is our view that systematic comparative studies are required to make such decisions. Fortunately, individual procedures for given problem behaviors and for social, communication and independent living skill-building have a wealth of well-documented data-based studies that help establish an evidence-based core of treatment strategies. At present, looking at which programs use the best available evidence-based strategies when these strategies are appropriate appears to us to be the best option in determining the quality of comprehensive treatment packages. These strategies have been reviewed at some length in the previous chapter.

Comparative treatment studies are insufficient at this writing and are unlikely to be available for years, if ever. Some direct tests of individual programs are available, although the studies are few and the methodological rigor is quire variable. In defense of those investigations we should note that it is much more difficult to adequately control a study of this sort compared to the example studies we described in the previous chapter. The former research tends to involve a few target behaviors with a few children over a relatively brief period of time. These comprehensive program studies are simply massive and require tremendous outlays of effort and resources on everyone's part. Thus, studies of this sort are easily criticized by the bystander but hard for researchers to carry out. However, those who have done research of this type are certainly deserving of credit and should be encouraged regardless of the inevitable methodological shortcomings.

Kasari (2002) provides an interesting review of the programmatic research studies available to date. She was able to find 10 papers that met minimal criteria that included using young children and which according to her assessment focused on all aspects of the child's development. Kasari (2002) makes a number of excellent points. She notes that many of these program studies use a manual, although treatment integrity checks were not uniform. Additionally, the training literature, particularly as it pertains to aberrant behavior, is evolving rapidly (see the functional assessment section in Chapter 4). Training strategies today may differ a good deal from those used 10 to 15 years ago. Thus, long-term studies may actually change training strategies as treatment evolves. As she points out, without careful documentation, the interventions used may blur over time.

We have begun our discussion of treatment with the procedures that have the greatest research support and have continued in descending order. Specific intervention targets clearly have the most data to support them. However, studies of comprehensive treatments have been promising and thus the amount of research on the topic is increasing. The next chapter will be on psychopharmacological treatments. Our views on this ranking of intervention approaches based on current acceptability is recognized by others. Jocelyn, Casiro, Beattie, Bow, and Kneisz (1998) note that "treatments most commonly used are educational and behavioral, since medically and psychopharmacologically oriented therapies have proven less successful in altering outcome." We concur with this assessment. Nonetheless, many other types of interventions have been used and pharmacology may, with further research, have a limited role in treating young children with ASD. We will very briefly cover some of the many unsubstantiated interventions, and then we will review the psychopharmacological literature in Chapter 6.

Unsubstantiated Treatment Models

Fortunately, most families utilize the more accepted, evidence-based interventions for young children with ASD (Richman, Reese, & Daniels, 1999). However, these treatments require a great deal of commitment on the part of the parents, the child and the trainers. Additionally, while improvement may occur, cure is certainly not guaranteed. As a result, a variety of therapies, usually endorsed via testimonials from a few parents, and of course the developers of the treatment, are routinely espoused. Cures are often promised with no peer-reviewed data to support the conclusions. And, while the interventions are often very expensive, a promise of rapid improvement is often made. The course of the therapy involves the hard sell to parents by "therapists" who, as noted, have no peer-reviewed research to support them, are out to make a name for themselves and in many instances make money in the process.

A little parent education provided by the responsible clinician will be helpful in steering parents towards evidence-based treatments. Any acceptable procedure should be available in the peer-reviewed literature. Over time, results should be replicated by independent investigators using the same or very similar client populations and training procedures. We believe we have covered the relevant training strategies with empirical support at this time in this book. We are not impressed by the claims made by the positive behavior supports and person-centered planning groups. These proponents are long on platitudes and rhetoric and short on data. Procedures such as gentle teaching argue for including parent and child goals, being nice to the person and so on, as if other strategies such as the many learning and education methods reviewed in this book do not also hold such values. These values are a given, but they do not promote active change in and of themselves. The research data clearly show the need for positive reinforcement and consequences for maladaptive behavior. We would characterize this as training personnel responsibility.

In sum, then, treatment developers who claim cure with no peer-reviewed database, who tend to downplay the empirical data that exist, and who exclusively use testimonials to support their treatment will most likely fail in the end. Solid programs based on sound evidence-based methods tend not to be glamorous. The methods require a great deal of work and planning over a long period of time. Positive reinforcement, skill-building, consequences for maladaptive behaviors, slow but steady treatment gains and no promise of an easy cure are hallmarks of the best treatments for ASD available today. Even under these circumstances cure may not occur, but more likely parents will observe an improvement in many areas that approach but fall short of "normal" development. The old saying that if it sounds too good to be true it probably is certainly fits when choosing a treatment for young children with ASD.

Conclusion

We are highly encouraged by developments in the last two decades of research on early intervention for children with ASD. The knowledge base should continue to expand rapidly. The near future appears to be dominated by learning theory and education-based interventions. One model may not fit all. Rather, different models of training and their variants are likely to emerge. Still, at the core, training strategies are the methods discussed in Chapter 4. These techniques have been put together in various packages to meet the needs of a given child based on the context of what the parents and community are comfortable with and can perform effectively.

We would be remiss if we did not also acknowledge the invaluable work of various parent groups, such as the Autism Society of America. Parent groups have been at the forefront in getting state and federal agencies to fund the research and training programs that are available around the country. Federal law in the form of the Individuals with Disabilities Education Act (IDEA) has been instrumental in providing the needed leverage to move local bureaucratic inertia in a way that has resulted in more and better services. Often times, a disconnect exists between the available research and the funds and motivation needed to implement these methods on a broad scale for a large number of children. In sum, the future for children with ASD appears to be brighter than ever before, largely due to the factors discussed above.

Chapter 6

Pharmacological Treatment

Pharmacotherapy has had a controversial history in the treatment of ASD. One of the main reasons parent and professional advocates have insisted on the disorder being viewed as a developmental condition rather than a mental health disorder is the past history of overmedication. These treatments have often produced serious short- and long-term side-effects, many of which are irreversible. Fairly or unfairly, many drugs prescribed for children with ASD were rushed into use with claims of potentially great improvement. To date, these hopes have not been fulfilled. Rather, what parents often observed were sedated individuals who still displayed many maladaptive and other dysfunctional behaviors, and who now also had a great deal of difficulty engaging in positive skill-building. Further, those prescribing the drugs often did not know or failed to report to parents the possible short- and long-term side-effects of their treatments. As a result, it is not uncommon to find early intervention programs that have a no-psychotropic-drug policy. This approach may be throwing the baby out with the bath water. However, past history has led to this reaction or over-reaction, depending on how one views these decisions. Thus, medicating symptoms of ASD has proven to be quite controversial.

Early History

In the early 1960s, a label of "autistic schizophrenic" children was common (Freedman, Ebin, & Wilson, 1962a). This conceptual model allowed for the application of treatments that were in vogue at the time for psychoses. One primary drug therapy researched during this period was LSD-25, whose psychedelic properties had been discovered in 1943 by Hoffman (Bender, Faretra, & Cobrinik, 1963). Although the claims made then are now generally regarded as nonsense, many professionals at the time believed that LSD-25 could facilitate other psychiatric interventions, heighten perceptual awareness, increase rapport, and break through the repressive ego defenses (Busch & Johnson, 1950). When the drug was used as a treatment for mental health conditions, it was usually combined, at weekly intervals, with psychotherapy. This latter treatment typically was psychodynamic in theoretical orientation, and for reasons noted earlier also created a great deal of consternation for many advocates for individuals with ASD.

As a result of these developments and the attitude toward LSD-25 in the psychiatric community at the time, it was not surprising that application to children soon followed. Freedman, Ebin, and Wilson (1962b) did just that, giving LSD to 12 "autistic schizophrenic" children under 12 years of age at a day school in New York. Ten children were given one dose and two others were given two doses of LSD. The researcher reported mood swings, vocalizations that were not typical for the children under normal conditions, and some changes in social contact. The authors conceptualized these behaviors as negative and attributable to the lack of developing tolerance to the treatment. Despite these results, the authors conducted a series of studies using LSD with "autistic schizophrenic" children. Among the favorable behavioral signs they reported in these latter reports were that children showed no serious side-effects, and no evidence of severe disturbance or toxicity. They argued from a psychodynamic formulation that children showed disturbances in awareness; they were unable to form identifications or meaningful interpersonal relationships or to break through autistic defenses. The purpose of the medication would then be to facilitate these efforts during therapy and real world experiences (Bender et al., 1963).

Bender and associates (1963) conducted an early LSD study and were very positive about the drug. They reported children changing their responses to the environment, becoming happy, laughing frequently, becoming more alert, aware and interested in others, showing appropriate changes in facial expressions, being able to understand and follow directions more readily, all in the context of children who previously had been very withdrawn and regressed. Professional personnel and parents were reported to be "enthusiastic" about the changes in the children. Another interesting interpretation of their observations was the reporting of mildly aggressive pushing, biting, and pinching of others. The researchers interpreted these as positive behaviors since the children were now "making contact with the environment." In addition to these anecdotal reports, noticeable shifts on pretest–posttest Rorschach scores were noted. (The Rorschach is not an appropriate measure of change for ASD, but that is a topic for another book.)

Given the glowing initial reports, why then did LSD research and treatment stop over the next few years? Mogar and Aldrich (1969) reported that at the end of the decade LSD-25 had been by far the most frequently studied psychedelic agent in "psychotic" children. They report seven studies employing a total of 91 children. Perhaps one reason for the lack of additional study was that the research was poorly done. Sufficient methodological controls, reliable and appropriate dependent variables, no systematic assessment of side-effects via operationally defined behaviors and psychometrically sound checklists, and the failure to attain adequate follow-up were some of the methodological shortcomings. Most importantly, however, the final result was that the drug did not positively affect autism and it produced many harmful side-effects.

We have chosen to discuss the LSD experience for several historical reasons. First, autism treatment is filled with interventions that are considered promising, but within a few years fade and are replaced with other "fad" treatments that promise marked improvement or cure. Thus, the LSD experience is a model of an intervention where claims were made but little long-term benefits resulted. LSD as a treatment for ASD is now a distant memory in the pantheon of interventions for ASD. Many more interventions are likely to fall by the wayside without adequate attention from researchers and clinicians. How do professionals and parents avoid such pitfalls? We give two suggestions: well-controlled research data and time. The criticisms of the LSD research on methodological grounds by Mogar and Aldrich (1969) is instructive since, as we have noted, these errors continue to be made presently with other interventions.

This historical point is pertinent to all therapies for children, but particularly drugs. Just because initial claims are that the treatment is not harmful, does not always mean that such a view is accurate. Often, initial treatments are of short duration and little systematic long-term follow-up occurs. Over time, the true nature and effectiveness of the intervention emerges. Thus, the later finding that LSD could be a very dangerous drug, with severe side-effects such as Post Traumatic Stress Disorder (PTSD) type flashbacks, should be instructive. Researchers, clinicians, and parents should be very cautious in advancing potential treatments until sufficient data have been published in peer-reviewed journals using adequate research designs and describing the context of the pertinent literature in the area. Unfortunately, this lesson does not seem to have been learned as of this writing.

Current Medication Practices

We must start by telling the reader that we are not particularly enamored with the notion of giving psychotropic drugs to young children with ASD. Not that many years ago, professionals who developed drug practices argued that only adolescents and adults would be the recipients of these powerful medications. Those in favor of prescribing drugs to younger and younger children argue currently that newer medications have fewer side-effects and are more symptom-specific, thus justifying their use. We are not convinced. For example, how can researchers know that minimal long-term side-effects are present when the drug has not been available long enough to measure such side-effects long term? However, the reader should be informed that there are many professionals who are encouraged by recent research on pharmacotherapy for young children with ASD and highly endorse this treatment approach.

We do not suggest that drug therapy does not have a role for individuals with ASD. Our contention is that such treatments should on the whole be reserved for older persons (late adolescents and adults). The second parameter would be that pharmacotherapy might be more appropriate for those children with ASD who have other mental health disorders as well. In this case, more conventional research support for specific drug use exists. DeLong and Nohira (1994), for example, suggested that ASD might be related to bipolar disorder, while Bolton, Pickles, and Murphy (1998) argue for a link with affective disorders. Similarly, Morgan, Roy, and Chance (2003), in a study of 164 adults with ASD, found that 41% of the sample evinced one of a number of mental health disorders, such as bipolar disorder, schizophrenia or major depression. Morgan et al. (2003) also found that 52% of their sample were on psychotropic medication and 40% of that group had ASD as their only mental health diagnosis.

Comorbid conditions are common in the developmentally disabled population. Therefore, mental health disorders co-occurring with ASD would not be unexpected. Obviously, ASD alone is viewed by some as sufficient reason to prescribe these drugs in many persons. For example, nearly one fourth of the children identified by Curtis et al. (2005) as receiving atypical antipsychotics were 9 years old or younger, with nearly 80% of these children being boys. A child with psychotic features as a second diagnosis might benefit from an antipsychotic drug, or a child with ASD who also had an anxiety disorder might benefit from an antianxiety drug. However, it is highly unlikely that even a few children under age 9 would evince such disorders.

In one of the more visible recent drug studies, McCracken et al. (2002) suggest that children with ASD may "benefit" from atypical antipsychotics if they have serious behavioral disturbances, such as tantrums, self-injury, and aggression. McCracken et al. (2002) studied 101 children averaging 8.8 years of age for 8 weeks. The authors concluded that risperidone was effective and "well tolerated" for the treatment of aggression, self-injury, and tantrums in children. Frankly, we consider this study, which included a number of prominent researchers in the field, a wrong turn in treatment options. The authors noted that given the short period of treatment, an evaluation of adverse side-effects of atypical antipsychotic medications, such as tardive dyskinesia (TD), could not be addressed. We refer the reader to research conducted in Europe by Geddes, Freemantle, and Harrison (2000), who found that atypical antipsychotics produced as many of the same long-term side-effects as typical antipsychotic drugs.

The field of developmental disabilities has had a long history of behavior problems being "treated" as we would argue by chemically restraining the person. Aggression and self-injury are not forms of psychopathology and have been particularly vulnerable to this drug overuse issue. In most instances, these problem behaviors have clear environmental causes that lead to effective psychological interventions. When a child does not receive consistent consequences for aggression or inadvertently receives a great deal of attention for the misbehavior, pharmacotherapy is not the appropriate treatment. Rather, clearer rules and consequences for socially unacceptable behaviors are needed. We argue that antipsychotic drugs should be limited to the extremely rare case of an individual with ASD and psychosis. Additionally, we are of the opinion that 4-year-old children should not be receiving antipsychotic medications.

A press release by one of the five universities that participated in the study by McCracken et al. (2002) concluded that Risperidone "is safe for children and reduces severe behavioral symptoms in youths with autism." The authors of this paper simply cannot know that at this time. The authors go on to say in the press release that ASD is an "orphan population because their relatively small number has resulted in little research being conducted in the past on the disorder." We could not disagree more. Relative to other psychological disorders, ASD is one of the most heavily researched areas in psychology, special education, and psychiatry. Literally hundreds of studies have been published with a substantial number of these being in the area of treatment development, as we noted earlier in this book. We refer the reader to Chapters 4 and 5 for an overview of this research.

We also have a number of concerns about the methodology of this study and pharmacotherapy research in ASD and ID in general. First, measures designed specifically to assess symptoms of ASD, not behavior problems in general, should be used as the primary outcome measure in ASD research. Second, measures of achievement and adaptive functioning should be assessed, as has been the case in the comprehensive treatment packages presented in Chapter 5. Third, operationally defined target behaviors should be used to measure outcome. Fourth, systematic scales designed to measure side-effect profiles of antipsychotic medications should be used during the initial study and in follow-up over the months and years that follow. Firth, functional analyses should be conducted on all disruptive or aberrant behaviors, such as self-injury, aggression, and noncompliance, to ensure that environmental factors are not maintaining the behaviors. Sixth, measures of psychopathology should be administered to ensure that a mental health disorder with psychotic features is present before an antipsychotic drug is prescribed. There are necessary factors required for identifying the nature of the problem and adequately measuring the effects and side-effects of these medications.

Debates about the intensity of behavioral interventions, which particular strategy is best and so on, pale in comparison to the research issues in pharmacotherapy, such as methodological shortcomings and potential side-effects. Our opinion is that the cure is worse than the problem with antipsychotic drug treatment of children with ASD at this time. At a minimum, researchers promoting use of such drugs in this population should be advocating their use as an adjunct to learning theory and educational approaches in only the most extreme cases. Even then, we strongly question the need for these powerful drugs in such young children.

Numerous methodological problems are associated with the research available to demonstrate the efficacy of psychotropic drug use for children with ASD. Luiselli, Blew, Keane, Thibadeau, and Halzman (2000) point out that these studies are rarely assessed in the long term (and we mean months, not years, when in fact years also need to be studied), and the studies do not identify specific target behavior symptoms (e.g. stereotypies, activity level) for assessment. However, we would argue that the Lusielli et al. (2000) paper further compounds the problem by "treating" aggression in a 12-year-old boy with ASD using pharmacotherapy. They use what is described as an open label study. Unfortunately, open label implies no systematic control of conditions within or across participants. We do not believe these papers should be published in science-based journals.

Another problem with the papers described above and many other pharmacology papers is that the focus is almost exclusively on symptom reduction. Additionally, as noted, these symptoms are often not part of the disorder per se, but are behavior problems, such as self-injury and aggression, which are seen in equally high rates in children with ID and in other populations. These behaviors are not unique to ASD. This approach is dangerous in our view since the possibility of promoting a model of behavior suppression (chemical restraint) will produce the same "positive effects" unless prosocial skills are monitored and increase (e.g. social and communication skills). Thus, what is being described as "effective" intervention, based on trial runs so far, could have their effects just as easily explained as sedation of the child. The first author of this book refers to this treatment model as rock therapy, since under this methodological approach a rock would be a patient success: no behavior problems.

This line of investigation, which now includes more and more "problem behaviors" treated at younger and younger ages, has led the field of psychiatry/psychology to the point where papers appear with titles such as "The use of psychotropic medication in preschoolers: Some recent developments" (Minde, 1998). Sadly then, we are at the point where some researchers are compelled to make points such as "psychotropic drugs should be used in preschoolers only as last resort and for brief periods" since for many these drugs are now seen as the first line of intervention. We agree with Minde (1998). However, the tide appears to be going against this view. For example, *The Wall Street Journal* (Abboud, 2005) published an article entitled "Treating children for bipolar disorder: Doctors try powerful drugs on kids as young as age 4; An overlap with ADHD." The reporter discussed the use of Seroquel and Risperdal "with rapidly increasing rates of bipolar being diagnosed" in these very young children. One study at Massachusetts General Hospital treated 39 children age 4 to 6 years with antipsychotic drugs. Key symptoms being described as bipolar were aggression or irritability. Again, we do not see these as core features of bipolar disorder in the same way that aggression and self-injury are not core features of ASD. Some psychiatrists noted that these "symptoms" also occur in depression, autism, and ID. We would also add that they can appear in typically developing children. Finally, bipolar disorder, which is one of the primary "fad" diagnoses presently, cannot be reliably diagnosed in young children. No scales have been normed nor have the symptoms been adequately defined for this population. Additionally, in all the studies noted, none of the researchers conducted an adequate functional analysis to determine if the behavior problems were environmentally caused before resorting to medication. We would argue that if Billy "acts out" because he does not like sitting next to Tom, move him next to Sally, rather than giving him an antipsychotic drug. We fear the overuse of antipsychotic drugs given that little is known about the safety, dosing, and efficacy in preschool children (Greenhill, 1998). Preliminary reports of possible irreversible neurological damage in children with disorders such as TD (Tsai, 1999b) with these drugs gives us even further concerns about their use.

We will now do a selective review of some of the drugs that have been commonly used, or are commonly used to treat ASD. A substantial number of drugs have had one or two studies published with individuals with ASD as the participants. Often these applications have been with adults versus children or vice versa. Therefore, we have selected what we consider to be the drugs that are more likely to be used in practice for young children with ASD.

Antipsychotic Medications

Children with ASD are not psychotic. Nonetheless, antipsychotic medications have been among the most frequently used psychotropic drugs in this group of children. Additionally, while consensus exists that ASD is a neurological disorder, no biological markers and thus no biological treatments linked to "cause" are currently available (Tsai, 1999a). Despite this, at least one third of people with ASD are on psychotropic drugs or vitamins for ASD (Aman, Van Bourgondien, Wolford, & Sarphare, 1995).

Haloperidol (Haldol) was the antipsychotic of choice in the early period of pharmacology in ASD. During the 1970s to 1990s some studies emerged which hypothesized its effectiveness. The drug is a dopamine antagonist, the system of the brain affecting motor movements. Thus, the drug, as in the risperidone study reported earlier, supposedly decreases hyperactivity and motor movements that can lead to aggression, self-injury, and other aberrant behavior. Typical of these studies were two done by Anderson and associates (1984, 1989). In the first study of 40 children aged 2 to 7 with ASD, the researchers alternated 4-week treatment phases of Haldol, no Haldol, Haldol, no Haldol. The authors reported significant decreases in maladaptive behavior, although only checklist data (no behavioral observation data, functional assessments, etc.) were obtained. Additionally, no positive behavior increases were noted. Rather, suppression of behavior was the primary outcome. Interestingly, the authors reported no adverse side-effects of the drug, although little was done to systematically address this variable. In the second study, Anderson et al. (1989) replicated these same findings with 45 children evincing ASD, aged 2 to 8 years old. They stated that the children showed decreases in hyperactivity, temper tantrums, withdrawal, and stereotypies. They reported no adverse side-effects on learning. Later, researchers pointed out that this set of "typical antipsychotic drugs" does adversely affect learning and long term produces many irreversible side-effects, such as TD and dyskinesia. Thus, Haldol is now out of favor as a treatment for ASD. We find it perplexing that Haldol was seen as so promising, yet research on it was dropped, and researchers moved on to another drug class. Looking through the treatment literature on pharmacology with ASD, one sees this pattern repeated with other drugs and drug classes.

The development of atypical antipsychotics held the promise of providing the therapeutic effects while minimizing the adverse side-effects produced by Haldol and other typical antipsychotic drugs. As noted, however, Geddes et al. (2000) and others have found that long term these atypical antipsychotic drugs appear to produce many of the same side-effects as their conventional counterparts. If indeed this is the case, the pattern seen with Haldol, where it was believed to produce great positive effects but few side-effects, only for it to emerge that marked side-effects are present, may be repeated with the atypical antipsychotics and drug classes that followed. Also, with such young children, where a developing nervous system must be considered, little or no hope of discontinuing the drug over time exists. Additionally, even if the drug works, it works only when it is being taken. Therefore, if such drugs produce chronic neurological disorders, these children are candidates for the most severe side-effects in the long term, since they will take the drugs for the longest time period and we know time and dose are linked to risk of irreversible neurological side-effects. We urge caution in prescribing in the meantime since we know dose and length of administration are major risk factors. Only 30–40 years on will sufficient long-term data be available to test this long-term side-effect hypothesis.

Fenfluramine

As we proceed, the reader will notice a pattern with drugs from varying classes. Each medication has a different theory of biochemical action that occurs for children with ASD. The theories are based on the drug action promoted for the specific drug class being prescribed. All of these theories cannot be correct. And, given the poor record of drug effectiveness to date, we wonder if this theoretical model of identifying an etiology is appropriate for ASD.

Fenfluramine is an atypical phenylethylamine anorexigenic drug, which reduces brain serotonin (5-HT) and serotonin's major metabolite (5-HIAA). The proponents of fenfluramine, of course, suggest a dysfunctional serotonergic system resulting in the same maladaptive behaviors of tantrums, hyperactivity, self-injury, and aggression noted above with antipsychotics where a different drug action is proposed. At present, we do not know if any of these drug action theories are accurate (nor does anyone else). Additionally, it does not necessarily follow that the maladaptive behaviors have a biological cause unless functional assessment is conducted to demonstrate no environmental cause. Even if pharmacologically based treatment appears to be the only acceptable explanation in a given instance, it does not prove the chemical action theory proposed. For example, we know that Lesch–Nyhan Syndrome has a biological cause based on genetic markers. The most effective intervention for the intensive self-injury these persons display is behavior modification. Obviously, this does not produce a causal link confirming that Lesch–Nyhan Syndrome is environmentally caused. However, a little more caution and a much sounder methodological approach to the problem appear to be in order.

One of the early studies on fenfluramine for ASD was conducted by Anderson and associates (1984). They treated 10 children with ASD ranging from 5 to 13 years of age for 16 weeks with fenfluramine. Anderson et al. (1984) concluded that the children improved in overactivity, distractibility, and affect. No marked side-effects were reported. Similarly, Ritvo et al. (1984) studied 14 outpatients with ASD and reported improvements in social awareness, eye contact, attention to school work, decreased hyperactivity, repetitive behaviors such as hand flapping and spinning, and improved sleep. Thus, the researchers who published these two studies reported positive benefits of fenfluramine for ASD.

Despite these early positive reports, negative data soon began to appear at an increasing rate. For example, concerns were expressed about its safety (Pranzatelli & Snodgrass, 1985; Schuster, Lewis, & Seiden, 1986). Similarly, Yarbrough, Santat, Perel, Webster, & Lombardi (1987) found a variety of adverse side-effects in a sample of 20 people with ASD aged 9 to 28 years of age. Primary difficulties included insomnia, increased tension, agitation, aggression, and hyperirritability. Additionally, no significant improvement was noted in any of the 21 variables such as sensory-motor behavior, sensory responses, relationships to people or improved language were noted. Ekman and associates (1989) found equally discouraging results. They treated 13 children with ASD, who ranged in age from $1\frac{1}{2}$ to $10\frac{1}{2}$ years, from the Gothenburg region of Sweden. They concluded that they were not able to confirm a specific positive effect of fenfluramine on maladaptive or adaptive behavior. Similarly, no improvement in intellectual functioning was noted. This latter finding has also been reported elsewhere (August et al., 1984; Ho, Lockitch, Eaves, & Jacobson, 1986; Klykylo, Feldis, O'Grady, Ross, & Halloran, 1985). Finally, Ekman and associates note that "from a clinical point of view, the improvements on fenfluramine were too few to recommend the drug for the general treatment of infantile autism."

How do researchers and clinicians reconcile this common pattern of early success followed by the sobering reality of drug ineffectiveness? We believe a good deal of the explanation is motivated by good intentions. Researchers, clinicians, and parents are desperate for improvement or cure. Often, this inadvertently leads to a less than critical analysis of the new treatment. Related to this point is that in the rush to find effective treatments, early studies on a given intervention fall short on methodological grounds. Often "open studies" are employed and systematic evaluation of side-effects is not pursued. Based on the "course" of research over time, we conclude that fenfluramine does not appear to be a viable clinical intervention for children with ASD. As a result, the hunt for an effective drug therapy has continued with other pharmacological methods.

Naltrexone

Neonatal rats and chicks exposed to substantial amounts of opiates were observed in the laboratory to evince "autistic like symptoms." Thus, it seemed to some researchers that a natural progression would be to use naltrexone, an opiate blocker, to treat persons with ASD. Campbell et al. (1990) tested this theory on behavioral and learning problems of 18 children with ASD from 3 to 8 years old. They obtained mixed results across their dependent measures. Some reports of reduced fidgeting, hyperactivity, and hostility, and changes in socialization, communication, object relations, and attention were noted (Bouvard et al., 1995). The gains were typically described as marginal, or results were "mixed." We should note that the half-life of naltrexone is only a few hours. Thus, it would be hard to demonstrate much improvement, if improvement occurred without frequent dosing. This factor further complicates the potential benefits of this drug for children with ASD.

Several other researchers have published studies describing the effects of naltrexone as modest or mixed for persons with ASD. For example, Kolmen, Feldman, Harden, and Janosky (1997) noted modest improvements in behavior problems but none in learning for 11 of 24 children. On the other hand, Williems-Swinkels, Buitelaar, and Van Engeland (1996) described teachers' reports of 23 children with ASD. The authors reported decreased hyperactivity and irritability but no improvement in social skills and stereotypies. Williams, Allard, Sears, Dalrymple, and Bloom (2001) present even less promising results for naltrexone as a treatment for ASD. These authors treated 8 boys with ASD ranging in age from 2 years, 10 months to 9 years, 2 months, with a mean of 4 years of age. Williams and associates (2001) found no difference on videotaped social imitations, stereotypies or attention problems. Generally speaking, they reported no positive effects.

Zingarelli et al. (1992) found similarly disappointing results with naltrexone. The "autistic behavior" in eight adults ranging from 19 to 39 years of age was treated with the medication. The authors determined that naltrexone had no clinical effect on self-injury or the idiosyncratic maladaptive mannerisms that were monitored. One could argue that more advanced age and the occurrence of maladaptive behaviors over a longer period of time strengthened these behaviors to a point where they were unresponsive to medication. Young children are more likely to be responsive to psychological interventions and thus may also respond better to pharmacotherapy. However, we consider this argument a stretch in this instance. We believe it is more appropriate to focus on the vulnerability of small children and a developing nervous system to these drug therapies. Additionally, the majority of the studies reported little or no positive effect with naltrexone. Thus, the data are mostly negative with this drug as a treatment for ASD.

While results are also variable for aberrant behavior, self-injury is one problem behavior that does appears to respond to naltrexone in some instances. This conclusion appears reasonable since some forms of self-injury are clearly linked to environmental antecedents, such as attention, and would account for some nonresponders. Persons with a diagnosis of ASD and those with ID have been effectively treated in some cases with this drug (Barrett, Feinstein, & Hole, 1989; Campbell et al., 1990; Herman et al., 1987). In summary, in the main, effects of naltrexone appear to be minimal and mixed. Additionally, a variety of side-effects are likely to occur. Thus, naltrexone does not appear to be an appropriate drug to treat ASD, particularly in light of the numerous effective psychological interventions, particularly for maladaptive behaviors, currently available. The exception may be in instances of self-injury when a clear antecedent event cannot be identified.

Fluoxetine

Fluoxetine, a selective 5-HT reuptake inhibitor, is yet another drug that has been tried in people with ASD. Fluoxetine has been demonstrated to be an effective intervention for depression and obsessive-compulsive disorder. This drug is seen as an adjunct in treating children with ASD to control disruptive and interfering behaviors. A few studies have been done using this medication with ASD. For example, McDougle et al. (1996) treated repetitive and other obsessive-compulsive behaviors in ASD. Fatemi, Realmuto, Khan, and Thursas (1998) also used fluoxetine to treat ASD. Seven adolescents and young adults were treated for 1.3 to 32 months. The authors reported improvement on irritability, lethargy, stereotypies, and inappropriate speech as measured with the Aberrant Behavior Checklist. A number of side-effects were also reported. These problems included initial appetite suppression, vivid dreams, and hyperactivity.

One study that is particularly relevant to our topic was conducted by DeLong, Teague, and Kamran (1998). They treated 47 children aged 2 to 7 years. However, this study was open label. In our view, this means, as noted earlier, that the results must be viewed with suspicion since inadequate methodology is in place. The authors reported improvement in 11 of the children via the development of appropriate, responsive language and social interactions. They stated that the children were animated and vivacious, and their movements normalized. The authors also suggest that the children were aware of their surroundings, and the researchers state that problem-solving and contextual cognitive function improved. How was this series of remarkably positive results determined? According to the authors, by assessing testing done by "various examiners" using "various instruments" and by retrospective data collection of independent evaluation and progress reports of language pathologists, speech therapists, and psychologists. In other words, unsystematic and inconsistent information collected by people of varying qualifications with no systematic training in data collection. Furthermore, the data collected to evaluate the treatment outcomes of this study were not designed for this use. Therefore, even with a more reliable, valid, and systematic data collection approach, there is still no guarantee that the data methods would be sensitive to the desired treatment changes the authors wished to assess.

At this stage, we would describe the results obtained for fluoxetine as highly questionable. Few studies have been done to demonstrate systematic positive effects. As a result, we are not of the opinion that a compelling case for the use of this drug with young children with ASD has been established. However, it should also be clear that results are minimal at best for the drugs we have discussed, and more methodologically sound research is needed if these drugs are to be considered viable treatments for children with ASD.

Clonidine

Norepinephrine agonists such as amphetamines or methylephenidate (MPH) appear to worsen the behavior of individuals with ASD in many instances. One study found modest gains for some clients with ASD who were administered MPH (Quintana, Birmaher, & Stedge, 1995). However, this study does not represent the conventional wisdom in the field. Because these stimulants are typically viewed as contraindicated, researchers have proposed that norepinephrine antagonists such as clonidine may be effective as therapeutic agents. The study by Frankhauser, Karumanchi, German, Yates, and Karumanchi (1992) is typical of the literature, which again is sparse. They treated seven children with ASD aged 5 to 12 years of age and two adults aged 25 and 33. Behaviors treated were hyperarousal responses including stereotypies, hypervigilance, and hyperactivity. We would concur that a drug class that could decrease these symptoms without producing serious side-effects would be a major aid in overall management of some children with ASD where these particular maladaptive behaviors are most common and intense. Many of the previous studies that target self-injury and aggression typically have identifiable environmental cause, such as escape from demands or activities and attention. However, the maladaptive symptoms targeted here form a core of temperament factors that could exacerbate behaviors such as self-injury or aggression that may be triggered by environmental factors. Thus, while hyper-arousal can be exacerbated by environmental factors it may have a more readily identifiable biological substrate. As a result, theoretically at least, these researchers may have a good point in our view with medications being seen as an adjunct to behavior therapies for some problems in the ASD population.

When Frankhauser et al. (1992) reported that clonidine treatment resulted in significant improvement in social relations for "some" of the participants, we were hopeful. Little additional research is available, which suggests that less promising findings were likely found in other clinical use. Rarely do negative results get reported in journals. Nonetheless, we do concur that further exploration and/or development of drugs, if not this particular one, which addresses the hyperarousal issue would be worth pursuing. In this area we believe medication has a potentially positive role to play.

Secretin

One of the newer and more controversial treatments in recent years for children with ASD is secretin. The drug has received a great deal of attention in the press. Horvath et al. (1998) studied three children with ASD. The children supposedly improved dramatically in a range of behavioral domains as well as in expressive language. Unfortunately, the study was seriously flawed. No systematic evaluation of treatment effects was used nor were standard research methods to control for potential effects of a variety of other factors employed.

In another study, Richman, Reese, and Daniels (1999) reported data on secretin dosing performed intravenously at 20 clinical units per kilogram of body weight (intravenous secretin has a 2-minute half-life). They tested only one person, a 4-year-old boy diagnosed with ASD using a pre- and posttest design. However, this methodology is inadequate to demonstrate experimental control. The standard for single case research, except where extraordinarily rare disorders are treated (e.g. Lesch–Nyhan Syndrome), requires at least two people so that the results can be replicated (generalized) across individuals. Information was collected on three areas: communication, repetitive behavior and interests, and impaired social interactions. No improvements were noted at 2 weeks or 3 months. These findings are consistent with most of the research on the topic. However, again we would warn that the methodological shortcoming of this study compromises the conclusion that can be made about secretin. Given the extremely short half-life of the drug, it would seem rather unlikely that any positive effects would be seen in a study that lasted days let alone weeks without multiple drug administrations.

Perry and Bangaru (1998) also used secretin with six children evincing ASD. They found language improvement in only one of the six cases. These authors concluded by cautioning against the purported effectiveness of secretin and stressed that gains appeared modest at best, despite claims to the contrary on the internet and in the popular press, where secretin had been touted as the next wonder drug.

A particularly interesting paper on the topic was conducted by Chez et al. (2000). The results stirred up something of a hornet's nest, with parent groups critiquing the negative findings while stressing that secretin is a safe and beneficial treatment for autism (Rimland, 2000). Chez and associates (2000) treated 56 children with an average age of 6.4 years. Diagnoses were either PDD or ASD. The children received one injection of secretin at 2 IU/kg. Children were assessed by their parents on CARS at baseline and follow-up at 3 to 6 weeks. The authors reported transient changes in speech and behavior in some children. They concluded that these changes were not meaningful and reiterated in a rebuttal letter to Rimland (2000) that they could not justify the use of secretin. The researchers suggested that if the intervention were worthwhile and beneficial then the treatment needed to be documented in a peer review journal (Chez & Buchanan, 2000). First, no control group was used and many basic rules for a minimal research design were not followed. Second, parents (as opposed to blind raters) were used. They knew when the secretin was administered and no reliability data were taken on the single dependent variable, the CARS. Direct observational data on specific target behaviors in this type of research as a second dependent variable, and a systematic means of measuring side-effects, should have been employed. However, this was another negative finding regarding secretin and more reports, with better methodology but the same results, were soon to follow, piling up a formidable negative view of secretin.

Molloy et al. (2002) in one such study looked at 42 children with ASD. One group received 2.0 IU/kg of intravenous synthetic human secretin at the first visit. An equal volume of placebo was administered at 6 weeks. A second group received these two injections in the reverse order. Standard assessments of language, behavior, and symptoms of ASD were evaluated at 1, 3, 6, 9, and 12 weeks. No effects of note were observed and the authors concluded that secretin was not effective as a treatment for ASD.

Carey et al. (2002) studied eight children with ASD using a double-blind, placebo-controlled dosing method for secretin. Using the Aberrant Behavior Checklist (ABC), the authors reported no effect of this treatment. No improvement was also reported by Sandler et al. (1999) with 60 children aged 2 to 14 years with ASD. Sandler et al. (1999) also used a double-blind, placebo-controlled method, which is the gold standard for drug research. The ABC was the primary means of assessing impairment over the 4 weeks of the study. Finally, Corbett et al. (2001) also conducted a double-blind, placebo-controlled study of secretin over a 16-week period. These researchers used one intravenous dose of secretin for 12 children with ASD ranging in age from 4 to 12 years. Measures of social skills, communication, affect, language, gastrointestinal symptoms, and a neurological evaluation demonstrated no appreciable effects.

These data and other relevant studies culminated in a recent review paper by Sturmey (2005). Sturmey reviewed 15 double-blind trials of secretin and concluded that almost none reported any significant effects and none of the authors concluded that secretin was effective. Most of these studies used multiple measures of ASD, socialization, communication and problem behaviors. These and the studies reported above vary in the rigor of the methodology. However, in scientific terms, it is remarkable to see so many papers showing no effect. These data indicate to us the incredible momentum that can be built up around a therapy when advocacy groups and the popular press continue to laud its effectiveness despite the lack of empirical support. We also have spent some time reviewing secretin since it exemplifies many interventions in the ASD field. Desperate parents are hoping for a cure. Of course, the parents cannot be blamed for this view. However, the old adage that if it sounds too good to be true it probably is, fits here. Patience is needed in evaluating possible early intervention programs for ASD. The professional community should not endorse any treatment until adequate documentation of effectiveness via methodologically sound studies can be performed.

Conclusions

The general conclusion regarding pharmacology is that it has a very limited role to play with young children evincing ASD at this time. Antipsychotic drugs recommendations appear to be over the top. Limited effectiveness outside of sedation has been demonstrated, and long-term serious side-effects for small children are very possible, even in the most positive scenario. Most of the other medications also have only a few poorly controlled studies to support their viability. The most and best studies on one drug involve secretin where the results are uniformly negative.

We also stress that researchers, parents, and clinicians must consider possible drug effects in the broader context. At present, many learning-based strategies have proven very effective. Additionally, there is the considerable safety issue regarding long-term adverse side-effects with these medications. Given this scenario, even assuming positive drug effects, there is little rationale for their use at this time. The exception may be anxiety, hypersensitivity or obsessive-compulsive symptoms, where medication may serve an adjunctive role to behavior modification and educational methods. However, these medications as add-ons would need to be in extreme cases and in instances where the child has severe symptoms and has not responded to learning-based methods alone. The research has not been done on this topic. Thus, at present our point would have to be considered speculative.

References

AACAP. (1999). Practice parameters for the assessment and treatment of children, adolescents and adults with autism and other Pervasive Developmental Disorders. *Journal of the American Academy of Child and Adolescent Psychiatry, 38*, 325–545.

Abboud, L. (2005, May 25). Treating children for bipolar disorder: Doctors try powerful drugs on kids as young as age 4; An overlap with ADHD. *The Wall Street Journal*, p. D1.

Adams, C., & Bishop, D. M. V. (1989). Controversial characteristics of children with semantic-pragmatic disorders I: Exchange structure, turn-taking, repairs and cohesion. *British Journal of Disorders of Communication, 24*, 211–239.

Aikman, G., Garbutt, U., & Furniss, F. (2003). Brief probes: A model for analyzing the function of disruptive behaviour in the natural environment. *Behavioural and Cognitive Psychology, 31*, 215–220.

Aldred, C., Pollard, C., & Adams, C. (2001). Child's talk for children with Autism and Pervasive Developmental Disorder. *International Journal of Language, 36*, 469–474.

Allyon, T., & Azrin, N. H. (1965). The measurement and reinforcement of behavior of psychotics. *Journal of the Experimental Analysis of Behavior, 8*, 357–383.

Allyon, T., & Azrin, N. H. (1968). *The token economy: A motivational system for therapy and rehabilitation.* New York: Appleton-Century-Crafts.

Aman, M. G., Van Bourgondien, M. E., Wolford, P. L., & Sarphare, G. (1995). Psychotropic and antipsychotic drugs in subjects with autism: Prevalence and patterns of use. *Journal of the American Academy of Child and Adolescent Psychiatry, 34*, 1672–1681.

American Psychiatric Association. (1952). *Diagnostic and statistical manual of mental disorders* (1st ed.). Washington, DC: Author.

American Psychiatric Association. (1980). *Diagnostic and statistical manual of mental disorders* (3rd ed.). Washington, DC: Author.

American Psychiatric Association. (1987). *Diagnostic and statistical manual of mental disorders* (3rd ed., revised). Washington, DC: Author.

American Psychiatric Association. (1994). *Diagnostic and statistical manual of mental disorders* (4th ed.). Washington, DC: Author.

American Psychiatric Association. (2000). *Diagnostic and statistical manual of mental disorders* (4th ed., Text Revision.). Washington, DC: Author.

Amir, R. E., Van den Veyver, I. B., Wan, M., Tran, C. Q., Francke, U. et al. (1999). RS is caused by mutations in X-linked MECP2, encoding methyl-CpG-binding protein 2. *Nature Genetics, 23*, 185–188.

Anderson, G. M., & Hoshino, Y. (1987). Neurochemical studies of autism. In D. J. Cohen, A. M. Donnellan, & R. Paul (eds), *Handbook of Autism and Pervasive Developmental Disorders* (pp. 166–191). New York: Wiley.

Anderson, G. M., & Hoshino, Y. (2005). Neurochemical studies of autism. In F. R. Volkmar, R. Paul, A. Klin, & D. J. Cohen (eds), *Handbook of Autism and Pervasive Developmental Disorders* (3rd ed.) (pp. 453–472). New York: Wiley.

Anderson, G. M., Minderaa, R. B., van Bentem, P. G., Volkmar, F. R., & Cohen, D. J. (1984). Platelet imipramine binding in autistic subjects. *Psychiatry Research, 11*, 133–141.

Anderson, L. T., Campbell, M., Adams, Small, A. M., Perry, R., & Shell, J. (1989). The effects of haloperidol on discrimination learning and behavioral symptoms in autistic children. *Journal of Autism and Developmental Disorders, 19*, 227–239.

Anderson, L. T., Campbell, M., Grega, D. M., Perry, R., Small, A. M., & Green, W. H. (1984). Haloperidol in the treatment of infantile autism: Effects on learning and behavioral symptoms. *American Journal of Psychiatry, 141*, 1195–1202.

Anderson, S. R., Avery, D. L., DiPietro, E. K., Edwards, G. C., & Christian, W. P. (1987). Intensive home-based early intervention with autistic children. *Education and Treatment of Children, 19*, 352–366.

Anderson, S. R., & Romanczyk, R. G. (1999). Early intervention for young children with autism: Continuum-based behavioral models. *Journal of the Association for Persons with Severe Handicaps, 24*, 162–173.

Applegate, H., Matson, J. L., & Cherry, K. E. (1999). An evaluation of functional variables affecting problem behaviors in adults with mental retardation using the Questions About Behavior Function scale (QABF). *Research in Developmental Disabilities, 20*, 229–238.

Asperger, H. (1944). Autistic psychopathy in children. In U. Frith (ed.), *Autism and Asperger's Syndrome* (pp. 37–92). Cambridge: Cambridge University Press.

August, G. J., Raz, W., Papanicoladu, A. C., Baird, T. D., Hirsch, S. L., & Hsu, L. L. (1984). Fenfluramine treatment of infantile autism: Neurochemical, electrophysiological and behavioral effects. *Journal of Nervous and Mental Disease, 172*, 604–612.

August, G. J., Stewart, M. A., & Tsai, L. (1981). The incidence of cognitive disabilities in the siblings of autistic children. *British Journal of Psychiatry, 138*, 416–422.

Azrin, W. H., & Foxx, R. M. (1971). A rapid method of toilet training the institutionalized retarded. *Journal of Applied Behavioral Analysis, 4*, 89–99.

Azrin, N. H., & Foxx, R. M. (1974). *Toilet training in less than a day.* New York: Pocket Books.

Bailey, A., LeCouteur, A., Gottesman, I., Bolton, P., Simonoff, E., Yuzda, F. Y. et al. (1995). Autism is a strongly genetic disorder: Evidence from a British twin study. *Psychological Medicine, 25*, 63–77.

Baird, T. D., & August, G. J. (1985). Familial heterogeneity in infantile autism. *Journal of Autism and Developmental Disorders, 15*, 315–321.

Baird, G., Charman, T., Baron-Cohen, S. Cox, A., Swettenham, J., Wheelwright, S. et al. (2000). A screening instrument for autism at 18 months of age: A 6-year follow-up study. *Journal of the American Academy of Child and Adolescent Psychiatry, 39*, 694–702.

Baron-Cohen, S., Allen, J., & Gillberg, C. (1992). Can autism be detected at 18 months? The needle, the haystack, and the CHAT. *British Journal of Psychiatry, 161*, 839–843.

Baron-Cohen, S., Cox, A., Baird, G., Swettenham, J., & Nightingale, N. (1996). Psychological markers in the detection of autism in infancy in a large population. *British Journal of Psychiatry, 168*, 158–163.

Barrera, R. D., Lobatos-Barrera, D., & Sulzer-Azaroff, B. (1980). A simultaneous treatment comparison of three expressive language training programs with a mute autistic child. *Journal of Autism and Developmental Disorders, 10*, 21–37.

Barrera, R. D., & Sulzer-Azaroff, B. (1983). An alternative treatment comparison of oral and total communication training programs with echolalic autistic children. *Journal of Applied Behavior Analysis, 16*, 379–394.

Barrett, R. P., Feinstein, C., & Hole, W. T. (1989). Effects of naloxone and naltrexone on self-injury: A double-blind placebo-controlled analysis. *American Journal of Mental Retardation, 93*, 644–651.

Bayley, N. (1993). *Manual for the Bayley Scales of Infant Development* (2nd ed.). New York: Psychological Corp.

Bellack, A. S., Turner, S. M., Hersen, M., & Luber, R. F. (1984). An examination of the efficacy of social skill straining for chronic schizophrenic patients. *Hospital and Community Psychiatry, 35*, 1023–1028.

Bender, L., Faretra, G., & Cobrinik, L. (1963). LSD and UML treatment of hospitalized disturbed children. *Recent Advances in Biological Psychiatry, 5*, 84–92.

Berkson, G. (1983). Repetitive stereotyped behaviors. *American Journal of Mental Deficiency, 88*, 239–246.

Bettelheim, B. (1967). *The empty fortress: Infantile autism and the birth of the self.* Oxford: Free Press of Glencoe.

Bibby, P., Eikeseth, S., Martin, S., Mudford, O. C., & Reeves, D. (2001). Progress and outcomes for children with autism receiving parent-managed intensive interventions. *Research in Developmental Disabilities, 22*, 425–447.

Bleuler, E. (1950). *Dementia praecox or the group of schizophrenias.* Oxford: International University Press.

Bolton, P., Macdonald, H., Pickles, A., Rios, P., Goode, S., Crowson, M. et al. (1994). A case-control family history study of autism. *Journal of Child Psychology and Psychiatry, 35*, 877–900.

Bolton, P. F., Pickles, A., & Murphy, M. (1998). Autism, affective and other psychiatric disorders: Patterns of familial aggregation. *Psychological Medicine, 28*, 385–395.

Bouvard, M. P., Leboyer, M., Launay, J. M., Recasens, C., Plumet, M. H., Waller-Perrotte, D. et al. (1995). Low-dose naltrexone effects on plasma chemistries and clinical symptoms in autism: A double-blind, placebo-controlled study. *Psychiatric Research, 58*, 191–201.

Bowman, E. P. (1988). Asperger's Syndrome and autism: The case for a connection. *British Journal of Psychiatry, 152*, 377–382.

Brady, D. D., & Smouse, A. D. (1978). A simultaneous comparison of three methods for language training with an autistic child: An experimental single case analysis. *Journal of Autism and Child Schizophrenia, 8*, 271–279.

British Medicines Commission Agency/Committee on Safety of Medicines. (1999). The safety of MMR vaccine. *Current Problems in Pharmacovigilance, 25*, 9–10.

Bryson, S. E., Rogers, S. J., & Fombonne, E. (2003). Autism Spectrum Disorder: Early detection, intervention, education, psychopharmacological management. *Canadian Journal of Psychiatry, 48*, 506–516.

Buffington, D. M., Krantz, P. J., McClannahan, L. E., & Poulson, C. L. (1998). Procedures for teaching appropriate gestural communication skills to children with autism. *Journal of Autism and Developmental Disorders, 28*, 535–545.

Burd, L., Fisher, W., & Kerbeshian, J. (1987). A prevalence study of Pervasive Developmental Disorders in North Dakota. *Journal of the American Academy of Child and Adolescent Psychiatry, 38*, 220–222.

Busch, A. K., & Johnson, V. C. (1950). LSD-25 as an aid in psychotherapy. *Diseases of the Nervous System, 11*, 241.

Cammisa, K. M., & Hobbs, S. H. (1993). Etiology of autism: A review of recent biogenic theories and research. *Occupational Therapy and Mental Health, 12*, (2), 39–67.

Campbell, M., Anderson, L., Small, A., Locascio, J., Lynch, N., & Choroco, M. (1990). Naltrexone in autistic children: A double-blind and placebo-controlled study. *Psychopharmacology Bulletin, 26*, 130–135.

Carey, T., Ratliff-Schaub, K., Funk, J., Weinle, C., Myers, M., & Jenks, J. (2002). Double-blind placebo-controlled trial of secretin: Effects on aberrant behavior in children with autism. *Journal of Autism and Developmental Disorders, 32*, 161–167.

Carr, E. G., & Durand, V. M. (1985). Reducing behavior problems through functional communication training. *Journal of Applied Behavior Analysis, 18*, 111–126.

Centers for Disease Control. (2003, January 15). *Measles, mumps and rubella vaccines: What you need to know*. Retrieved August 15, 2005, from http://www.cdc.gov/nip/publications/VIS/vis-mmr.txt.

Chakrabarti, S., & Fombonne, E. (2001). Pervasive Developmental Disorders in preschool children. *Journal of the American Medical Association, 285*, 3093–3099.

Chakrabarti, S., & Fombonne, E. (2005). Pervasive Developmental Disorders in preschool children: Confirmation of high prevalence. *American Journal of Psychiatry, 162*, 1133–1141.

Charlop, M. H., & Walsh, M. E. (1986). Increasing autistic children's spontaneous verbalizations of affection: An assessment of time delay and peer modeling procedures. *Journal of Applied Behavior Analysis, 19*, 307–314.

Charlop-Christy, M. H., & Haymes, L. K. (1996). Using obsessions as reinforcers with and without mild reductive procedures to decrease inappropriate behaviors of children with autism. *Journal of Autism and Developmental Disorders, 26*, 527–546.

Charman, T., & Baird, G. (2002). Practitioner review: Diagnosis of Autism Spectrum Disorder in 2- and 3-year-old children. *Journal of Child Psychology and Psychiatry, 43*, 289–305.

Chen, R. T., & DeStefano, F. (1998). Vaccine adverse events: Causal or coincidental? *The Lancet, 351*, 611–612.

Chez, M. B., & Buchanan, C. P. (2000). Reply to B. Rimland's "Comments on secretin and autism: A two-part clinical investigation". *Journal of Autism and Developmental Disorders, 30*, 97–98.

Chez, M. B., Buchanan, C. P., Bagan, B. T., Hammer, M. S., McCarthy, K. S., Ovrutskaya, I. et al. (2000). Secretin and autism: A two-part clinical investigation. *Journal of Autism and Developmental Disorders, 30*, 87–94.

Chomsky, N. (1967). A review of B. F. Skinner's "Verbal Behavior". In L. A. Jakobovits & M. S. Miron (eds), *Readings in the psychology of language* (pp. 142–143). New Jersey: Prentice-Hall.

Coe, D. A., Matson, J. L., Craigie, C. J., & Gossen, M. A. (1991). Sibling training of play skills to autistic children. *Child and Family Behavior Therapy, 13*, 13–40.

Cohen, D. J., Caparulo, B. K., Gold, J. R., Waldo, M. C., Shaywitz, B. A., Ruttenberg, B. A., & Rimland, B. (1978). Agreement in diagnosis: Clinical assessment and behavior rating scales for pervasively disturbed children. *Journal of the American Academy of Child Psychiatry, 17*, 589–603.

Cooper, J. R., Bloom, F. E., & Roth, R. H. (2003). *The biochemical basis of neuropharmacology* (8th ed.). New York: Oxford University Press.

Corbett, B., Khan, K., Czapansky-Beilman, D. Brady, N., Dropik, P., Zelinksy Goldman, D. et al. (2001). A double-blind, placebo-controlled crossover study investigating the effect of porcine secretin in children with autism. *Clinical Pediatrics, 40*, 327–331.

Creak, M. (1961). Schizophrenia syndrome in childhood: Progress report of a working party. *Cerebral Palsy Bulletin, 3*, 501–504.

Croen, L. A., Grether, J. K., Hoogstrate, J., & Selvin, S. (2002). The changing prevalence of autism in California. *Journal of Autism and Developmental Disorders, 32*, 207–215.

Curtis, L. H., Masselink, L. E., Østbye, T., Hutchinson, S., Dans, P. E., Wright, A. et al. (2005). Prevalence of atypical antipsychotic drug use among commercially insured youth in the United States. *Archives of Pediatric and Adolescent Medicine, 159*, 362–366.

Dales, L., Hammer, S. J., & Smith, N. J. (2001). Time trends in autism and in MMR immunization coverage in California. *Journal of the American Medical Association, 285*, 1183–1185.

De Giacomo, A., & Fombonne, E. (1998). Parental recognition of developmental abnormalities in autism. *European Child & Adolescent Psychiatry, 7*, 131–136.

DeBildt, A., Serra, M., Luteijn, E., Kraijer, D., Sytema, S., & Minderaa, R. (2005). Social skills in children with intellectual disabilities with and without autism. *Journal of Intellectual Disability Research, 49*, 317–328.

DeLeon, I. G., Neidert, P. L., Anders, B. M., & Rodriguez-Catter, V. (2001). Choices between positive and negative reinforcement during treatment for escape-maintained behavior. *Journal of Applied Behavior Analysis, 34*, 521–525.

DeLong, G. R., Teague, L. A., & Kamran, M. M. (1998). Effects of fluoxetine treatment in young children with idiopathic autism. *Developmental Medicine and Child Neurology, 40,* 551–562.

DeLong, R., & Nohira, C. (1994). Psychiatric family history and neurological disease in autistic spectrum disorders. *Developmental Medicine and Child Neurology, 36,* 441–448.

DeMyer, M., Barton, S., DeMyer, W. E., Norton, J. A., Allen, J., & Steele, R. (1973). Prognosis in autism: A follow-up study. *Journal of Autism and Childhood Schizophrenia, 3,* 199–246.

DeMyer, M. K., Churchill, D. W., Pontius, W., & Gilkey, K. M. (1971). A comparison of five diagnostic systems for childhood schizophrenia and infantile autism. *Journal of Autism and Childhood Schizophrenia, 1,* 175–189.

DiLalla, D. L., & Rogers, S. J. (1994). Domains of the Childhood Autism Rating Scale: Relevance for diagnosis and treatment. *Journal of Autism and Developmental Disorders, 24,* 115–128.

DiLavore, P. C., Lord, C., & Rutter, M. (1995). The Pre-Linguistic Autism Diagnostic Observation Schedule. *Journal of Autism and Developmental Disorders, 25,* 355–379.

Dunn, L. M., & Dunn, M. (1981). *Peabody Picture Vocabulary Test-Revised.* Circle Pines, MN: American Guidance Service.

Durand, V. M., & Carr, E. G. (1991). Functional communication training to reduce challenging behavior: Maintenance and applications in new settings. *Journal of Applied Behavior Analysis, 24,* 251–264.

Durand, V. M., & Crimmins, D. B. (1988). Identifying the variables maintaining self-injurious behavior. *Journal of Autism and Developmental Disorders, 18,* 99–117.

Egel, A. L. (1981). Reinforcement variation: Implications for motivating developmentally disabled children. *Journal of Applied Behavior Analysis, 14,* 345–350.

Eikeseth, S. (2001). Recent critiques of the UCLA young autism project. *Behavioral Interventions, 16,* 249–264.

Eikeseth, S., Smith, T., Jahr, E., & Eldevik, S. (2002). Intensive behavioral treatment at school for 4 to 7 year old children with autism. A 1-year comparison controlled study. *Behavior Modification, 26,* 49–68.

Eisenberg, L., & Kanner, L. (1956). Early infantile autism 1943–55. *American Journal of Orthopsychiatry, 26,* 556–566.

Ekman, G., Miranda-Linné, F., & Gillberg, C. (1989). Fenfluramine treatment of twenty children with autism. *Journal of Autism & Developmental Disorders, 19,* 511–532.

Ellis, A. (1961). Treatment of a psychopath with rational psychotherapy. *Journal of Psychology: Interdisciplinary and Applied, 51,* 141–150.

Eveloff, H. H. (1960). The autistic child. *Archives of General Psychiatry, 3,* 66–81.

Factor, D. C., Freeman, N. L., & Kardish, A. (1989). A comparison of DSM-II and DSM-III-R criteria for autism. *Journal of Autism and Developmental Disorders, 19,* 637–640.

Falcomata, T. S., Roane, H. S., & Hovanetz, A. N. (2004). An evaluation of response cost in the treatment of inappropriate vocalizations maintained by automatic reinforcement. *Journal of Applied Behavior Analysis, 37,* 83–87.

Fatemi, S. H., Realmuto, G. M., Khan, L., & Thursas, P. (1998). Fluoxetine in treatment of adolescent patients with autism: A longitudinal open trial. *Journal of Autism and Developmental Disorders, 28,* 303–307.

Favell, J. E., McGimsey, J. F., & Jones, M. L. (1978). The use of physical restraint in the treatment of self-injury and as positive reinforcement. *Journal of Applied Behavior Analysis, 11,* 225–241.

Ferster, C. B. (1961). Positive reinforcement and behavioral deficits of young children. *Child Development, 32,* 437–456.

Ferster, C. B., & DeMyer, M. K. (1961). The development of performances in autistic children in an automatically controlled environment. *Journal of Chronic Diseases, 13,* 312–345.

Filipek, P., Accardo, P. J., Baranek, G., Cook, E. H., Dawson, G., Gordon, B. et al. (1999). The screening and diagnosis of autistic spectrum disorders. *Journal of Autism and Developmental Disorders, 29*, 439–484.

Fish, B. (1976). Biological disorders in infants at risk for schizophrenia. In E. R. Ritvo (ed.), *Autism: Diagnosis, current research and management* (pp. 111–146). New York: Spectrum.

Folstein, S., & Rutter, M. (1977). Genetic influences and infantile autism. *Nature, 265*, 726–728.

Fombonne, E. (1999). The epidemiology of autism: A review. *Psychological Medicine, 29*, 769–786.

Fombonne, E. (2003). Epidemiological surveys of autism and other Pervasive Developmental Disorders: An update. *Journal of Autism and Developmental Disorders, 33*, 365–382.

Fombonne, E., & du Mazaubrun, C. (1992). Prevalence of infantile autism in four French regions. *Social Psychiatry and Psychiatric Epidemiology, 27*, 203–210.

Fombonne, E., du Mazaubrun, C., Cans, C., & Grandjean, H. (1997). Autism and associated medical disorders in a large French epidemiological sample. *Journal of the American Academy of Child and Adolescent Psychiatry, 36*, 1561–1569.

Fombonne, E., Simmons, H., Ford, T., Meltzer, H., & Goodman, R. (2003). Prevalence of Pervasive Developmental Disorders in the British nationwide survey of child mental health. *International Review of Psychiatry, 15*, 158–165.

Foxx, R. M. (2005). Severe aggressive and self-destructive behavior: The myth of the nonaversive treatment of severe behavior. In J. W. Jacobson, R. M. Foxx, & J. A. Mulick (eds), *Controversial therapies for developmental disabilities* (pp. 295–310). Mahwah, NJ: Lawrence Erlbaum Associates.

Foxx, R. M., & Azrin, N. H. (1973). The elimination of autistic self-stimulatory behavior by overcorrection. *Journal of Applied Behavior Analysis, 6*, 1–14.

Frankhauser, M. P., Karumanchi, V. C., German, M. L., Yates, A., & Karumanchi, S. D. (1992). A double-blind placebo-controlled study of the efficacy of transdermal clonidine in autism. *Journal of Clinical Psychiatry, 53*, 77–82.

Freedman, A. M., Ebin, E. V., & Wilson, E. A. (1962a). Autistic schizophrenic children: An experiment in the use of d-lysergic acid diethylamide (LSD-25). *Archives of General Psychiatry, 6*, 203–213.

Freedman, A. M., Ebin, E. V., & Wilson, E. A. (1962b). Autistic schizophrenia children. *Archives of General Psychiatry, 6*, 203–213.

Freeman, B. J., Ritvo, E. R., & Schroth, P. C. (1984). Behavior assessment of the syndrome of autism: Behavioral Observation System. *Journal of the American Academy of Child Psychiatry, 23*, 588–594.

Gardner, W. I., & Cole, C. L. (1987). Conduct problems. In C. Frame & J. L. Matson (eds), *Handbook of assessment in childhood psychopathology: Applied issues in differential diagnosis and treatment evaluation* (pp. 251–270). New York: Plenum Press.

Geddes, J., Freemantle, N., & Harrison, P. (2000). Atypical antipsychotics in the treatment of schizophrenia: Systematic overview and meta-regression analysis. *British Medical Journal, 312*, 1371–1376.

Gena, A., Krantz, P. J., McClannahan, L. E., & Poulson, C. L. (1996). Training and generalization of affective behavior displayed by youth with autism. *Journal of Applied Behavior Analysis, 29*, 291–304.

Gilham, J. E., Carter, A., Volkmar, F., & Sparrow, S. A. (2000). Toward a developmental operational definition of autism. *Journal of Autism and Developmental Disorders, 30*, 269–279.

Gillberg, C. (1987). Autistic symptoms in Rett Syndrome: The first two years according to mother reports. *Brain and Development, 9*, 499–501.

Gillberg, C., Terenius, L., & Lonnerholm, G. (1985). Endorphin activity in childhood psychosis. *Archives of General Psychiatry, 42*, 780–783.

Goldstein, H. (2002). Communication interaction for children with autism: A review of treatment efficacy. *Journal of Autism and Developmental Disabilities, 32*, 373–396.

Goldstein, H., & Ferrell, D. R. (1987). Augmenting communicative interaction between handicapped and nonhandicapped preschool children. *Journal of Speech and Hearing Disorders, 52*, 200–211.

Graff, R. B., & Green, G. (2004). Two methods for teaching simple visual discriminations to learner with severe disabilities. *Researchers in Developmental Disabilities, 25*, 295–307.

Grandin, T. (1995). The learning style of people with autism: An autobiography. In K. A. Quill (ed.), *Teaching children with autism: Strategies to enhance communication and socialization* (pp. 33–52). New York: Delmar.

Green, G. (1996). Early behavioral intervention for autism: What does research tell us? In C. Maurice, G. Green, & S. C. Luce (eds), *Behavioral intervention for young autistic children: A manual for parents and professionals* (pp. 29–44). Austin, TX: Pro-Ed.

Green, G. (2001). Behavior analytic instruction for learners with autism: Advances in stimulus control technology. *Focus on Autism and Other Developmental Disabilities, 16*, 72–85.

Green, G., Brennan, L. C., & Fein, D. (2002). Intensive behavioral treatment for a toddler at risk for autism. *Behavior Modification, 26*, 69–102.

Greenhill, L. L. (1998). The use of psychotropic medications in preschoolers: Indications, safety and efficacy. *Canadian Journal of Psychiatry, 43*, 576–581.

Gresham, F. M., & MacMillan, D. L. (1997a). Autistic recovery? An analysis and critique of the empirical evidence on the Early Intervention Project. *Behavioral Disorders, 22*, 185–201.

Gresham, F. M., & MacMillan, D. L. (1997b). Denial and defensiveness in the place of fact and reason: Rejoinder to Smith and Lovaas. *Behavioral Disorders, 22*, 219–230.

Guralnick, M. J. (1998). Effectiveness of early intervention for vulnerable children: A developmental perspective. *American Journal on Mental Retardation, 102*, 319–345.

Hagberg, B., Aicardi, J., Dias, K., & Ramos, O. (1983). A progressive Syndrome of autism, dementia, ataxia and loss of purposeful hand use in girls: Rett's Syndrome – report of 35 cases. *Annals of Neurology, 14*, 471–479.

Hall, S. (in press). Comparing descriptive, experimental and informant-based assessments of problem behaviors. *Research in Developmental Disabilities*.

Halsey, N. A., & Hyman, S. L. (2001). Measles-mumps-rubella vaccine and autistic spectrum disorder: Report from the New Challenges in Childhood Immunization Conference convened in Oak Brook, Illinois June 12–13, 2000. *Pediatrics, 107*, 84.

Hart, B., & Risley, T. R. (1975). Incidental teaching of language in preschool. *Journal of Applied Behavior Analysis, 8*, 411–420.

Herman, B., Hammock, K., Arthur-Smith, A., Egan, J., Chatoor, I., Werner, A. et al. (1987). Naltrexone decreases self-injurious behavior. *Annals of Neurology, 22*, 550–552.

Herrnstein, R. J., & Murray, C. (1994). *The bell curve: Intelligence and class structure in American life*. New York: Free Press.

Hersen, M., Eisler, R. M., & Miller, P. M. (1973). Development of assertive responses: Clinical measurement and research considerations. *Behaviour Research and Therapy, 11*, 505–521.

Hertzig, M. E., Snow, M. E., New, E., & Shapiro, T. (1990). DSM-III and DSM-III-R diagnosis of Autism and Pervasive Developmental Disorder in nursery school children. *Journal of the American Academy of Child and Adolescent Psychiatry, 29*, 123–126.

Hewett, F. M. (1965). Teaching speech to an autistic child through operant conditioning. *American Journal of Orthopsychiatry, 35*, 927–936.

Hingtgen, J. N., & Churchill, D. W. (1969). Identification of perceptual limitations in mute autistic children: Identification by the use of behavior modification. *Archives of General Psychiatry, 21*, 68–71.

Ho, H., Lockitch, G., Eaves, L., & Jacobson, B. (1986). Blood serotonin concentrations and fenfluramine therapy in autistic children. *Pediatric Pharmacology and Therapeutics, 108*, 465–469.

Hodgdon, L. Q. (1995). Solving social-behavioral problems through the use of visually supported communication. In K. A. Quill (ed.), *Teaching children with autism: Strategies to enhance communication and socialization* (pp. 265–286). New York: Delmar.

Horvath, K., Steffanatos, G., Sokolski, K., Watchel, R., Nabors, L., & Tildon, T. (1998). Improved social and language skills after secretin administration in patients with autistic spectrum disorders. *Journal of the Association for the Academy of Minority Physicians, 9*, 9–15.

Howlin, P. (1997). Prognosis in autism: Do specialist treatments affect long-term outcome? *European Child & Adolescent Psychiatry, 6*, 55–72.

Husted, J. R., Hall, P., & Agin, B. (1971). The effectiveness of time-out in reducing maladaptive behavior of autistic and retarded children. *Journal of Psychology: Interdisciplinary and Applied, 79*, 189–196.

Hwang, B., & Hughes, C. (2000). Increasing early social-communicative skills of preverbal preschool children with autism through social interactive training. *Journal of the Association for Persons with Severe Handicaps, 25*, 18–29.

Ingenmey, R., & Van Houten, R. (1991). Using time delay to promote spontaneous speech in an autistic child. *Journal of Applied Behavior Analysis, 24*, 591–596.

Iwata, B. A., Dorsey, M. F., Slifer, K. J., Bauman, K. E., & Richmond, G. S. (1982). Toward a functional analysis of self-injury. *Analysis and Intervention in Developmental Disabilities, 2*, 3–20.

Iwata, B. A., Pace, G. M., Dorsey, M. F., Zarcone, J. R., Vollmer, T. R., Smith R. G. et al. (1994). The functions of self-injurious behavior: An experimental epidemiological analysis. *Journal of Applied Behavior Analysis, 27*, 215–240.

Jocelyn, L. J., Casiro, O. G., Beattie, D., Bow, J., & Kneisz, J. (1998). Treatment of children with autism: A randomized controlled trial to evaluate a caregiver-based intervention program in community day-care centers. *Developmental and Behavioral Pediatrics, 19*, 326–334.

Jones, M. B., & Szatmari, P. (1988). Stoppage rules and genetic studies of autism. *Journal of Autism and Developmental Disorders, 18*, 31–40.

Jordan, R., & Jones, G. (1999). Review of research into educational interventions for children with autism in the UK. *Autism, 3*, 101–110.

Kanner, L. (1943). Autistic disturbances of affective contact. *Nervous Child, 2*, 217–250.

Kasari, C. (2002). Assessing change in early intervention programs for children with autism. *Journal of Autism and Developmental Disorders, 32*, 447–461.

Kawasaki, Y., Yokota, K., Shinomiya, M., Shimizu, Y., & Niwa, S. (1997). Brief report: Electroencephalographic paroxysmal activities in the frontal area emerged in middle childhood and during adolescence in a follow-up study of autism. *Journal of Autism and Developmental Disorders, 5*, 605–620.

Kazdin, A. E., Matson, J. L., & Esveldt-Dawson, K. (1984). The relationship of role-play assessment of children's social skills to multiple measures of social competence. *Behaviour Research and Therapy, 22*, 129–140.

Keen, D. (2005). The use of non-verbal repair strategies by children with autism. *Research in Developmental Disabilities, 26*, 243–254.

Kerbeshian, J., & Burd, L. (1986). Asperger's Syndrome and Tourette Syndrome. *British Journal of Psychiatry, 148*, 731–736.

Klinger, L. G., & Renner, P. (2000). Performance-based measures in autism: Implications for diagnosis, early detection, and identification of cognitive profiles. *Journal of Clinical Child Psychology, 29*, 479–492.

Klykylo, W. M., Feldis, D., O'Grady, D., Ross, D. L., & Halloran, C. (1985). Clinical effects of fenfluramine in ten autistic subjects. *Journal of Autism and Developmental Disorders, 15*, 417–423.

Knibbs, G. H. (1929). The International Classification of Disease and Causes of Death and its revision. *Medical Journal of Australia, 1*, 2–12.

Koegel, L. K., Camarata, S. M., Valdez-Menchaca, M., & Koegel, R. L. (1998). Setting generalization of question-asking by children with autism. *American Journal of Mental Retardation, 102*, 346–357.

Koegel, R. L., Bimbala, A., & Schreibman, L. (1996). Collateral effects of parent training on family interactions. *Journal of Autism and Developmental Disorders, 23*, 347–359.

Koegel, R. L., Koegel, L. K., & Brookman, L. I. (2003). Empirically supported pivotal response interventions for children with autism. In A. E. Kazdin & J. R. Weisz (eds), *Evidence-based psychotherapies for children and adolescents* (pp. 341–357). New York: Guilford Press.

Koegel, R. L., Koegel, L. K., & McNerney, E. K. (2001). Pivotal areas in intervention for autism. *Journal of Clinical Child Psychology, 30*, 19–32.

Koegel, R. L., O'Dell, M. C., & Koegel, L. K. (1987). A natural language teaching paradigm for nonverbal autistic children. *Journal of Autism and Developmental Disorders, 17*, 187–199.

Kolmen, B., Feldman, H., Harden, B., & Janosky, J. (1997). Naltrexone in young autistic children: Replication study and learning measures. *Journal of the American Academy of Child and Adolescent Psychiatry, 36*, 1570–1578.

Kraijer, D. W. (2000). Review of adaptive behavior studies in mentally retarded persons with Autism/Pervasive Developmental Disorder. *Journal of Autism and Developmental Disorders, 30*, 39–47.

Kravitz, H., & Boehm, J. J. (1971). Rhythmic habit patterns in infancy: Their sequence, age of onset, and frequency. *Child Development, 42*, 399–413.

Krug, D. A., Arick, J., & Almond, P. (1979). Autism screening instrument for educational planning background and development. In J. Gilliam (ed.), *Autism: Diagnosis, instruction, management and research*. Austin: University of Texas at Austin Press.

Krug, D. A., Arick, J., & Almond, P. (1980a). *Autism Screening Instrument for Educational Planning*. Portland: ASIEP Educational Co.

Krug, D. A., Arick, J., & Almond, P. (1980b). Behavior checklist for identifying severely handicapped individuals with high levels of autistic behavior. *Journal of Child Psychology and Psychiatry, 21*, 221–229.

Lam, K. S. L., Aman, M. G., Arnold, L. E. (in press). Neurochemical correlates of Autistic Disorder: A review of the literature. *Research in Developmental Disabilities*.

Larsen, F. W., & Mouridesen, S. E. (1997). The outcome in children with childhood autism and Asperger Syndrome originally diagnosed as psychotic. A 30-year follow-up study of subjects hospitalized as children. *European Journal of Child and Adolescent Psychiatry, 6*, 181–190.

Lauritsen, M. B., & Ewald, H. (2001). The genetics of autism. *Acta Psychiatrica Scandinavica, 103*, 411–427.

LaVigna, G. W., & Donnellan, A. M. (1986). *Alternatives to punishment: Solving behavior problems with non-aversive strategies*. New York: Irvington.

Layton, T. L. (1988). Language training with autistic children using four different modes of presentation. *Journal of Communication Disorders, 21*, 333–350.

LeCouteur, A., Bailey, A. J., Goode, S., Pickles, A., Robertson, S., Gottesman, I. et al. (1996). A broader phenotype of autism: The clinical spectrum in twins. *Journal of Child Psychology and Psychiatry, 37*, 785–801.

LeCouteur, A., Rutter, M., Lord, C., Rios, P., Robertson, S., Holdgrafer, M. et al. (1989). Autism Diagnostic Interview: A standardized investigator-based instrument. *Journal of Autism and Developmental Disorders, 19*, 363–387.

Lee, S., & Odom, S. L. (1996). The relationship between stereotypic behavior and peer social interactions for children with severe disabilities. *Journal of the Association for Persons with Severe Handicaps, 21*, 88–95.

Leiber, B. (1985). Rett Syndrome: A nosological entity. *Brain and Development, 7*, 275–276.

Levine, M. N. (1982). *Leiter International Performance Scale: A handbook*. Los Angeles: Western Psychological Services.

Lindsley, O. R. (1959). Reduction in rate of vocal psychotic symptoms by differential positive reinforcement. *Journal of the Experimental Analysis of Behavior, 2*, 269.

Liss, M., Harel, B., Fein, D., Allen, D., Dunn, M., Feinstein, C. et al. (2001). Predictors and correlates of adaptive functioning in children with developmental disorders. *Journal of Autism and Developmental Disorders, 31*, 219–230.

Lockyer, L., & Rutter, M. (1969). A five to fifteen-year follow-up study of infantile psychosis III—Psychological aspects. *British Journal of Psychiatry, 115*, 865–882.

Lord, C. (1997). Diagnostic instruments in Autism Spectrum Disorders. In D. J. Cohen & F. R. Volkmar (eds), *Handbook of Autism and Pervasive Developmental Disorders* (2nd ed.) (pp. 460–483). New York: Wiley.

Lord, C., & Corsello, C. (2005). Diagnostic instruments in autism spectrum disorders. In F. R. Volkmar, R. Paul, A. Klin, & D. J. Cohen (eds), *Handbook of Autism and Pervasive Developmental Disorders* (3rd ed.) (pp. 730–771). New York: Wiley.

Lord, C., Risi, S., Lambrecht, L., Cook, E. H., Leventhal, B. L., DiLavore, P. C. et al. (2000). The Autism Diagnostic Observation Schedule – Generic: A standard measure of social and communication deficits associated with the spectrum of autism. *Journal of Autism and Developmental Disorders, 30*, 205–223.

Lord, C., Rutter, M., Goode, S., Heemsbergen, J., Jordan, H., Mawhood, L. et al. (1989). Autism Diagnostic Observation Schedule: A standardized observation of communicative and social behavior. *Journal of Autism and Developmental Disorders, 19*, 185–212.

Lord, C., Rutter, M., Le Couteur, A. (1994). Autism Diagnostic Interview-Revised: A revised version of a diagnostic interview for caregivers of individuals with possible Pervasive Developmental Disorders. *Journal of Autism and Developmental Disorders, 24*, 659–685.

Lotter, V. (1966). Epidemiology of autistic conditions in young children: Prevalence. *Social Psychiatry, 1*, 124–127.

Lotter, V. (1967). Epidemiology of autistic conditions in young children II – Some characteristics of the parents and children. *Social Psychiatry, 1*, 163–173.

Lovaas, O. I. (1987). Behavioral treatment and normal educational and intellectual functioning in young autistic children. *Journal of Consulting and Clinical Psychology, 55*, 3–9.

Lovaas, O. I. (2003). *Teaching individuals with developmental delays: Basic intervention techniques.* Austin, TX: Pro-Ed.

Lovaas, O. I., Schaeffer, B., & Simmons, J. A. (1965). Experimental studies in childhood schizophrenia building social behaviors by use of electric shock. *Journal of Experimental Studies in Personality, 1*, 99–105.

Lovaas, O. I., & Smith, T. (1989). A comprehensive behavioral theory of autistic children; Paradigm for research and treatment. *Journal of Behavior Therapy and Experimental Psychiatry, 20*, 17–29.

Lovaas, O. I., & Smith, T. (2003). Early and intensive behavioral intervention in autism. In A. E. Kazdin & J. R. Weisz (eds), *Evidence-based psychotherapies for children and adolescents* (pp. 325–340). New York: Guilford Press.

Luiselli, J. K., Blew, P., Keane, J., Thibadeau, S., & Holzman, T. (2000). Pharmacotherapy for severe aggression in a child with autism: "Open-label" evaluation of multiple medications on response frequency and intensity of behavioral interventions. *Journal of Behaviour Therapy and Experimental Psychiatry, 31*, 219–230.

Maag, J. W., Rutherford, R. B., & Wolchik, S. A. (1986). Sensory extinction and overcorrection in suppressing self-stimulation: A preliminary comparison of efficacy and generalization. *Education and Treatment of Children, 9*, 189–201.

Maag, J. W., Rutherford, R. B., Wolchik, S. A., & Parks, B. T. (1986). Comparison of two short overcorrection procedures on the stereotypic behavior of autistic children. *Journal of Autism and Developmental Disorders, 16*, 83–87.

MacCorquodale, K. (1970). On Chomsky's review of Skinner's "Verbal Behavior". *Journal of the Experimental Analysis of Behavior, 13*, 83–99.

Magnusson, P., & Saemundsen, E. (2001). Prevalence of autism in Iceland. *Journal of ASD and Developmental Disorders, 31*, 153–163.

Mahoney, G., & Perales, F. (2003). Using relationship-focused interventions to enhance the social-emotional functioning of young children with Autism Spectrum Disorders. *Topics in Early Childhood Special Education, 23*, 77–89.

Malhorta, S., & Gupta, N. (2002). Childhood Disintegrative Disorders: Re-examination of the current concept. *European Child & Adolescent Psychiatry, 11*, 108–114.

Malhorta, S., & Singh, S. (1993). Disintegrative psychosis of childhood: An appraisal and case study. *Acta Paedopsychiatrica, 56*, 37–40.

Marcus, L. M., Lansing, M., Andrews, C. E., & Schopler, E. (1978). Improvement of teaching effectiveness in parents of autistic children. *Journal of the American Academy of Child and Adolescent Psychiatry, 17*, 625–639.

Margolies, P. J. (1977). Behavioral approaches to the treatment of early infantile autism: A review. *Psychological Bulletin, 84*, 249–264.

Masters, J. C., & Miller, D. E. (1970). Early infantile autism: A methodological critique. *Journal of Autism and Childhood Schizophrenia, 8*, 162–167.

Matson, J. L. (personal communication, October 23, 2004). On the nature and role of functional assessment: Strengths and weaknesses of the procedures.

Matson, J. L., Bamburg, J. W., Cherry, K. E., & Paclawskyj, T. R. (1999). A validity study on the Questions About Behavior Function (QABF) scale: Predicting treatment success for self-injury, aggression and stereotypies. *Research in Developmental Disabilities, 20*, 163–176.

Matson, J. L., Benevidez, D. A., Compton, L. S., Paclawskyj, T., & Baglio, C. (1996). Behavioral treatment of autistic persons: A review of research from 1980 to the present. *Research in Developmental Disabilities, 17*, 433–465.

Matson, J. L., Compton, L. S., & Sevin, J. A. (1991). Comparison and item analysis of the MESSY for autistic and normal children. *Research in Developmental Disabilities, 12*, 361–369.

Matson, J. L., Esveldt-Dawson, K., Andrasik, F., Ollendick, T. H., Petti, T. A., & Hersen, M. (1980). Observation and generalization effects of social skills with emotionally disturbed children. *Behavior Therapy, 11*, 522–531.

Matson, J. L., Kazdin, A. E., & Esveldt-Dawson, K. (1980). Training interpersonal skills among mentally retarded and socially dysfunctional children. *Behaviour Research and Therapy, 18*, 419–427.

Matson, J. L., Laud, R. B., & Matson, M. L. (eds). (2004). *Behavior modification for persons with developmental disabilities: Treatments and supports.* Kingston, NY: National Association for the Dually Diagnosed.

Matson, J. L., Mayville, S. B., Kuhn, D. E., Sturmey, P., Laud, R. B., & Cooper, C. (2005). The behavioral function of feeding problems as assessed by the Questions About Behavior Function (QABF). *Research in Developmental Disabilities, 26*, 399–408.

Matson, J. L., & Ollendick, T. H. (1977). Issues in toilet training. *Behavior Therapy, 8*, 549–553.

Matson, J. L., & Ollendick, T. H. (1989). *Enhancing children's social skills: Assessment and training.* New York: Pergamon Press.

Matson, J. L., Sevin, J. A., Box, M. L., Francis, K. L., & Sevin, B. M. (1993). An evaluation and comparison of two methods for increasing self-initiated verbalizations in autistic children. *Journal of Applied Behavior Analysis, 26*, 389–398.

Matson, J. L., Sevin, J. A., Fridley, D., & Love, S. R. (1990). Increasing spontaneous language in three autistic children. *Journal of Applied Behavior Analysis, 23*, 227–233.

Matson, J. L., Smiroldo, B. B., & Hastings, T. L. (1998). Validity of the Autism/Pervasive Developmental Disorder subscale of the Diagnostic Assessment for the Severely Handicapped-II. *Journal of Autism and Developmental Disorders, 28*, 77–81.

Matson, J. L., & Vollmer, T. R. (1995). *User's guide: Questions About Behavior Function (QABF).* Baton Rouge, LA: Disability Consultants, LLC.

McConnell, S. R. (2002). Interventions to facilitate social interaction for young children with autism: Review of available research and recommendations for educational intervention and future research. *Journal of Autism and Developmental Disorders, 32,* 351–372.

McCracken, J. T., McGough, J., Shah, B., Cronin, P., Hong, D., Aman, M. et al. (2002). Risperidone in children with autism and serious behavior problems. *New England Journal of Medicine, 347,* 314–321.

McDougle, C. J., Naylor, S. T., Cohen, D. J., Volkmar, F. R., Heninger, G. R., & Price, L. H. (1996). A double-blind placebo-controlled study of fluvoxamine in adults with Autistic Disorder. *Archives of General Psychiatry, 53,* 1001–1008.

McEachin, J. J., Smith, T., & Lovaas, O. I. (1993). Long-term outcome for children with autism who receive early intensive behavioral treatment. *American Journal of Mental Retardation, 97,* 359–372.

McGee, G. G., Krantz, P. J., & McClannahan, L. E. (1985). The facilitative effects of incidental teaching on preposition use by autistic children. *Journal of Applied Behavior Analysis, 18,* 17–31.

McKeegan, G. F., Estill, K., & Campbell, B. M. (1984). Brief report: Use of nonexclusionary time-out for the elimination of a stereotyped behavior. *Journal of Behavior Therapy & Experimental Psychiatry, 15,* 261–264.

Mesibov, G. B., Shea, V., & Schopler, E. (2005). *The TEACCH approach to Autism Spectrum Disorder.* New York: Springer.

Metz, B., Mulick, J. A., & Butter, E. M. (2005). Autism: A late 20th century fad magnet. In J. W. Jacobson, R. M. Foxx, & J. A. Mulick (eds), *Controversial therapies for developmental disabilities* (pp. 237–263). Mahwah, NJ: Lawrence Erlbaum Associates.

Meyers, L. H., & Evans, I. M. (1989). *Nonaversive intervention for behavior problems: A manual for home and community.* Baltimore: Brookes.

Michael, J. (1984). Verbal behavior. *Journal of the Experimental Analysis of Behavior, 42,* 363–376.

Milich, R., & Landau, S. (1982). Socialization and peer relations in hyperactive children. In K. Gadow & I. Bialer (eds), *Advances in learning and behavioral disabilities* (vol. 1) (pp. 283–339). Greenwich, CT: JAI Press.

Minde, K. (1998). The use of psychotropic medication in preschoolers: Some recent developments. *Canadian Journal of Psychiatry, 43,* 571–575.

Minshew, N. J. (1991). Indices of neural function in autism: Clinical and biological implications. *Pediatrics, 87,* 744–780.

Minshew, N. J., Sweeney, J. A., Bauman, M. L., & Webb, S. J. (2005). Neurologic aspects of autism. In F. R. Volkmar, R. Paul, A. Klin, & D. J. Cohen (eds), *Handbook of Autism and Pervasive Developmental Disorders* (3rd ed.) (pp. 473–514). New York: Wiley.

Miranda, P., & Mathy-Laikko, P. (1989). Augmentative and alternative communication for persons with severe congenital communication disorders: An introduction. *Augmentative and Alternative Communication, 5,* 3–13.

Mirenda-Linne, F. M., & Melin, L. (2002). A factor analytic study of the Autism Behavior Checklist. *Journal of Autism and Developmental Disorders, 32,* 181–188.

Moes, D. (1995). Parent education and parenting stress. In R. L. Koegel & L. K. Koegel (eds), *Teaching children with autism: Strategies for initiating positive interactions and improving learning opportunities* (pp. 79–93). Baltimore: Brookes.

Mogar, R. E., & Aldrich, R. W. (1969). The use of psychedelic agents with autistic schizophrenic children. *Psychedelic Review, 19,* 5–13.

Mohr, C., & Sharpley, C. F. (1985). Elimination of self-injurious behaviour in an autistic child by use of overcorrection. *Behaviour Change, 2,* 143–147.

Molloy, C. A., Manning-Courtney, P., Swayne, S., Bean, J., Brown, J. M., Murray, D. S. et al. (2002). Lack of benefit of intravenous synthetic human secretin in the treatment of autism. *Journal of Autism and Developmental Disorders, 32*, 545–551.

Morgan, C. N., Roy, M., & Chance, P. (2003). Psychiatric comorbidity and medication use in autism: A community survey. *Psychiatric Bulletin, 27*, 378–381.

Morgan, S. (1988). Diagnostic assessment of autism: A review of objective scales. *Journal of Psycheducational Assessment, 6*, 130–151.

Mudford, O. C. (2004). Autism and Pervasive Developmental Disorders. In J. L. Matson, R. B. Laud, & M. L. Matson (eds), *Behavior Modification for persons with developmental disabilities: Treatments and supports* (vol. 2) (pp. 213–252). Kingston, NY: National Association for the Dually Diagnosed Press.

Mueser, K. T., & Bellack, A. S. (1989). Social learning treatment for chronic schizophrenia and autism. In J. L. Matson (ed.), *Chronic schizophrenia and adult autism* (pp. 275–310). New York: Springer Publishing.

Murch, S. H., Anthony, A., Casson, D. H., Malik, M., Berelowitz, M., Dhillon, A. P. et al. (2004). Retraction of an interpretation. *Lancet, 363*, 750.

National Institutes of Health. (1989). *Treatment of destructive behaviors in persons with developmental disabilities.* NIH Consensus Development Conference, Washington, DC: US Department of Health and Human Services.

National Research Council. (2001). *Educating children with autism.* Washington, DC: National Academy Press.

Newman, B., Needleman, M., Reinecke, D. R., & Robek, A. (2002). The effect of providing choices on skill acquisition and competing behavior of children with autism during discrete trial instruction. *Behavioral Interventions, 17*, 31–41.

Newton, J. T., & Sturmey, P. (1991). The Motivation Assessment Scale: Interrater reliability and internal consistency in a British sample. *Journal of Mental Deficiency Research, 35*, 472–474.

Nicholl, A., Elliman, D., & Ross, E. (1998). MMR vaccination and autism 1998. *British Medical Journal, 316*, 715–716.

Nicholson, J., Konstantinidi, E., & Furniss, F. (in press). On some psychometric properties of the Questions About Behavior Function (QABF). *Research in Developmental Disabilities.*

Njardvik, V., Matson, J. L., & Cherry, K. E. (1999). A comparison of social skills in adults with Autistic Disorder, Pervasive Developmental Disorder Not Otherwise Specified and ID. *Journal of Autism and Developmental Disorders, 29*, 287–295.

O'Brien, S., & Repp, A. C. (1990). Reinforcement-based reductive procedures: A review of 20 years of their use with persons with severe or profound retardation. *Journal of the Association for Persons with Severe Handicaps, 15*, 148–159.

Olsson, I., Steffenburg, S., & Gillberg, C. (1988). Epilepsy in autism and autistic-like conditions: A population-based study. *Archives of Neurology, 45*, 666–668.

O'Neill, R. E., Horner, R. H., Albin, R. W., Storey, K., & Sprague, J. R. (1991). *Functional analysis of problem behavior: A practical guide.* Sycamore, IL: Sycamore Publications.

Ozonoff, S., & Cathcart, K. (1998). Effectiveness of a home program intervention for young children with autism. *Journal of Autism and Developmental Disorders, 28*, 25–32.

Ozonoff, S., Rogers, S. J., & Pennington, B. F. (1991). Asperger's Syndrome: Evidence of an empirical distinction from high-functioning autism. *Journal of Child Psychology and Psychiatry, 32*, (7), 1107–1122.

Paclawskyj, T. R., Matson, J. L., Rush, K. S., Smalls, Y., & Vollmer, T. R. (2001). Assessment of the convergent validity of the Questions About Behavior Function Scale with analogue functional analysis and the Motivation Assessment Scale. *Journal of Intellectual Disability Research, 45*, 485–494.

Parks, S. L. (1988). Psychometric instruments available for the assessment of autistic children. In E. Schopler & G. B. Mesibov (eds), *Diagnosis and assessment in autism* (pp. 123–136). New York: Plenum Press.

Pauls, D. L. (1987). The familiality of autism and related disorders: A review of the evidence. In D. J. Cohen, A. M. Donnellan, & R. Paul (eds), *Handbook of autism and developmental disorders* (pp. 192–207). New York: John Wiley & Sons.

Pelios, L. V., MacDuff, G. S., & Axelrod, S. (2003). The effects of a treatment package in establishing independent academic work skills in children with autism. *Education and Treatment of Children, 26*, 1–21.

Peltola, H., Patja, A., Leinikki, P., Valle, M., Davidkin, I., & Paunio, M. (1998). No evidence for measles, mumps, and rubella vaccine-associated inflammatory bowel disease or autism in a 14-year prospective study. *The Lancet, 351*, 1327–1328.

Perry, R., & Bangaru, B. S. (1998). Secretin and autism. *Journal of Child and Adolescent Psychopharmacology, 8*, 247–248.

Phelps, L., & Grabowski, J. (1991). Autism: Etiology, differential diagnosis, and behavioral assessment update. *Journal of Psychopathology and Behavioral Assessment, 13*, 107–125.

Pierce, K., & Schreibman, L. (1995). Increasing complex play in children with autism via peer-implemented Pivotal Response Training. *Journal of Applied Behavior Analysis, 28*, 295–295.

Piven, J., Gayle, J., Chase, G. A., Fink, B., Landa, R., Wzorek, M. M. et al. (1990). A family history study of neuropsychiatric disorders in the adult siblings of autistic individuals. *Journal of the American Academy of Child and Adolescent Psychiatry, 29*, 177–183.

Pranzatelli, M. R., & Snodgrass, S. R. (1985). Fenfluramine therapy for autism. *Journal of Autism and Developmental Disorders, 15*, 439–441.

Prior, M. R. (1987). Biological and neuropsychological approaches to childhood autism. *British Journal of Psychiatry, 150*, 8–17.

Quintana, H., Birmaher, B., & Stedge, D. (1995). Use of methylphenidate in the treatment of children with Autistic Disorder. *Journal of Autism and Developmental Disorders, 25*, 283–294.

Rett, A. (1979). Cerebral atrophy associated with hyperammonaemia. In P. J. Vinken & G. W. Bruyn (eds), *Handbook of Clinical Neurology* (vol. 29) (pp. 305–329). Amsterdam: North-Holland Publishing Company.

Ricciardi, J. N., & Luiselli, J. K. (2003). Behavioral intervention to eliminate socially mediated urinary incontinence in a child with autism. *Child and Family Behavior Therapy, 25*, 53–63.

Richman, D. M., Reese, R. M., & Daniels, D. (1999). Use of evidence-based practice as a method for evaluating the effects of Secretin on a child with autism. *Focus on Autism and Other Developmental Disabilities, 14*, 204–211.

Rimland, B. (1964). *Infantile autism: The syndrome and its implications for a neural theory of behavior.* Englewood Cliffs: Prentice-Hall.

Rimland, B. (1968). On the objective diagnosis of infantile autism. *Acta Paedopsychiatrica, 35*, 146–161.

Rimland, B. (1971). The differentiation of childhood psychoses: An analysis of checklist for 2,218 psychotic children. *Journal of Autism and Childhood Schizophrenia, 8*, 162–167.

Rimland, B. (2000). Comments on secretin and autism: A two-part clinical investigation by M. G. Chez et al. *Journal of Autism and Developmental Disorders, 30*, 95.

Rincover, A. (1978). Sensory extinction: a procedure form eliminating self-stimulatory behavior in developmentally disabled children. *Journal of Abnormal Child Psychology, 6*, 299–310.

Ritvo, E. R. (1978). National Society for Autistic Children definition of the syndrome of autism. *Journal of Autism and Childhood Schizophrenia, 8*, 162–169.

Ritvo, E. R., Freeman, B. J., Mason-Brothers, A., Mo, A., & Ritvo, A. M. (1985). Evidence for autosomal recessive inheritance in 46 families with multiple incidence of autism. *American Journal of Psychiatry, 142*, 187–192.

Ritvo, E. R., Freeman, B. J., Yuwiler, A., Geller, E., Yokota, A., Schroth, P. et al. (1984). Study of fenfluramine in outpatients with the syndrome of autism. *Journal of Pediatrics, 105,* 823–828.

Rogers, S. J. (1998). Empirically supported comprehensive treatments for young children with autism. *Journal of Clinical Child Psychology, 27,* 168–179.

Rogers, S. J., & DiLalla, D. (1990). Age of symptom onset in young children with Pervasive Developmental Disorders. *Journal of the American Academy of Child and Adolescent Psychiatry, 29,* 863–872.

Ross, D. L., Klykylo, W. M., & Hitzmann, R. (1985). Cerebrospinal fluid indoleamine and monoamine effects in fenfluramine treatment of autism. *Annals of Neurology, 18,* 394.

Royko, M. (May 29, 1986). A brain disorder in bureaucracy. *Chicago Tribune,* p. 3.

Rutherford, A. (2003). Skinner boxes for psychotics: operant conditioning at Metropolitan State Hospital. *Behavior Analyst, 26,* 267–279.

Ruttenberg, B. A., Dratman, M. L., Frankno, J., & Wenar, C. (1966). An instrument for evaluating autistic children. *Journal of the American Academy of Child Psychiatry, 5,* 453–478.

Ruttenberg, B. A., Kalish, B. I., Wenar, C., & Wolf, E. G. (1977). *Behavior rating instrument for autistic and other atypical children* (Rev. ed.). Philadelphia: Developmental Center for Autistic Children.

Rutter, M. (1967). Psychotic disorders in early childhood. In A. J. Coppen & A. Walk (eds), *Recent developments in schizophrenia* (pp. 133–158). Ashford: Headley Brothers/RMPA.

Rutter, M. (1968). Concepts of autism: A review of research. *Journal of Child Psychology and Psychiatry, 9,* 1–25.

Rutter, M. (1970). Autistic children: Infancy to adulthood. *Seminal of Psychiatry, 2,* 435–450.

Rutter, M. (1978a). Diagnosis and definition of childhood autism. *Journal of Autism and Childhood Schizophrenia, 8,* 139–161.

Rutter, M. (1978b). Diagnosis and definition. In M. Rutter & E. Schopler (eds), *Autism: A reappraisal of concepts and treatment.* New York: Plenum Press.

Rutter, M. (1985). Infantile autism and other Pervasive Developmental Disorders. In M. Rutter & L. Hervov (eds), *Child and adolescent psychiatry: Modern approaches* (2nd ed.). Oxford: Blackwell Scientific Publications.

Rutter, M. (2005). Genetic influences and autism. In F. Volkmar, R. Paul, A. Klin, & D. Cohen (eds), *Handbook of Autism and Pervasive Developmental Disorders* (3rd ed.) (pp. 425–452). New York: John Wiley.

Rutter, M., & Lockyer, L. (1967). A five to fifteen-year follow-up study of infantile psychosis I—Description of sample. *British Journal of Psychiatry, 113,* 1169–1182.

Sahley, T. L., & Panksepp, J. (1987). Brain opioids and ASD: An updated analysis of possible linkages. *Journal of Autism and Developmental Disorders, 17,* 201–206.

Sainato, D. M., Goldstein, H., & Strain, P. S. (1992). Effects of self-monitoring on preschool children's use of social interaction strategies with their handicapped peers. *Journal of Applied Behavior Analysis, 25,* 127–142.

Sandler, A. D., Sutton, K. A., DeWeese, J., Girardi, M. A., Sheppard, V., & Bodfish, J. W. (1999). Lack of benefit of a single dose of synthetic human secretin in the treatment of Autism and Pervasive Developmental Disorder. *New England Journal of Medicine, 341,* 1801–1806.

Sandman, C. A., Barron, J. L., Chizcdemet, A., & Demet, E. M. (1991). Brief report – Plasma beta-endorphin and cortisol levels in autistic patients. *Journal of Autism and Developmental Disorders, 21,* 83–87.

Sandyk, R., & Gillman, M. A. (1986). Infantile ASD: A dysfunction of the opioids? *Medical Hypotheses, 19,* 41–45.

Sasso, G. M., Garrison-Harrell, L., & Rogers, L. (1994). The conceptualization of socialization and autism. In T. Scruggs & M. Mastropieri (eds), *Relevant research issues in developmental disabilities* (pp. 161–175). New York: Plenum Press.

Scambler, D., Rogers, S. J., & Wehner, E. A. (2001). Can the Checklist for Autism in Toddlers differentiate young children with autism from those with developmental delays? *Journal of the American Academy of Child & Adolescent Psychiatry, 40*, 1457–1463.

Scarr, S. (1992). Developmental theories for 1990s: Development and individual differences. *Child Development, 63*, 1–9.

Schopler, E. (1978). On confusion in the diagnosis of autism. *Journal of Autism and Childhood Schizophrenia, 8*, 137–138.

Schopler, E. (1987). Specific and nonspecific factors in the effectiveness of a treatment system. *American Psychologist, 42*, 376–383.

Schopler, E. (1989). Principles for directing both educational treatment and research. In C. Gillberg (ed.), *Diagnosis and treatment of autism*. New York: Plenum Press.

Schopler, E. (1994). A statewide program for the treatment and education of autistic and related communication handicapped children (TEACCH). *Psychoses and Pervasive Disorders, 3*, 91–103.

Schopler, E., Brehm, S. S., Kinsbourne, M., & Reichler, R. J. (1971). Effect of treatment structure on development in autistic children. *Archives of General Psychiatry, 24*, 415–421.

Schopler, E., Mesibov, G. B., & Hearsey, K. (1995). Structured teaching in the TEACCH system. In E. Schopler & G. B. Mesibov (eds), *Learning and cognition in autism* (pp. 243–268). New York: Plenum Press.

Schopler, E., Reichler, R. J., DeVellis, R. F., & Daly, K. (1980). Toward objective classification of childhood autism: Childhood Autism Rating Scale (CARS). *Journal of Autism and Developmental Disorders, 10*, 91–103.

Schopler, E., Reichler, R. J., & Renner, B. R. (1988). *The Childhood Autism Rating Scale (CARS)*. Los Angeles: Western Psychological Services.

Schreibman, L. (1988). *Autism*. New York: Sage Publications.

Schuster, C. R., Lewis, M., & Seiden, L. S. (1986). Fenfluramine: Neurotoxicity. *Psychopharmacology Bulletin, 22*, 148–151.

Scott, J. (1996). Recruiting, selecting, and training teaching assistants. In C. Maurice, G. Green, & S. C. Luce (eds), *Behavioral interventions for young children with autism: A manual for parents and professionals* (pp. 231–240). Austin, TX: Pro-Ed.

Sevin, J. A., Matson, J. L., Coe, D. A., Fee, V. E., & Sevin, B. M. (1991). A comparison and evaluation of three commonly used autism scales. *Journal of Autism and Developmental Disorders, 21*, 417–432.

Sevin, J. A., Matson, J. L., Coe, D., Love, S. R., Matese, M., & Benavidez, D. A. (1995). Empirically derived subtypes of Pervasive Developmental Disorder. *Journal of Autism and Developmental Disorders, 25*, 561–578.

Shahbazian, M. D., & Zoghbi, H. Y. (2002). Rett Syndrome and the MeCP2: Linking epigenetics and neuronal function. *American Journal of Human Genetics, 71*, 1259–1272.

Shearer, D. D., Kohler, F. W., Buchan, K. A., & McCullough, K. M. (1996). Promoting independent interactions between preschoolers with autism and their nondisabled peers: An analysis of self-monitoring. *Early Education and Development, 7*, 205–220.

Sheinkopf, S. J., & Siegel, B. (1998). Home based behavioral treatment of young autistic children. *Journal of Autism and Developmental Disorders, 28*, 15–24.

Short, A. B. (1984). Short-term treatment outcome using parents as co-therapists for their own autistic children. *Journal of Child Psychology and Psychiatry, 25*, 443–448.

Short, C. B., & Schopler, E. (1988). Factors relating to age of onset in autism. *Journal of Autism and Developmental Disorders, 18*, 207–216.

Siegel, B., Pliner, C., Eschler, J., & Elliot, G. (1988). How children with autism are diagnosed: Difficulties in identification of children with multiple developmental delays. *Journal of Developmental and Behavioral Pediatrics, 9*, 199–204.

Sigman, M., & Kasari, C. (1994). *Social referencing, shared attention and empathy in infants.* Paper presented at the Ninth International Conference on Infant Studies, Paris, France.

Skinner, B. F. (1957). *Verbal behavior.* Englewood Cliffs, NJ: Prentice-Hall.

Smalley, S. L., Asarnow, R. L., & Spence, M. A. (1988). Autism and genetics: A decade of research. *Archives of General Psychiatry, 45*, 958–961.

Smith, T., Groen, A. D., & Wynn, J. W. (2000). Randomized trial of intensive early intervention for children with Pervasive Developmental Disorder. *American Journal of Mental Retardation, 105*, 269–285.

Stone, W. L., Coonrod, E. E., & Ousley, O. Y. (2000). Brief report: Screening Tool for Autism in Two-Year-Olds (STAT): Development and preliminary data. *Journal of Autism and Developmental Disorders, 30*, 607–612.

Stone, W. L., Coonrod, E. E., Turner, L. M., & Pozdol, S. L. (2004). Psychometric properties of the STAT for early autism screening. *Journal of Autism and Developmental Disorders, 34*, 691–701.

Strain, P. S. (1977). Effects of peer social initiations on withdrawn preschool children: Some training and generalization effects. *Journal of Abnormal Child Psychology, 5*, 445–455.

Strain, P. S. (1983). Identification of social skills curriculum targets for severely handicapped children in mainstream preschools. *Applied Research in Mental Retardation, 4*, 369–382.

Strain, P. S., & Danko, C. D. (1995). Caregivers' encouragement of positive interactions between preschoolers with autism and their siblings. *Journal of Emotional and Behavioral Disorders, 3*, 2–12.

Strain, P. S., Kohler, F. W., Storey, K., & Danko, C. D. (1994). Teaching preschoolers with autism to self-monitor their social interactions: An analysis of results in home and school settings. *Journal of Emotional and Behavioral Disorders, 2*, 78–88.

Strain, P. S., Shores, R. E., & Timm, M. A. (1977). Effects of peer initiations on social behavior of withdrawn preschoolers. *Journal of Applied Behavior Analysis, 10*, 289–298.

Stratton, K., Gable, A., Shetty, P., & McCormick, M. (2001). *Immunization safety review: Measles-mumps-rubella vaccine and autism.* Washington, DC: National Academy Press.

Sturmey, P. (1996). *Functional analysis in clinical psychology.* Chichester: John Wiley & Sons.

Sturmey, P. (2005). Secretin is an ineffective treatment for pervasive developmental disabilities: A review of 15 double-blind randomized controlled trials. *Research in Developmental Disabilities, 26*, 87–97.

Sturmey, P., & Sevin, J. A. (1994). Defining and assessing autism. In J. L. Matson (ed.), *Autism in children and adults: Etiology, assessment, and intervention* (pp. 13–36). Pacific Grove, CA: Brooks/Cole.

Sundberg, M. L., & Michael, J. (2001). The benefits of Skinner's analysis of verbal behavior for children with autism. *Behavior Modification, 25*, 698–724.

Symes, M. D., & Hastings, R. P. (in press). Early intensive behavioral interventions for children with autism: Therapists' perspectives on achieving procedural fidelity. *Research in Developmental Disabilities.*

Szatmari, P., Archer, L., Fisman, S., Streiner, D. L., & Wilson, F. (1995). Asperger's Syndrome and autism: Differences in behavior, cognition and adaptive functioning. *Journal of the American Academy of Child and Adolescent Psychiatry, 34*, (12), 1662–1671.

Szatmari, P., Bartolucci, G., & Bremner, R. (1989). Asperger's Syndrome and autism: Comparison of early history and outcome. *Developmental Medicine and Child Neurology, 31*, 709–720.

Tager-Flusberg, H., Joseph, R., & Folstein, S. (2001). Current directions in research on autism. *Mental Retardation and Developmental Disabilities Research Reviews, 7*, 21–29.

Taras, M., Matson, J. L., & Leary, C. (1988). Training social interpersonal skills in two autistic children. *Journal of Behavior Therapy and Experimental Psychiatry, 19*, 275–280.

Taylor, B. A., Hoch, H., Potter, B., Rodriguez, A., Spinnato, D., & Kalaigian, M. (in press). Manipulating establishing operations to promote initiations. *Research in Developmental Disabilities.*

Taylor, B., Miller, E., Farrington, C. P., Petropoulos, M., Favot-Mayaud, I., Li, J. et al. (1999). Autism and measles, mumps, and rubella vaccine: No epidemiological evidence for a causal association. *The Lancet, 353*, 2026–2029.

Teal, M. B., & Wiebe, M. J. (1986). A validity analysis of selected instruments used to assess autism. *Journal of Autism and Developmental Disorders, 16*, 485–494.

Thompson, R. H., & Iwata, B. A. (2005). A review of reinforcement control procedures. *Journal of Applied Behavior Analysis, 38*, 257–278.

Treffert, D. A. (1970). Epidemiology of infantile autism. *Archives of General Psychiatry, 22*, 431–438.

Trevanthan, E., & Naidu, S. (1988). The clinical recognition and differential diagnosis of Rett Syndrome. *Journal of Child Neurology, 3*, (Suppl), S6–S16.

Tsai, L. Y. (1999a). Psychopharmacology in autism. *Psychosomatic Medicine, 61*, 651–665.

Tsai, L. Y. (1999b). Recent neurobiological research in autism. In D. B. Zager (ed.), *Autism: Identification, education, and treatment*. Mahwah, NJ: Lawrence Erlbaum Associates.

Tsai, L. Y., Stewart, M. A., & August, G. (1981). Implications of sex differences in the familial transmission of infantile autism. *Journal of Autism and Developmental Disorders, 11*, 165–173.

Van Acker, R. (1991). Rett Syndrome: A review of current knowledge. *Journal of Autism and Developmental Disorders, 21*, 381–406.

Van Houten, R., Axelrod, A., Bailey, J. S., Favell, J. E., Foxx, R. M., Iwata, B. A. et al. (1988). The right to effective treatment. *Journal of Applied Behavior Analysis, 21*, 381–384.

Volkmar, F. R. (1992). Childhood Disintegrative Disorder: Issues for DSM-IV. *Journal of Autism and Developmental Disorders, 22*, 625–642.

Volkmar, F. R., & Anderson, G. M. (1989). Neurochemical perspectives on infantile autism. In G. Dawson (ed.), *Autism: Nature, diagnosis, and treatment* (pp. 208–224). New York: Guilford Press.

Volkmar, F. R., Bregman, J., Cohen, D. J., & Cicchetti, D. V. (1988). DSM-III and DSM-III-R diagnoses of autism. *American Journal of Psychiatry, 145*, 1404–1408.

Volkmar, F. R., Cicchetti, D. V., Bregman, J., & Cohen, D. J. (1992a). Three diagnostic systems for autism: DSM-III, DSM-III-R, and ICD-10. *Journal of Autism and Developmental Disorders, 22*, 483–492.

Volkmar, F. R., Cicchetti, D. V., Bregman, J., & Cohen, D. J. (1992b). Developmental aspects of DSM-III-R criteria for autism. *Journal of Autism and Developmental Disorders, 22*, 657–662.

Volkmar, F. R., Cicchetti, D. V., Dykens, E., Sparrow, S. S., Leckman, J., & Cohen, D. J. (1988). An evaluation of the Autism Behavior Checklist. *Journal of Autism and Developmental Disorders, 18*, 81–97.

Volkmar, F. R., & Cohen, D. J. (1989). Disintegrative disorder of "late-onset autism"? *Journal of Child Psychology and Psychiatry, 30*, 717–724.

Volkmar, F. R., Klin, A., Marans, W., & Cohen, D. J. (1996). The Pervasive Developmental Disorders: Diagnosis and assessment. *Mental Retardation, 5*, 963–976.

Volkmar, F. R., Klin, A., Marans, W., & Cohen, D. J. (1997). Childhood Disintegrative Disorder. In D. J. Cohen & F. R. Volkmar (eds), *Handbook of Autism and Pervasive Developmental Disorders* (2nd ed.) (pp. 47–59). New York: Wiley.

Volkmar, F. R., Klin, A., Schultz, R., Bronen, R., Marans, W. D., Sparrow, S. et al. (1996). Asperger's Syndrome. *Journal of the American Academy of Child and Adolescent Psychiatry, 35*, (1), 118–123.

Volkmar, F. R., Klin, A., Siegel, B., Szatmari, P., Lord, C., Campbell, M. et al. (1994). Field trial for Autistic Disorder in DSM-IV. *American Journal of Psychiatry, 151*, 1361–1367.

Volkmar, F. R., & Rutter, M. (1995). Childhood Disintegrative Disorder: Results of the DSM-IV autism field trial. *Journal of the American Academy of Child and Adolescent Psychiatry, 34*, 1092–1095.

Wadden, N. P. K., Bryson, S. E., & Rodger, R. S. (1991). A closer look at the Autism Behavior Checklist: Discriminant validity and factor structure. *Journal of Autism and Developmental Disorders, 21*, 529–541.

Wakefield, A. J., Murch, S. H., Anthony, A., Linnell, J., Casson, D. M., Malik, M. et al. (1998). Ileal-lymphoid-nodular hyperplasia, non-specific colitis, and Pervasive Developmental Disorder in children. *The Lancet, 351*, 637–641.

Wechsler, D. (1949). *Manual for the Wechsler Intelligence Scale for Children.* New York: Psychological Corp.

Wechsler, D. (1989). *Manual for the Wechsler Preschool and Primary Scale of Intelligence-Revised.* San Antonio, TX: Psychological Corp.

Williams, P. G., Allard, A. M., Sears, L., Dalrymple, N., & Bloom, A. S. (2001). Brief report: Case reports on Naltrexone use in children with autism: Controlled observations regarding benefits and practical issue of medication management. *Journal of Autism and Developmental Disorders, 31*, 103–108.

Williems-Swinkels, S. H. N., Buitelaar, J., & van Engeland, H. (1996). The effects of chronic Naltrexone treatment in young children: A double-blind, placebo-controlled crossover study. *Biological Psychiatry, 39*, 1023–1031.

Wing, L. (1981). Asperger's Syndrome: A clinical account. *Psychological Medicine, 11*, 115–130.

Wing, L. (1997). The autistic spectrum. *The Lancet, 350*, 1761–1766.

Wing, L., & Atwood, A. (1987). Syndromes of autism and atypical development. In D. J. Cohen & A. M. Donnellan (eds), *Handbook of Autism and Pervasive Developmental Disorders* (pp. 3–19). New York: Wiley.

Wing, L., & Potter, D. (2002). The epidemiology of autistic spectrum disorders: Is the prevalence rising? *Mental Retardation and Developmental Disabilities Research Review, 8*, 151–161.

Wolf, E. G., Wenar, C., & Ruttenberg, B. A. (1972). A comparison of personality variables in autistic and mentally retarded children. *Journal of Autism and Childhood Schizophrenia, 2*, 92–108.

Wolf, M. M., Risley, T., & Mees, H. (1964). Application of operant conditioning procedures to the behavior problems of an autistic child. *Behavior Research and Therapy, 1*, 305–312.

World Health Organization. (1948). *Manual of the international statistical classification of disease, injuries, and causes of death, Sixth Revision.* Geneva: Author.

World Health Organization. (1996). *Multiaxial classification of child and adolescent psychiatric disorders: The ICD-10 classification of mental and behavioral disorders in children and adolescents.* Geneva: Author.

World Health Organization. (2005). *History of the development of the ICD.* Retrieved August 15, 2005, from http://www.who.int/classification/icd/en/

Yarbrough, E., Santat, V., Perel, I., Webster, C., & Lombardi, R. (1987). Effects of fenfluramine on autistic individuals residing in a state developmental center. *Journal of Autism and Developmental Disorders, 17*, 313–314.

Yeargin-Allsopp, M., Rice, C., Karapurkar, T., Doernberg, N., Boyle, C., & Murphy, C. (2003). Prevalence of autism in a US metropolitan area. *Journal of the American Medical Association, 289*, 49–55.

Yoder, P. J., & Layton, T. L. (1988). Speech following sign language training in autistic children with minimal verbal language. *Journal of Autism and Developmental Disorders, 18*, 217–229.

Yuwiler, A., Geller, E., & Ritvo, E. (1985). Biochemical studies of autism. In E. Lajtha (ed.), *Handbook of neurochemistry* (pp. 671–691). New York: Plenum.

Zarcone, J. R., Rodgers, T. A., Iwata, B. A., Rourke, D. A., & Dorsey, M. F. (1991). Reliability analysis of the Motivation Assessment Scale: A failure to replicate. *Research in Developmental Disabilities, 12*, 349–360.

Zingarelli, G., Ellman, G., Hom, A., Wymore, M., Heidorn, S., & Chicz-DeMet, A. (1992). Clinical effects of Naltrexone on autistic behavior. *American Journal of Mental Retardation, 97*, 57–63.

Author Index

Subject Index